The Snopes Dilemma

THE SNOPES DILEMMA:
Faulkner's Trilogy

JAMES GRAY WATSON

UNIVERSITY OF MIAMI PRESS

Coral Gables, Florida

Copyright © 1968 by
James Gray Watson
Library of Congress Catalog Card Number 72–102699
ISBN 0-87024-150-8

Designed by Bernard Lipsky

Manufactured in the United States of America

For Ann

Contents

Acknowledgments

Quotations from *Sanctuary*, *The Hamlet*, *The Town*, and *The Mansion*, by William Faulkner, are protected by copyright and have been reprinted by permission of the Estate of William Faulkner and Random House, Inc., and Chatlo and Windus, London.

My indebtedness to a number of critics whose work with Faulkner precedes this study will easily be seen. I am particularly obliged to Warren Beck, whose articles and book on the trilogy first helped to form my own thinking, and to Cleanth Brooks and Olga W. Vickery, whose evocative studies of the Faulkner canon I find endlessly rewarding. In a more general way, I am equally indebted to Robert L. Gale, Professor of English at the University of Pittsburgh, whose firm friendship and tireless professional guidance were invaluable to me in the preparation of this manuscript. Finally, I would like to thank Mr. Francis Bloodgood, of the University of Tulsa, for the many hours he spent with me in preparing this book for publication.

Tulsa, Oklahoma
Spring, 1970

Introduction

"The Human Heart in Conflict"

IN HIS much-quoted Nobel Prize address in 1950, Faulkner asserted that it is "the problems of the human heart in conflict with itself which alone can make good writing because only that is worth writing about." [1] Often in the next twelve years he was to iterate his commitment to writing of and from the heart. His subject, he contended at the University of Virginia, was not ideas but people, not moral or social standards but "men and women, human beings, the human heart in conflict with its self, with its fellows, or with its environment." [2] He went so far as to say that "maybe the writer has no concept of morality at all, only an integrity to hold always to what he believes to be the facts and truths of human behavior, not moral standards at all." [3] For him the task was one of optimism and hope. It was his conviction that "man will not merely endure: he will prevail," and he left no room in his work for the glorification of "anything but the old verities and truths of the heart: . . . love and honor and pity and pride and compassion and sacrifice." [4] His fiction repeatedly dramatizes his belief that mere conformity to society's artificially established codes and traditions has no moral significance. Morality demands a sensitivity and responsiveness to "the old universal truths" housed in each man's heart, and only by so responding can man fulfill his human potential to live morally. At the center of much of Faulkner's major work is the continuing conflict involved in man's choosing between the exercise of the "verities" and those elements in his makeup and environment that threaten them with extinction. Nowhere in the Faulkner canon is this conflict more integral than in the Snopes trilogy, where principled opposition to amoral aggression is sustained as the basis for structural and thematic unity.

At the center of the conflict, and of the trilogy, is the ominous figure of Flem Snopes. Lacking those primary human responses that Faulkner considered essential to moral existence, Flem is a character so completely resistant to moral definition as to be literally inhuman. Motivated by an unappeasable natural appetite for money, power, and position, he recognizes no imperatives of the heart but conforms instead to the inflexible codes of increasingly subtle social units. As he rises steadily from tenant farm to bank presidency, efficacy is his only determinant of right conduct and finance his basis of personal identity. As Warren Beck correctly says, Flem is the "paragon of the simple life, the extreme instance of that class of the unresponsive, the humanly undeveloped to whom the appeals of civility, ameliorative concession, and graciousness are inaudible." [5] As such, Flem poses a devastating threat to principled existence that cannot go unchallenged by men committed to justice and equity in human affairs. Because his every action violates human verities, each demands a counterreaction from the moral world; the more excruciating the injury, the more intense must be the response to it. It is the sustention of this confrontation, in its meditative as well as dramatic modes, that unifies the trilogy in theme as well as in structure. Whereas morality, by virtue of its endless variations because of individual interpretation and revaluative action, is regenerative, amorality is self-destructive, eliciting by its nature those responses that ultimately destroy it.

Snopeses, Faulkner said, "were simply an invention of mine to tell a story of man in his struggle," [6] and in the trilogy this struggle is dramatized as the "Snopes dilemma" (*The Mansion*, p. 322).[7] In the steadily modifying context of *The Hamlet*, *The Town*, and *The Mansion*, the recurrence of character, action, and event establishes Flem Snopes as the unchanging amoral archetype in contrast to which the range and opulent complexity of the moral world are revealed. Throughout, the responses of the principals confronted with the threat of Snopesism are reinforced by those of the multitude of minor characters, similarly confronted, who populate the trilogy. In his own way, each is faced with the "Snopes dilemma" because each must ultimately choose between asserting moral "verities" and submitting to amoral Snopesism. No less than Ratliff's does Mrs. Littlejohn's concern for the idiot, Ike, signal her capacity for compassion. Nor is Mrs. Armstid's humble suit against Flem any less an assertion of her pride in her identity as a human being than is Mink's determination to murder him. The injuries incurred at Flem's hands are grievous, yet they invoke individual affirmations of humanity which, tightly controlled, lucidly detailed, and unified by mutual opposition to a common aggressor, merge ultimately to project a cumulative portrait of man's regenerative moral nature.

The Snopes Dilemma

I.

The Hamlet

"Flem":
"The Usurpation of an Heirship"

MEMBERS of the Snopes clan begin working their way into Faulkner's fiction on an experimental basis well before the publication of *The Hamlet* in 1940, and there is evidence from the manuscript fragment "Father Abraham" that Faulkner was seriously at work on a Snopes novel sometime between the completion of *Sartoris* in 1927 and *The Sound and the Fury* in 1928. In an interview at the University of Virginia, Faulkner stated that *The Hamlet* was begun during the 1920s as "mostly short stories. In 1940 I got it pulled together." [1] In his 1945 correspondence with Malcolm Cowley, he revealed that

THE HAMLET was incepted as a novel. When I began it, it produced Spotted Horses, went no further. About two years later suddenly I had The HOUND, then JAMSHYD'S COURTYARD, mainly because SPOTTED HORSES had created a character I fell in love with: the itinerant sewing machine agent named Suratt. . . . Meanwhile my book [*Sartoris*] had created Snopes and his clan, who produced stories in their saga which are to fall in a later volume: MULE IN THE YARD, BRASS, etc. This over about ten years, until one day I decided I had better start on the first volume or I'd never get any of it down. So I wrote an induction toward the spotted horse story, which included BARN BURNING and WASH, which I discovered had no place in that book at all. Spotted horses became a longer story, picked up the HOUND (rewritten and much longer and with the character's name changed from Cotton to Snopes) and went on with JAMSHYD'S COURTYARD.[2]

In addition to these stories, an account is given in *Sartoris* of Flem's rise from dirt farmer to vice-president of the Jefferson bank, and Ab Snopes appears in *The Unvanquished* (1938) as Granny Millard's agent in the mule-trading business.

A relatively complete treatment of these Snopes tales, their publication history, and the means by which they were incorporated into the first novel of the trilogy *Snopes* has been supplied recently by Michael Millgate.[3] Their significance lies in the fact that Faulkner was experimenting with Snopeses prior to writing *The Hamlet*, but, as Millgate points out, it was not until *The Hamlet* that Snopeses were developed beyond the poor-white trash and tall-tale characters of the early fiction into a distinct breed, fully drawn and organic to the fiction. With consistent descriptive imagery, delayed and progressive contrast, and sensitive dramatic and thematic confrontation, Faulkner has created what Beck calls an "opulently detailed yet scrupulous fable of the human condition, with recurrent conflict between ruthless aggression and a principled resistance which is only partially successful, barely forestalling despair." [4] Against Flem Snopes's frightening rapacity and insensitivity to the claims of humanity, the community acts and reacts with fear and cunning and rage, weaving by indirection a complex fiber of morality, which, though frustrated and often distorted, is enduring. Flem's opponents without exception become his victims, only to rise again or be replaced by others as the struggle continues. While Flem's successes are inevitable, they are self-annihilating, and the rejuvenatory nature of the moral world is revealed in the temporariness of its defeats. Irving Howe has said of Popeye in *Sanctuary* that he is "less a man than a visitation." [5] The statement is also descriptive of Flem's impact on the community of *The Hamlet*, a community that, in reaction to Flem Snopes, is self-revealing.

This self-revelation is most often progressive and partial and delayed, building in contrast and irony, and boiling to the surface in moments of greatest individual stress. This is the case with the initial introduction of Ab Snopes. Tucked into the northern corner of Yoknapatawpha County, Frenchman's Bend is a self-reliant community, "hill-cradled and remote . . . straddling into two counties and owning allegiance to neither" (p. 3).[6] Originally the site of a pre-Civil War plantation, the Bend is now populated by the yeoman sharecroppers and farmers who trace their origins to "England and the Scottish and Welsh Marches" (p. 4). This inbred community of soil-bound men and women "supported their own churches and schools . . . married and committed infrequent adulteries and more frequent homicides among themselves and were their own courts judges and executioners. They were Protestants and Democrats and prolific; there was not one Negro landowner in the entire section" (pp. 4–5). The leading citizen of this community is Will Varner.

> He was the largest landholder and beat superviser in one county and Justice of the Peace in the next and election commissioner in both, and hence the fountainhead if not of law at least of advice and suggestion to a countryside which would have repudiated the term constituency if they had ever heard it, which came to him, not in the attitude of *What must I do* but *What do you think you think you would like for me to do if you was able to make me do it.* He was a farmer, a usurer, a veterinarian; Judge Benbow of Jefferson once said of him that a milder-mannered man never bled a mule or stuffed a ballot box. He owned most of the good land in the country and held mortgages on most of the rest. He owned the store and the cotton gin and the combined grist mill and blacksmith shop in the village proper and it was considered, to put it mildly, bad luck for a man of the neighborhood to do his trading or gin his cotton or grind his meal or shoe his stock anywhere else. (p. 5)

Varner's second in command is his bachelor son, Jody, "a prime bulging man, slightly thyroidic. . . . a big man, already promising a considerable belly in ten or twelve years" (p. 6). A lesser luminary than his hardy, Rabelaisian father, Jody "dealt mostly in foreclosed mortgages, and the gin, and oversaw the scattered farm holdings which his father at first and later the two of them together had been acquiring during the last forty years" (p. 7). To him Ab Snopes applies for a farm to sharecrop, appearing suddenly, "silhouetted by the open door, a man smaller than common, in a wide hat and a frock coat too large for him, standing with a curious planted stiffness" (p. 7). In description and behavior Ab is immediately set off from those elements of the community that are known, familiar, and predictable. His is a voice "not harsh exactly, or not deliberately harsh so much as rusty from infrequent use" (p. 7), a "lifeless voice," a "dead voice," "inflectionless" (p. 8). He comes not from the East, as did the residents, but from the West, uniquely counts himself among his own field hands, and declines to bargain over the rental rate, accepting Jody's usurious terms in the attitude of *"What must I do,"* which is repudiated by the general countryside. He is alien, and there is an element of threat in his eyes, "a cold opague gray between shaggy graying irascible brows and a short scrabble of iron-gray beard as tight and knotted as a sheep's coat" (p. 8), and his stiff, limping gait. To hear his footsteps "you'd think he weighed two hundred pounds" (p. 9).

It develops, moreover, that Ab "was mixed up in that burnt barn of a fellow named Harris over in Grenier County two years ago" (p. 9), an insight supplied by Vernon Tull with a hesitancy and unwillingness to become involved at which Jody scoffs. For his own part, Jody's reaction is to capitalize on Ab's reputation as a barn burner in order to cheat him of his crop. In answer to his father's warning to "stay clear of them folks" (p. 12), Jody replies, "Hell fire, he'll have to [leave]! He cant fight it! He dont dare!" (p. 11).

Ironically, Ab never gets the opportunity to "fight it" because Jody's plan is never put into action. Intervening is the character Faulkner fell in love with, the itinerant sewing machine agent named V. K. Ratliff. As Jody listens in apoplectic horror, Ratliff tells him that it was not simply one barn that Ab was suspected of burning and tried for, but two, and that Ab's son, Flem, had returned to the scene of the second fire and commented to the enraged owner "That ere hay goes fast" (p. 17). The tale itself is in the tall-tale tradition of country humor and is successful even as a digression to frighten the self-assured Jody. But though Ratliff baits Jody "in a tone of absolutely creamlike innocence" (p. 14), Ratliff "was not laughing. The shrewd brown face was as bland and smooth as ever beneath the shrewd impenetrable eyes" (p.

14). In telling this tale, Ratliff establishes his intimate acquaintance with Snopes history and his ability as a commentator on Snopeses generally. He epitomizes "a type Faulkner strongly believes in, the exceptional common man, unsophisticated but intelligent, responsible, principled, and plainly capable on a number of sectors. . . . the practical humorous critic of men and affairs, whose most casual remarks may be double-edged. The keenness is extreme, too; duplicity is met as such and penetrated by a superior device, in which *de facto* recognition of mischief is accorded so easily that it seems almost an acceptance, under which shield of appearance an uncompromising conviction strikes quick and true." [7]

Through the barn-burning tale, the danger implicit in Ab's description and reputation is expanded and detailed to produce a dramatic effect on Ab's first opponent. In effect, Jody is totally disarmed by being forewarned. He approaches Ab's farm "breathing hard through his nose and even sweating a little" (p. 18), watching the perfectly blank house, as blank as Ab's own countenance, "with wire-taut wariness, as if he were approaching an ambush" (p. 19). His silently repeated "Hell fire! Hell fire!" takes on a new and ironic significance, "as though [he were] proving to himself what even a second's laxity of attention might bring him to" (p. 20). The positions of the first interview are reversed here, and it is now Jody who assumes the attitude of *"What must I do"* and puts himself at Ab's command. Jody says, "Anything that comes up, all you got to do is come down to the store. No, you dont even need to do that: just send me word and I'll ride right up here as quick as I can get here. You understand? Anything, just anything you dont like——(pp. 20–21).

Jody's cunning revives briefly in his interview with Flem, but now his misapprehension of the danger of dealing with Snopeses has implications that go far beyond the loss of a barn to fire. Flem is a more rapacious opponent than his father, and, whereas the latter is content to be left alone to farm, the former abjures farming: "Aint no benefit in farming. I figure on getting out of it as soon as I can" (p. 23). His speech is sprinkled with threatening innuendoes. In reference to tobacco he says, "I chew up a nickel now and then until the suption is out of it. But I aint never lit a match to one yet" (p. 23). "One" may refer to tobacco, barns, nickels, or all three. Like Ab, Flem is set off from the community by his physical appearance, but, unlike his father, there is nothing overtly threatening about him. Rather, with eyes "the color of stagnant water" set in a face "as blank as a pan of uncooked dough" (p. 22), he is the very absence of those qualities that find expression in Ab's features and gait. Inscrutable, he belies understanding. He guarantees nothing yet gains himself a place in the store. Instinctively he avoids commitment: to Jody for a guarantee of fire insurance, to his father for the benefits that Jody has promised will accrue if no fires are set. Impenetrable, intransigent, noncommittal, he is the essence of the alien; and Jody, confronted by this specter, is very soon pleading "All right. . . . Next fall. When he has made his crop. . . . All right. . . . Next week then. You'll give me that long, wont you?" (p. 23).

Speaking of Ab's function in *The Hamlet*, Beck says that "this notorious barn burner Ab, still a dour and compulsively quarrelsome fellow, has his primary importance as a factor in Flem's gambit to become clerk in Varner's store." [8] Actually, his function is a good bit more subtle and extensive. When Ratliff and Will Varner get together to discuss the new clerk, they assume that Jody's fear of Ab is the sole reason that Flem was able to insinuate himself into the store. They do not recognize that Flem is the more lethal of the two Snopeses, and they mistake Jody's desperate "I had to! I had to hire him! I had to, I tell you!" (p. 27) as a reaction to Ab alone. Their concern is solely for "this here firefighter," of whom Ratliff says "It wasnt proved. . . . Of course, that's the trouble. If a fellow's got to choose between a man that is a murderer and one he just thinks maybe is, he'll choose the murderer. At least then he will know exactly where he's at. His attention aint going to wander then" (p. 26). While they admit the danger represented by Ab, however, they state, somewhat hopefully that "he aint naturally mean. He's just soured" (p. 27). And while they first believe there is little to worry about, for "it's just Flem that Jody mixed up with" (p. 27), Ratliff concludes that "there aint but two men I know can risk fooling with them folks. And just one of them is named Varner and his front name aint Jody." To Varner's question "And who's the other one?" Ratliff replies pleasantly, "That aint been proved yet neither" (p. 28).

Ab's part in the novel is developed further when Ratliff, having missed the significance of Flem, devotes a long tale to Ab's trade with Pat Stamper. While the townsmen apprehensively watch the front of Varner's store, worrying about the new clerk in the only store with which they dare to deal, Ratliff again explains that Ab is not "naturally mean" and then proceeds to tell a tale which mellows and to some extent justifies Ab's behavior. In the process he greatly reduces the stature of Ab's threat by showing him to have possessed pride, family feeling, and the admiration of the young Ratliff himself. At the same time, however, he unknowingly establishes the grounds that will frighteningly increase Flem's stature by contrast. In telling this long tale, Ratliff not only demonstrates how far afield even he can wander from the central issues when dealing with Ab, but he also helps to pave the way for Flem's more devastating impact on the community and on Ratliff himself. His fallibility here as a commentator on and interpreter of Snopesism has a definite significance for his later not altogether successful interventions against Flem's ravages in Frenchman's Bend, and his story establishes some impressions of the lesser Snopeses, against whom Flem will be recurrently contrasted. The story is capped by Ratliff's final interview with Ab, wherein the qualities he has ascribed to him are borne out in Ab's response to their former friendship. Immediately thereafter, however, Flem gains ascendancy as the archetypal Snopes, and Ab disappears from the novel. He has indeed served as a major factor in Flem's gambit to gain a clerkship in Varner's store, but he has also served to decoy Ratliff's attention away from Flem and, by contrast with Flem, to deepen and intensify the amorality of Flem at the point when he is first introduced to the community.

Although Ratliff momentarily focuses his attention on the lesser Snopes, he is not so unconcerned or incurious as to be absent when Flem arrives in Frenchman's Bend on his first day as Varner's clerk. On this day, and indeed for a full week thereafter, Ratliff is one of the group of loungers who view with curiosity and increasing alarm the settling-in of Flem Snopes. Nor is Flem's potential for harm confined to the immediate locale of Frenchman's Bend. It is felt throughout the county. "By the end of that first week they had all come in and seen him, not only those who in future would have to deal through him for food and supplies but some who had never traded with the Varners and never would— the men, the women, the children—the infants who had never before crossed the doorsteps beyond which they had been born, the sick and the aged who otherwise might never have crossed them but once more—coming on horses and mules and by wagonsful" (p. 52). If this is exaggeration it is justified by the portrait of the man they have come to see. In his zebra-striped shirt of bolt cloth, "cut and stitched by hand and by a stiff and unaccustomed hand too" (p. 51), Flem is something of a grotesque copy of Jody Varner. New to life in even so small a town as Frenchman's Bend, Flem slavishly imitates the former storekeeper. The contrast his attire bears to the "perfectly clean faded shirt[s]" (p. 15) that Ratliff makes by hand also sets him apart. By the end of the first day, in fact, Flem's sweat-stained shirt images the alien and dangerous nature of its wearer. "It was as though its wearer, entering though he had into a new life and milieu already channelled to compulsions and customs fixed long before his advent, had nevertheless established in it even on that first day his own particular soiling groove" (p. 51).

Physically, too, he is the center of the community's alarmed attention. "Like half-wild cattle following word of the advent of a strange beast upon their range" (p. 52), the countryside comes warily to look at the new clerk "with whom in the future they would have to deal for the necessities of living" (p. 52). Throughout this examination, Flem maintains his impenetrable, blankly noncommittal visage. In his description now, the threat is explicit.

> He did not speak. If he ever looked at them individually, that one did not discern it—a thick squat soft man of no establishable age between twenty and thirty, with a broad still face containing a tight seam of mouth stained slightly at the corners with tobacco, and eyes the color of stagnant water, and projecting from among the other features in startling and sudden paradox, a tiny predatory nose like the beak of a small hawk. It was as though the original nose had been left off by the original designer or craftsman and the unfinished job taken over by someone of a radically different school or perhaps by some viciously maniacal humorist or perhaps by one who had had only time to clap into the center of the face a frantic and desperate warning. (pp. 51–52)

From the interior of the store, the listeners hear only Jody Varner's "heavy bass matter-of-fact murmur, still talking apparently to itself for all the audible answer it ever got" (p. 53), and when Will Varner arrives "it was not the clerk who now discovered at last whom he was working for, but Will Varner who discovered who was working for him" (p. 53): Flem charges Will for a plug of his own tobacco.

Ratliff's subsequent departure from Frenchman's Bend and the detailed description of his complicated trading expedition into Tennessee prepare the way for a Ratliff-Flem contrast which is central to their ensuing opposition: the barter-trade theme. Pressed for funds by his Memphis wholesaler and unable to collect until harvest time on the notes he has taken, Ratliff shrewdly parlays the note of a kinsman into a sound profit. Unlike Pat Stamper's dealings with Ab Snopes, Ratliff's gains are accomplished with fairness and concern for those with whom he trades. When he returns to the hamlet in November, he finds that Flem Snopes has developed a scrupulous "fairness" of his own, although it can hardly be said to be tempered with concern. Whereas Jody Varner had charged high rates of interest, he gave long credit. He made money errors in his favor, but let a customer get away with a spool of thread or a tin of snuff now and then. The new clerk "never made mistakes in any matter pertaining to money" (p. 56). Flem has never been caught overcharging and, like the man choosing between a murderer and a suspected murderer in Ratliff's earlier metaphor, the community would rather that he were caught. " 'You mean aint nobody caught him *once* even?' 'No,' Bookwright said, 'And folks dont like it. Otherwise, how can you tell?' " (p. 57).

Furthermore, Flem is unwilling to grant credit, even refusing it to a man "who had been into and out of the store's debt at least once a year for the last fifteen" (p. 57). Because Flem lacks human concern and is as yet unaware of the interest to be gleaned from granting credit, there is nothing in him to which borrowers can appeal.

But Flem is never slow to see advantage or opportunity. In hollow imitation of the Varners, he astonishes the community by appearing one Sunday at church, his now clean white shirt complemented by a necktie—"a tiny machine-made black bow which snapped together at the back with a metal fastener. It was not two inches long and with the exception of the one which Will Varner

himself wore to church it was the only tie in the whole Frenchman's Bend country" (pp. 57–58). In this tie and in the burgeoning ambition that its imitation of Varner represents, another danger sign is established. It is "a tiny viciously depthless cryptically
balanced splash like an enigmatic punctuation symbol against the
expanse of white shirt which gave him Jody Varner's look of
ceremonial heterodoxy raised to its tenth power and which postulated to those who had been present on that day that quality of
outrageous overstatement of physical displacement which the
sound of his father's stiff foot made on the gallery of the store that
afternoon in the spring" (p. 58). Flem is to wear this tie, or one
like it, every day for the rest of his life. He soon moves to town
and as the summer passes through the "dead slack days of August," Will and Jody leave the store entirely to the clerk, and it
"actually seemed as if not only the guiding power but the proprietorial and revenue-deriving as well was concentrated in that squat
reticent figure in the steadily-soiling white shirts and the minute
invulnerable bow, which in those abeyant days lurked among the
ultimate shadows of the deserted and rich-odored interior with a
good deal of the quality of a spider of that bulbous blond omnivorous though non-poisonous species" (p. 58). With the coming
of September and the harvest, it is Flem who runs the gin while
Jody replaces him in the store, speaking now in "short surly
grunts" (p. 60). Will Varner and Flem, resembling "the white
trader and his native parrot-taught headman in an African outpost"
(p. 61), carry the ledgers that Jody was not allowed to handle.
Jody has been dispossessed of his privileges as Will's son as efficiently as he had planned to dispossess Ab of his crop, and at
the same season of the year. "This was the time they referred to
later, two and three years later, when they told one another: 'That
was when he passed Jody,' though it was Ratliff who amended it:
'You mean, that was when Jody begun to find it out'" (p. 60).

    The "parrot-taught headman," pagan and inscrutable, continues
his secret machinations in the community throughout the winter,
and Ratliff, "speculate, curious, shrewd, and inscrutable himself"
(p. 62), recovering from an operation in Jefferson, muses on
Flem's successes. Flem has made "a considerable cash loan, security
and interest not specified," parlayed a "considerable herd of scrub
cattle" into "a herd of good Herefords" (p. 61), and replaced the

village blacksmith, Trumbull, with a cousin, Eckrum Snopes. Eckrum is himself responsible to a second cousin, I. O., Flem's epigrammatic agent. These two are the first in a long line of Snopes "cousins" to invade the hamlet, apparently at Flem's bidding, and they represent nearly polar opposites on the scale of Snopesism. Eck is a "young, well-made, muscle-bound man" with "an open equable face beginning less than an inch below his hairline" (p. 62), whose proclivities as a breeder indicate to the community that there is "considerably more force and motion to his private life, his sex life anyway, than would appear on the surface of his public one" (p. 66). He is "accommodating and unfailingly pleasant and even generous" (p. 66). Conversely, I.O. is "a frail man none of whose garments seemed to belong to him, with a talkative weasel's face" (p. 63) and "bright darting eyes" (p. 65). Both provide strong contrasts to Flem, as did Ab before them. Eck's simple openness is the antithesis of Flem's dark inscrutability, while I.O.'s shallow, meaningless chatter emphasizes Flem's perpetual silence. I.O.'s speech of greeting to the community is a masterpiece of absurdity:

> Well, gentlemen, off with the old and on with the new. Competition is the life of trade, and though a chain aint no stronger than its weakest link, I don't think you'll find the boy yonder [Eck] no weak reed to have to lean on once he catches onto it. It's the old shop, the old stand; it's just a new broom in it and maybe you cant teach a old dog new tricks but you can teach a new young willing one anything. Just give him time; a penny on the waters pays interest when the flood turns. Well, well; all pleasure and no work, as the follow says, might make Jack so sharp he might cut his-self. I bid you good morning, gentlemen. (p. 65)

The images of investment, trade, and business, which are here so jumbled, set off the skillful intricacy of Flem's next transaction. In a series of manipulations that parallel Ratliff's earlier ones with sewing machines and mules, Flem buys and sells blacksmith shops in a deal so complex that "even Ratliff had lost count of what profit Snopes might have made" (p. 67). This successful transaction recalls Ab's unsuccessful deal with Pat Stamper, in contrast to which Flem's stature is inevitably increased, and sets the stage for the next business deal, in which the canny Ratliff tests Flem's lately acquired skills in a trade involving goats. The ominous note on which this next deal ends is also sounded here, prefiguring the outcome of that trade by suggesting a distinction between the tools available to the two traders. Whereas Ratliff conducted his mule trade with no adverse effects to anyone, collecting his due from his kinsman and building from it, Flem's blacksmith shop trade is founded on the dispossession of the long-established Trumbull and the manipulation of Flem's kinsmen. Musing upon Jody's probable reaction to Flem's blacksmith shop transaction and to the influx of yet more Snopeses, Ratliff imagines Jody in a state of desperate frustration at having risked "fooling with them folks."

> He could almost see it—in the store, at night, the door barred on the inside and the lamp burning above the desk where the clerk sat, chewing steadily, while Jody Varner stood over him, in no condition to sit down, with a good deal more in his eyes than had been in them last fall, shaking, trembling, saying in a shaking voice: "I want to make one pure and simple demand of you and I want a pure and simple Yes and No for a answer: How many more is there? How much longer is this going on? Just what is it going to cost me to protect one goddamn barn full of hay?" (p. 67)

Despite the fact that the answers demanded of Flem are the only ones he ever gives, there are no "Yes and No" answers to these questions. There can be no communication between the moral world and Flem. For Jody, as for Ratliff, comprehension of the "Snopes dilemma" will have to be found in confrontation with Snopesism.

Ratliff's engagement of Flem is the goat trade, while it does not prove definitely whether or not he can risk "fooling" with Snopeses, does delineate clearly Flem's ruthlessness and insensitivity to moral claims and forces on Ratliff a reassessment of his previous observations. "The Snopes dilemma" has intensified during Ratliff's absence from Frenchman's Bend, and the sewing-machine agent, intent initially on no more than "the pleasure of the shrewd dealing which far transcended mere gross profit" (p. 68), is discovered rising to a moral challenge. In Tull's and Bookwright's story of Flem's usurious exploitation of the helplessly naive Negroes, Ratliff sees the frightening scope of Flem's cupidity. Bookwright reports, "The fireman wanted to borrow some money, said Quick wouldn't let him have it. 'Go to Mr Snopes at the store,' the other nigger says. 'He will lend it to you. He lent me five dollars over two years ago and all I does, every Saturday night I goes to the store and pays him a dime. He aint even mentioned that five dollars' " (p. 70). Unlike Flem's transactions with the blacksmith shop, "the first which he not only admitted but affirmed" (p. 66), this one is secret. The parties involved are grossly mismatched, and the profit is unconscionably large. In essence, it violates Ratliff's sense of fellow-feeling and the unwritten customs of fair trading by which he makes his living.

> "Well well well," he said. "So he's working the top and the bottom both at the same time. At that rate it will be a while yet before he has to fall back on you ordinary white folks in the middle. . . . Aint none of you folks out there done nothing about it?" he said.
> "What could we do?" Tull said. "It aint right. But it aint none of our business."
> "I believe I would think of something if I lived there," Ratliff said.
> "Yes," Bookwright said. . . . "And wind up with one of them bow ties in place of your buckboard and team. You'd have room to wear it."
> "Sho now," Ratliff said. "Maybe you're right." He stopped looking at them now and raised his spoon, but lowered it again. "This here cup seems to have a draft in it," he said to the counterman. "Maybe you better warm it up a little. It might freeze and bust, and I would have to pay for the cup too." (p. 71)

Moral principles, when allowed to go untested against the cold, aggressive challenge of amorality, will freeze. Unwilling to sacrifice his principles, Ratliff must intervene against Flem by outtrading him. As Beck points out, "paired with pity . . . resistance to evil can make a stand well this side of terror, in a genuine righteous wrath held behind the mask of irony." [9]

The specific details of the goat trade and the profits realized and losses suffered by each side have been amply treated by Cleanth Brooks.[10] The significance of the trade, however, lies not so much in Ratliff's practice of the "science and pastime of skullduggery" (p. 82) as in the effects that his practice of them produce on the community and himself. Whereas Bookwright earlier neglects to intervene on behalf of the Negroes and warns Ratliff sarcastically that he ought to return to the Bend "nekkid" so that he will not "notice the cold coming back" (p. 71), Bookwright's present concern for Ratliff is sincere and approaches intervention on his behalf. " 'Go buy your goats,' Bookwright said. 'Wait till after that to do your eating' " (p. 82). Ratliff says of him, "he done all he could to warn me. He went as far and even further than a man can let his-self go in another man's trade" (p. 82). Since Ratliff has purposely spread the news that there is a buyer for fifty goats, however, this warning too goes unheeded. Ratliff permits Flem to buy the goats and then gets them from Flem by using the promissory notes he received from Flem's cousin, Mink, and Mink's threat to burn Flem's barn if the notes are not honored.

At this point Ratliff has shown himself to be the superior trader; it remains for him to demonstrate his moral superiority to Flem. When he recognizes that the Isaac Snopes whose note he holds is the idiot, "something black blew in him, a suffocation, a sickness, nausea" (p. 85). Forsaking all thought of profit, Ratliff burns Ike's note to save the idiot from Flem's further exploitation. He tells himself, "Only thank God men have done learned how to forget quick what they aint brave enough to try to cure" (p. 86). He gives up his profit, and more, to Mrs. Littlejohn to make up the amount of Ike's inheritance and the interest that it should have been gathering and, still insisting that "it aint been proved yet" (p. 87), muses on his now clearer perception of Flem's amorality: "I just never went far enough, he thought. I quit too soon. I went as far as one Snopes will set fire to another Snopes's barn and both Snopeses know it, and that was all right. But I stopped there. I never went on to where the first Snopes will turn around and stomp the fire out so he can sue that second Snopes for the reward and both Snopeses know that too" (p. 88). Through his direct engagement with Snopesism, Ratliff achieves insights that mere commenting and observing could not supply. The forces of amorality, by their machinations in the community, have forced a reaction from that community through which its morality is revealed. While Flem avoids financial loss, reasserting his amorality by the constant sale and resale of his idiot cousin's inheritance, Ratliff gives up his financial advantage and asserts his morality by intervening against Flem and saving Ike from him. His right to claim that he may be able to "risk fooling with them folks" lies in the fact that he has scored a moral victory and, temporary though it may be, a victory in the name of morality.

Nonetheless, the inexorable Flem Snopes continues his rapacious "grazing" (p. 70) through Frenchman's Bend totally unchecked. Having symbolically withstood the moral world's only serious opposition in the person of Ratliff, Flem expands his field of vision. "Those who watched the clerk now saw, not the petty dispossession of a blacksmith, but the usurpation of an heirship" (p. 88). Flem takes over the ledgers himself, moves into the Varner household, and rides about the countryside with Will, not on horseback as Jody used to do, but in a new runabout buggy purchased by Varner for the purpose. While his cousin Mink's argument with Houston rages in front of the store, Flem is seated with Will Varner in the yard of the Old Frenchman place. Ratliff's informant adds, "as if in trivial afterthought: 'It was Flem Snopes that was setting in the flour barrel' " (p. 91).

"Eula": "The Crippled Vulcan to that Venus"

IN BOOK two of *The Hamlet*, the narrative emphasis temporarily changes from moral to physical response as the community is confronted with the primal sexuality of Eula Varner. In her overripe pubescence is embodied all that is alluring, maddening, and ruinous to animal man. She is "supine and female and soft and immovable" (p. 98), an almost grotesquely sexual figure of whom "even at nine and ten and eleven, there was too much—too much of leg, too much of breast, too much of buttock; too much of mammalian female meat" (p. 100). Her appeal is such that she transcends time and space, assuming the nearly mythical stature of ultimate and unattainable physicality.

> Her entire appearance suggested some symbology out of the old Dionysic times—honey in sunlight and bursting grapes,

the writhen bleeding of the crushed fecundated vine beneath
the hard rapacious trampling goat-hoof. She seemed to be
not a living integer of her contemporary scene, but rather
to exist in a teeming vacuum in which her days followed one
another as though behind sound-proof glass, where she seemed
to listen in sullen bemusement, with a weary wisdom heired of
all mammalian maturity, to the enlarging of her own organs.
(p. 95)

So imaged, Eula provides a focus for community response.

As Eula transcends her environment, so her significance to the
novel transcends the mere fact of her sexuality and the reactions
of the community to her. The Eula-Labove and Eula-McCarron
episodes provide the intense atmosphere of physical response
against which Flem Snopes is ultimately contrasted. Absent from
the narrative while the seduction of Eula runs its course in lust,
madness, and frustration, Flem's inhumanity is reaffirmed finally
by his insensitivity to Eula and his exploitation of the passions
that she inspires in other men. The more mythic Eula becomes, the
more these passions are heightened and Flem's impact on the community is intensified.

Despite the fact that Flem is not an active presence until the
end of this book, there are numerous implications throughout
that prefigure his reappearance. By reference to him, Eula's age is
established: "When Flem Snopes came to clerk in her father's
store, Eula Varner was not quite thirteen" (p. 95). She is heralded,
furthermore, by her brother, Jody, whose reactions to her provide the initial means by which her sexuality is established just as
his reactions to Flem established the element of Snopes's threat.
Through Jody's fear, Flem gained a clerkship. Jody sends Eula to
school with equally desperate results, crying to his father and
mother that "she's just like a dog! Soon as she passes anything in
long pants she begins to give off something. You can smell it! You
can smell it ten feet away!" (p. 99). Reacting in fear to Flem's
impenetrability, he reacts with "raging impotence" (p. 101) to
Eula's obliviousness to her own appeal, his acute awareness of her
heightening her mythic sexuality. He imagines himself "transport-
ing not only across the village's horizon but across the embracing
proscenium of the entire inhabited world like the sun itself, a
kaleidoscopic convolution of mammalian ellipses" (p. 100). Jody

is Eula's self-appointed chaperone, and it is his fate, therefore, to undergo self-inflicted misery, victimized by forces that he can neither control nor comprehend. Insofar as he is victimized by both Flem and Eula, he provides a medium through which the two are implicitly contrasted. Though absent, Flem is a felt presence throughout.

The contrasts by which Flem's presence is felt find increased scope in the brilliantly done Labove episode. Structurally, the introduction of Labove closely parallels the introduction of Flem, and there are a number of narrative similarities between them that call for their comparison and contrast. Both are sons of poor dirt farmers whose fathers' encounters with Varner men precede their own and shape their futures. In the case of Flem, Ab is totally inhospitable and Flem himself is only a face that Jody glimpses in the window of the "broken-backed cabin" (p. 18). The senior Labove is Will Varner's "host" (p. 103) at the "bleak puncheon-floored cabin" (p. 102) and speaks freely and proudly of his self-sacrificing son. Flem avoids a commitment to his family by dealing with Jody out of sight of his father's cabin, and he gains his place in the Varner employ by exploiting Jody's fear. Labove generously sends his family football shoes and permits himself to be exploited by taking the position as Varner's schoolmaster. Flem's physical appearance suggests alien impenetrability, flat and expressionless. Labove's face tells a great deal about him.

> He [Varner] saw approaching on foot across the yard the man whom he had never seen before but knew at once—a man who was not thin so much as actually gaunt, with straight black hair coarse as a horse's tail and high Indian cheekbones and quiet pale hard eyes and the long nose of thought but with the slightly curved nostrils of pride and the thin lips of secret and ruthless ambition. It was a forensic face, the face of invincible conviction in the power of words as a principle worth dying for if necessary. A thousand years ago it would have been a monk's, a militant fanatic who would have turned his uncompromising back upon the world with actual joy and gone to a desert and passed the rest of his days and nights calmly and without an instant's self-doubt battling, not to save humanity about which he would have cared nothing, for whose sufferings he would have had nothing but contempt, but with his own fierce and unappeasable natural appetites. (p. 105)

The contrasts implicit in these parallels link Flem and Labove in much the same way that Flem and Eula are linked through Jody. The theme of love, which is first sounded in Labove's subsequent reactions to Eula, therefore, has definite reference to Flem. As Ann Hayes points out, "by what Labove is and understands, by what Eula is, Faulkner implies what Flem is not." [11] Flem's only goal is self-aggrandizement. Labove too lives solely for the day when he will pass through "the last door and . . . [face] the straight hard road with nothing between him and his goal save himself" (p. 116). When that time comes, however, he, unlike Flem, is touched by another person and finds himself helplessly "drawn back into the radius and impact of an eleven-year-old girl who, even while sitting with veiled eyes against the sun like a cat on the schoolhouse steps at recess and eating a cold potato, postulated that ungirdled quality of the very goddesses in his Homer and Thucydides: of being at once corrupt and immaculate, at once virgins and the mothers of warriors and of grown men" (p. 113).

To Labove, Eula is "the drowsing maidenhead symbol's self" (p. 114), bringing into "the bleak, ill-lighted, poorly-heated room dedicated to the harsh functioning of Protestant primary education a moist blast of spring's liquorish corruption, a pagan triumphal prostration before the supreme primal uterus" (pp. 113–114). To this man of "fierce and unappeasable natural appetites" (p. 105), she is the one thing that even his monastic determination cannot resist. His immediate reaction to her is desperation: "No. No. Not here. Dont leave her here" (p. 113). For two years he watches the reactions of his students to her "with what he thought was only rage" (p. 115). It is not until he is confronted with Eula's uterine symbol, a sweet potato, that he realizes "it was not on the school steps but in his mind that she had constantly been for two years now, that it had not been rage at all but terror, and that the vision of that gate which he had held up to himself as a goal was not a goal but just a point to reach, as the man fleeing a holocaust runs not for a prize but to escape destruction" (pp. 116–117). Arming himself with what sexual experience he can, he forfeits his virginity in a Memphis brothel, knowing at the time that "this would not help him either" (p. 117). In the face of Eula's "weary wisdom" it is his fate to be destroyed. "His was that quality lacking which no man can ever be completely brave or completely craven: the ability to see both sides of the crisis and visualize himself as already vanquished—itself inherent with its own failure and disaster" (p. 117).

Brooks says of Labove that "his is a special kind of lust, a lust in the head as well as in the glands, and it is perverse and obsessive." [12] In the next three years, he becomes "the monk indeed . . . the virile anchorite of old time" (p. 118), to whom the village is at once Gethsemane and Golgotha. As his stoic resistance intensifies, distortions are produced. He is imaged as a satyr, "his legs haired-over like those of a faun" (p. 118). It is his desire to possess Eula not as a wife but "one time as a man with a gangrened hand or foot thirsts after the axe-stroke which will leave him comparatively whole again" (p. 118). Wallowing his face against her seat in the schoolroom, he alternately longs to hurt Eula and to be hurt by her, to rape her and to be raped. "He was mad. He knew it" (p. 119).

In the perverse atmosphere of such distortions, it is fitting that Labove's vision of Eula's marriage be based on a grotesque paradox. The opposites that he imagines juxtaposed bear a distinct thematic relationship to the contrasts on which the earlier episodes are based, and prefigure, structurally as well as thematically, the fate to which Eula is to be subjected. Though mad, Labove perceives that the love goddess's consort ironically will be impotent.

> He could almost see the husband which she would someday have. He would be a dwarf, a gnome, without glands or desire, who would be no more a physical factor in her life than the owner's name on the fly-leaf of a book. There it was again, out of the books again, the dead defacement of type which had already betrayed him: the crippled Vulcan to that Venus, who would not possess her but merely own her by the single strength which power gave, the dead power of money, wealth, gewgaws, baubles, as he might own, not a picture, statue: a field, say. He saw it: the fine land rich and fecund and foul and eternal and impervious to him who claimed title to it, oblivious, drawing to itself tenfold the quantity of living seed its owner's whole life could have secreted and compounded, producing a thousand-fold the harvest he could ever hope to gather and save. (pp. 118–119)

The descriptions of Eula's future husband as a "dwarf" and of his relationship to her as her owner suggest direct references to Flem Snopes, the squat owner of herds and fields. In the dwarf's asexuality and exploitation of the land, the scope of Flem's amorality is further expanded.

Moreover, by imaging the "field" as impervious and "him who claimed title to it" as impotent, Labove ironically suggests his own inability to possess Eula. Like Flem, who has become a storekeeper, Labove has forsaken the land and farming and forfeited, thereby, the right to plow. His attack on Eula thus results in his own figurative emasculation. In an expansion of his metaphoric desire for relief from his obsession, Labove finds his "axe" and hacks "in almost an orgasm of joy at the dangling nerves and tendons of the gangrened member long after the first bungling blow" (p. 120). The "priapic hullabaloo" (p. 121) of the combat between Labove and Eula, however, is shattered by Eula's instinctive, passion-killing reaction: "Stop pawing me. . . . You old headless horseman Ichabod Crane" (p. 122). Her imperviousness to his advances denies him not only "penetration" but the "katharsis" of fighting her brother. Eula does not even think enough of Labove's attack on her to consider it worth mentioning to Jody. The bullet for which Labove longs, which will provide "proof in the eyes and beliefs of living men that that happened which did not" (p. 123), remains as bloodless as that which failed to harm the Negro of his memory. Denied even the recognition of having attempted an assault on Eula, Labove suffers an uncompromising defeat. Leaving Frenchman's Bend he leaves behind him the books in which he found the mythical figures to whom he compared Eula.

With the departure of Labove, the tone of the narrative shifts. Released from the vividly hallucinatory scrutiny of the anchorite, Eula becomes the center of adolescent attention. That which, in Labove's single response, was obsessive lust, is turned to passionate pride by the collective response of the community. This is not to suggest, however, that Eula's sexuality is any less insistent. Rather, it is reaffirmed by what Beck calls "a recurrence in modifying context." [13] In contrast to Labove's solitary and introverted longing through "the iron winter nights" (p. 118), the youths of the village swarm "through that spring [of the year Labove fled] and through the long succeeding summer of her fourteenth year . . . like wasps about the ripe peach which her full damp mouth resembled" (p. 127). Eula matures and develops now in the seasonal cycle of the fields to which the schoolmaster has compared her. She is seen with the "loud knot of loutish and belligerent adolescents" for the last time "in early September" (p. 129). By the "second spring," when she is fifteen, they have been replaced by young "men," who erupt "into her placid orbit like a stampede of wild cattle, trampling ruthlessly aside the children of last summer's yesterday" (p. 129). These, too, are dispossessed in their turn: "By the third summer the trace-galled mules had given way to the trotting horses and the buggies" (p. 131).

Each dispossession of a group of suitors is marked by the increased physical maturity and sophistication of the dispossesors. The accompanying intensification of each group's reaction to losing Eula is in direct proportion to the capacity of that group to feel the force of her appeal. The farm boys of the second summer court her collectively, "doggedly and vainly sitting each other out" (p. 130), and fight each other "with bare fists . . . silently and savagely and wash the blood off in the water and mount again and ride their separate ways, with their skinned knuckles and split lips and black eyes and for the time being freed even of rage and frustration and desire, beneath the cold moon, across the planted land" (p. 131). Replaced in the next summer, they jealously unite to protect from others what they themselves have not been able to attain. This alliance and the distinctions between its membership and those outsiders to whom it is in opposition suggest the scope of Eula's growing appeal within the community. Imaged in terms of the fertile summer fields, her growth is set forth dramatically through the increasingly intense reactions she elicits. In the face of her impassivity, desire turns to rage, frustration to protectiveness.

This uniquely moral atmosphere is further distorted during the summer of Eula's sixteenth year by the arrival of Hoake McCarron. One of the three suitors to appear in this third spring, McCarron soon establishes his preeminence when "last summer's vain and raging jetsam . . . divined or at least believed that there had never been but one buggy all the time" (p. 133). For his role as Eula's primary suitor, he is eminently qualified. In appearance "bold and handsome too . . . a little swaggering and definitely spoiled" (p. 135), he is the son of a dashing gambler and has the reputation of having seduced his college instructor's young wife. "This was he against whom, following the rout of the Memphis drummer, the youths of last summer's trace-galled mules rose in embattled concert to defend that [Eula's virginity] in which apparently they and the brother [Jody] both had no belief, even though they themselves had failed signally to disprove it" (p. 136). McCarron meets their every challenge with an almost preordained success, running them down with his mare, whipping them away from his buggy, and finally, pistol in hand, cursing them "in a pleasant, drawling, conversational voice," daring "any two of them to meet him down the road" (p. 136).

Rendered thus impotent by McCarron's ridicule, the youths abjure Jody's assistance in protecting Eula and send the adversary a "formal warning" (p. 136), a challenge, in a last, desperate effort to vindicate their manhood. Their frustration now approaches the pitch of Labove's before them.

> They could have told the brother but they did not, not because the brother would more than likely have turned upon the informers with physical violence. Like the teacher Labove, they would have welcomed that, they would have accepted that with actual joy. As with Labove, it would at least have been the same living flesh warm under furious impact, bruising, scoriating, springing blood, which, like Labove, was what they actually desired now whether they knew it or not. It was because they were already insulated against acceptance of the idea of telling him by the fact that their rage would be wasted then upon the agent of their vengeance and not the betrayer; they would have met the profferer of a mortal affronting and injury with their hands bound up in boxing gloves. So they sent McCarron a formal warning in writing with their names signed. (pp. 136–137)

Since the youths assume that McCarron has already accomplished the seduction of Eula, they must avenge not only the seduction but the affront to their manhood that it represents. This can only be accomplished in direct conflict with the "betrayer."

Ironically, the ensuing combat at the ford brings about the end that it was to avenge. Eula herself defeats three of the attackers, "springing from the buggy and with the reversed whip beating three of them back while her companion used the reversed pistol-butt against the wagon-spoke and the brass knuckles of the other two" (pp. 137–138). It is not until "later, years later" (p. 137) that this humiliation is related. In addition, this final extreme of violence provides the background of passionate response against which Eula at last takes a lover. Having been wakened from apathy for the first time by the battle at the ford, Eula remains sufficiently roused to "support, with her own braced arm from underneath, . . . [McCarron's] injured side" (p. 139) while he makes love to her. She takes as active a part in spotting her dress with her own blood as she did in spotting it with the blood of McCarron's attackers.

With the final arousal of "the drowsing maidenhead symbol's self" (p. 114), the intense atmosphere of physical reaction gives way to the comedy of emotional release. All three suitors of the third summer flee from Frenchman's Bend. "Although one of the three knew certainly one who was guilty, and the other two knew collectively two who were not, all three of them fled, secretly and by back roads probably, with saddle-bags or single hurried portmanteaus for traveling fast. One of them went because of what he believed the Varner men would do. The other two fled because they knew that the Varners would not do it. . . . By fleeing too, they put in a final and despairing bid for the guilt they had not compassed, the glorious shame of the ruin they did not do" (p. 140). In the highly burlesque scene that follows Jody's discovery of this "ruin," Eula is again the impassive and unconcerned figure of female stasis. To Jody's raving, she replies, "Stop shoving me. . . . I dont feel good" (p. 141). Mrs. Varner's concern is solely for the interruption of her nap: " 'Hold him till I get a stick of stove wood,' she gasped. 'I'll fix him. I'll fix both of them. Turning up pregnant and yelling and cursing here in the house when I am trying to take a nap!' " (p. 142). Will Varner finally quiets his "huge, bull-goaded, impotent and outraged" son with the comment, "Hell and damnation, all this hullabaloo and uproar because one confounded running bitch finally foxed herself. What did you expect—that she would spend the rest of her life just running water through it?" (pp. 143–144).

This crude bit of fatherly practicality is significant, as well, because of the setting in which it occurs. Jody and his father argue in "the ground-floor room which Varner still called his office though for the last two years now the clerk, Snopes, had slept on a cot in it" (p. 142). In the context of an argument between the eminently practical Will Varner and his raging, frustrated son, the juxtaposition of business office and Snopes domain signals the expedient to which Varner is quick to resort. Two days later Flem Snopes appears. Faintly "chewing," Flem seats himself in the buggy, not beside Eula but beside her physical property, a suitcase, and spits over the wheel of the moving buggy, holding his own suitcase on his knees "like the coffin of a baby's funeral" (p. 145). In Jefferson, they visit the bank and the chancery clerk's office before they do the justice of the peace. The entire affair is no more than a business transaction in which Flem trades his availability for a large check and the deed to the Old Frenchman place. He exploits Will Varner's need for a son-in-law in much the same way that he exploited Jody's fear of fire to gain a place as clerk in the store. In the process Varner proves himself unable to "risk fooling with them folks." Whereas Flem greets the loungers on the gallery with a jerk of his head "exactly as Will Varner himself did it" (p. 144) and proprietarily enters the store, Will only calls "a general greeting, short, perfectly inflectionless, unreadable" (p. 145) and remains in the buggy. Telling of what he saw in Jefferson, Vernon Tull is embarrassed to admit that Will Varner had to pay for the marriage license as well as for Eula's husband.

    In addition to the impact on Tull, Bookwright, and Armstid of Flem's bettering Will Varner, the marriage transaction greatly increases the scope of Flem's inhumanity. In contrast to the community's increasingly intense physical reactions to Eula's primal sexuality, Flem is physically insensible to her. There is such a complete absence of physical response in him, indeed, that Eula herself, at the age of fourteen, "knew him so well that she never had to look at him anymore" (p. 145). "In the rich deshabille . . . as if she had just been surprised from a couch of illicit love by a police raid, she would meet and pass him returning to his noon meal, in the hall, and he had never been" (p. 146). Without sexual responses, Flem does not exist for her. His impotence, while not amoral in itself, reinforces his amorality by rendering him yet more immune to appeals other than his own rapacity. By amorally exploiting Eula's pregnancy, Flem actually exploits her bravery and passion with McCarron and betrays the marshalled passions of the entire community. Having traded for her, Flem is not a husband but an owner, possessing her, as in Labove's tortured vision, "as he might own, not a picture, statue: a field, say" (pp. 118–119).

Now, as Beck points out, "murmurs of regret move across the community," [14] and V. K. Ratliff reappears to elucidate them with detached reflection. Seeing Eula depart on the train, "the calm beautiful mask beneath the Sunday hat . . . looking at nothing" (p. 147), he recalls Frenchman's Bend as it had been during the last heroic summer and describes it now as having lost the focus for response.

> If he had lived in Frenchman's Bend itself during that spring and summer, he would have known no more—a little lost village, nameless, without grace, forsaken, yet which wombed once by chance and accident one blind seed of the spendthrift Olympian ejaculation and, did not even know it, without tumescence conceived and bore—one bright brief summer, concentric, during which three fairly well-horsed buggies stood in steady rotation along a picket fence or spun along adjacent roads between the homes and the crossroads stores and the schoolhouses and churches where people gathered for pleasure or at least for escape, and then overnight and simultaneously were seen no more; then eccentric: buggies gone, vanished—a lean, loose-jointed, cotton-socked, shrewd, ruthless old man, the splendid girl with her beautiful masklike face, the froglike creature which barely reached her shoulder, cashing a check, buying a license, taking a train—a word, a single will to believe born of envy and old deathless regret, murmured from cabin to cabin above the washing pots and the sewing, from wagon to horseman in roads and lanes or from rider to halted plow in field furrows; the word, the dream and wish of all male under sun capable of harm—the young who only dreamed yet of the ruins they were still incapable of; the sick and the maimed sweating in sleepless beds, impotent for the harm they willed to do; the old, now-glandless earth-creeping, the very buds and blossoms, the garlands of whose yellowed triumphs had long fallen into the profitless dust, embalmed now and no more dead to the living world if they were sealed in buried vaults, behind the impregnable matronly calico of others' grandchildren's

grandmothers—the word, with its implications of lost triumphs
and defeats of unimaginable splendor—and which best: to have
that word, that dream and hope for future, or to have had need
to flee that word and dream, for past. (pp. 147–148)

The loss of Eula to what Labove envisioned as "a dwarf, a gnome,
without glands or desire" (p. 118) and to him whom Ratliff regards as a "froglike creature" is thus, in Ratliff's reflections,
mourned by the entire community with a singular sense of loss
commensurate with the pride and passion she formerly inspired.
In the backwash of passion spent and betrayed, even the proud
buggies of that heroic summer's suitors decay in sheds, gathering
dust, roosted in by chickens, and at last sold "to a Negro farm-
hand" (p. 148): "spilling children, no longer glittering, its wheels
wired upright in succession by crossed barrel staves until staves
and delicate wheels both vanished, translated apparently in motion at some point into stout, not new, slightly smaller wagon
wheels . . . [drawn by] a succession of spavined and bony horses
and mules in wire-and rope-patched harness" (p. 148).

Appropriately, the loss of Eula is accompanied also by a change
of season. The girl who ripened like a planted field through repeated springs and summers is gone: "it was now September. . . .
The air was hot, vivid and breathless—a final fierce concentration
of the doomed and dying summer" (pp. 148–149). This change is
not altogether to be regretted, however, for September, while it
marks the end of summer, and of Eula, also brings the harvest
season to the farm country of Frenchman's Bend. Returning, Ratliff drives past cotton "open and spilling into the fields. . . . the
constant surf of bursting bolls like piles in surf" (p. 148). Characteristically mulling over previous perceptions, he remembers
again "the bank, the courthouse, the station" (p. 149), sees again
"the calm beautiful mask . . . beyond a moving pane of glass,
then gone" (p. 149). In the context of the changing seasons, the
community's defeat seems less permanent, the loss of Eula less
extreme: "it was just meat, just gal-meat he thought, and God
knows there was a plenty of that, yesterday and tomorrow too"
(p. 149). He remembers the train window and Eula's face looking
out, a face that "had not been tragic, and now . . . was not even
damned" (p. 149), and suddenly Eula is associated with "the train

itself, which had served its day and schedule and so, despite the hard cars, the locomotive, no more existed" (p. 149). She is in Ratliff's refined perception "only another mortal natural enemy of the masculine race" (p. 149), moving in retrograde from existence to memory, "merely a part, a figment, of the concentric flotsam and jetsam of the translation" (p. 149). The moral universe is rejuvenatory, flowing from present to past, from future to present in a concentric unity. Juxtaposed against this translational cycle, standing outside it unaffected, "there remained only the straw bag, the minute tie, the constant jaw" (p. 149) of Flem Snopes.

In what Beck calls "the surrealistic mystery-play of Flem in hell," [15] Ratliff illumines the full implications of such amorality by taking to its logical conclusion the inevitability of Flem's successes. As is so often the case with Ratliff when he is affected by outraged indignation, his insights take the form of ironic country humor. In hell the devils discover that there is nothing left of the soul Flem traded them except *"a little kind of dried-up smear under one edge* [of the matchbox]" (pp. 149–150). Characteristically, Flem demands *"no more and no less than his legal interest according to what the banking and the civil laws states in black and white is hisn"* (p. 150). Moral law is never mentioned. Bribes are ineffectual: for the *"gratifications"* he requires only a spittoon, for the *"vanities"* only a bow tie. Figuratively a creation of the devil, Flem demands not paradise, but hell, and gets it. In the end Satan proves to be no more worthy to "risk fooling with them folks" than are the residents of Frenchman's Bend. " *'Who are you?'* he [Satan] *says, choking and gasping and his eyes a-popping up at him setting there with that straw suitcase on the Throne among the bright, crown-shaped flames. 'Take Paradise!' the Prince screams. 'Take it! Take it!' And the wind roars up and the dark roars down and the Prince scrabbling across the floor, clawing and scrabbling at that locked door, screaming. . . ."* (p. 153).

Narrated by the self-appointed commentator on men and affairs in Frenchman's Bend, and following as it does his compassionate reflections on Flem's "grazing up" of the mythically sexual Eula, this imaginative vision expresses the contrast between the amoral Flem and the moral community in which he performs his rapacious machinations. The inevitability of his successes and the cold assurance with which he accepts them reveal the humanity of his victims and the depth of emotion accompanying their defeats. The "surrealistic mystery-play" is in fact a bitter metaphoric iteration of Flem's career to date and of the "scrabbling" and "screaming" by which his rise is marked.

"The Long Summer": "The Old Job at the Old Stand"

IN BOOK three of *The Hamlet*, "The Long Summer," the implications of the betrayal of human passion represented in Flem's marriage to Eula are dramatically illustrated in the stories of Ike Snopes, Houston, and Mink Snopes. No matter how grotesque their situations or how self-interested their motives, Ike, Houston, and Mink exhibit the same fundamental passions that Eula, though not herself passionate, inspires in the community. Each, in varying degrees, is a responsive, generous, and dedicated lover possessed of an innate sense of honor. As such, each is vulnerable to betrayal by the same forces that betray Eula's suitors and the community. Whereas Eula's remote impassivity precludes community involvement with her, the common ground of emotion which the community shares with Ike, Houston, and Mink presupposes involvement. Thus, the exploitation of Eula is mourned, but only mourned, because by her nature she is beyond the scope of the community's affective intervention. Since, by their basic humanity, Ike, Houston, and Mink are well within the scope of possible intervention, their exploitation poses a challenge to the moral world. Intervention on their behalf will constitute moral affirmation; failure to intervene will signify self-betrayal and a denial of principled existence. Ultimately, then, the choice is between actively asserting morality and passively surrendering it.

Characteristically, it is V. K. Ratliff who recognizes and then rises to meet this moral challenge. In the aftermath of Eula's departure from Frenchman's Bend, he turns his attention to Will Varner, for whom, because of his part in the transaction, Eula's marriage to Flem represents compromise and defeat. Not only is Varner once again astride his horse rather than sitting in the buggy that he and Flem had driven, but he has given up the Old Frenchman place as well. To Ratliff, who was "a good deal nearer his [Varner's] son in spirit and intellect and physical appearance too than any of his own get" (p. 158), Varner's forfeiture of the very symbol of his proprietorship of Frenchman's Bend is a bitter disappointment, even though the price was "necessity and not cash" (p. 157). Eula's marriage to Flem is a "waste," "useless squandering" (p. 159), but Varner's willingness to give her to Flem signifies his capitulation to Snopesism, and Ratliff meets his old friend now "like a caller in a house of death" (p. 157). Snopeses abound. Although Flem himself is in Texas, his holdings in the community and the abundance of lesser Snopeses are constant reminders of him. Mink Snopes still tenant-farms Varner land, I. O. Snopes teaches in the Varner school, and in the Varner store there is a second Snopes clerk: "the new clerk exactly like the old one [Flem] but a little smaller, a little compacter, as if they had both been cut with the same die but in inverse order to appearance, the last first and after the edges of the die were dulled and spread a little—with his [the new clerk's] little, full, bright-pink mouth like a kitten's button and his bright, quick, amoral eyes like a chipmunk and his air of merry and incorrigible and unflagging conviction of the inherent constant active dishonesty of all men, including himself" (p. 160). This is Lump Snopes, whom Flem installed in the store in his place while Will Varner waited with his daughter in the wagon that would take them to Jefferson.

As these Snopeses spill from the store following Mink's unsuccessful suit against Houston, Ratliff's disappointment with Will Varner turns to indignant anger at the leniency shown Snopeses. Mink is fined only three dollars pasturage to reclaim his cow, and I. O.'s fine is no more than "the considerable balance of one uncompleted speech" (p. 161). Varner's adjudication of the case is as absent of justice as the suit itself and testifies, if not to his acceptance of Snopesism, at least to his unwillingness or inability to resist it. As T. Y. Greet correctly points out, "Ratliff, still rankled by the sacrifice of Eula, seizes at once on I. O.'s idiom for the most scathing comment he has yet made." [16]

> "Well well," Ratliff said. "Well well well. So Will couldn't do nothing to the next succeeding Snopes [I. O.] but stop him from talking. Not that any more would have done any good.

Snopes can come and Snopes can go, but Will Varner looks
like he is fixing to snopes forever. Or Varner will Snopes
forever—take your pick. What is it the fellow says? off with the
old and on with the new; the old job at the old stand, maybe
a new fellow doing the jobbing but it's the same old stern
getting reamed out?" Bookwright was looking at him.
    "If you would stand closer to the door, he could hear you
a heap better," he said.
    "Sholy," Ratliff said. "Big ears have little pitchers, the world
beats a track to the rich man's hog-pen but it aint every family
has a new lawyer, not to mention a prophet. Waste not want
not, except that a full waist dont need no prophet to prophesy
a profit and just whose." Now they were all watching him—
the smooth, impenetrable face with something about the eyes
and the lines beside the mouth which they could not read.
    "Look here," Bookwright said. "What's the matter with you?"
(pp. 161–162)

Following this public contumely, Ratliff illustrates the ramifications of Varner's surrender by picturing forth the sexual habits of
the creature whose machinations that surrender implicitly sanctions. Eula's treatment, even to the store-shelf setting, will be
exactly that which Ratliff imagines the ignorant Negress to have
received at Flem's hands behind the counter of the store. By comparing her to a Negress paying with her body for a tin of lard,
Ratliff at once diminishes Eula's sexuality as a factor in Flem's
life and reinforces the profit motive as a basis for all of Flem's
responses. The animal imagery Ratliff uses to describe the Negress,
moreover, prefigures the Ike-cow relationship and provides contrasts to it. The Negress is a "black brute from the field with the
field sweat still drying on her that she dont know it's sweat she
smells because she aint never smelled nothing else, just like a mule
dont know it's mule he smells for the same reason" (p. 164). Flem's
union with her is base, vulgar, even usurious, and is described in
raw, brutal terms that are totally antithetical to the poetry of Ike's
love affair. The story is even interrupted by a reference to Ike in
Lump Snopes's announcement of the salacious occurrence now
taking place in Mrs. Littlejohn's barn.
    Finally, the extent of Ratliff's outrage and its end result are
suggested in the fact that he chooses as Flem's helpless victim a
Negress. Negroes, as Ratliff comments earlier after hearing the

story of Flem's usurious treatment of the Negro sawmill workers, are at "the bottom" of the social scale (p. 71), and the exploitation of their helplessness is a particularly grievous affront to human dignity that demands retribution. In the case of the sawmill workers, Ratliff is further incensed by the unwillingness of Tull and Bookwright to intervene and so asserts his own will through the medium of the goat trade. Here, in the only other story in the novel in which a Negro takes a significant part, Ratliff is equally aroused, and Tull and Bookwright, by their passive acceptance of what they recognize to be cruel inhumanity toward Ike, counterpoint Ratliff's mood as before.

> "Go on and see it," Bookwright said again, harshly and violently.
> "It looks like I'll have to, since aint nobody going to tell me," Ratliff said. He moved toward the steps. The group was now well on ahead, hurrying along the fence. Ratliff began to descend. He was still talking. He continued to talk as he went down the steps, not looking back; nobody could have told whether he was actually talking to the men behind him or not, if he was talking to anyone or not: "—goes and puts the bar up on the inside and comes back and this here black brute from the field with the field sweat still drying on her. . . ." (p. 164)

This mood requires only an actual victim of Snopes exploitation to turn Ratliff's verbalized reflections to active self-assertion.

Now when the atmosphere of dangerous unrest is at an intense pitch, September gives way to an earlier season when "winter became spring and the spring itself advanced" (p. 164), and the loveless relationships previously recounted find contrasts in the idyll of Ike and the cow. As Brooks points out, this love affair is "grotesque and terrible," and yet "there is more here than the mere needs of blind animality." [17] The bare fact of the idiot's sodomy is pathetic, even repulsive, but the poetry given this story obscures no depravity. Rather, it elevates Ike's inchoate virtues of gentleness, love, and devotion to a standard against which all other lovers are implicitly judged. In Melvin Backman's words, "Ike Snopes [is] the truest lover in the novel. For Labove and McCarron love was lust, for Flem a commodity to be bartered. Only in an idiot's passion has Faulkner found an unbrutalized and

uncorrupted love, as if the idiot represented a state of nature." [18]
   In moral terms Ike does indeed represent a "state of nature."
In the same way that Eula represents an unattainable ideal and
Flem unfathomable inhumanity, Ike is the embodiment of the
primordial natural love that is the basis of fellow-feeling and community. Lacking the capacity for such love, Eula and Flem stand
outside the human community, impenetrable figures whose stature
is conveyed largely through external description and the reactions
of the community to them. In contrast, Ike's love is demonstrated
in terms of his own clearly visible actions, and he has an emotional inner life, which, though obscured from community view
by the fact that he is an idiot, is artlessly open and finds expression
in the lyricism that is its mode. Its metaphor is the natural world.
Terror exists "only during that moment after the false dawn,
that interval's second between it and the moment which birds and
animals know: when the night at last succumbs to day" (p. 165).
Anticipation comes with "the growing visibility, the graduation
from gray through primrose to the morning's ultimate gold" as he
lies in the "creekside mist . . . in the drenched myriad waking life
of grasses" (p. 165). Joy is sensory, "smelling and even tasting the
rich, slow, warm barn-reek milk-reek, the flowing immemorial
female, hearing the slow planting and the plopping suck of each
deliberate cloven mud-spreading hoof, invisible still in the mist
loud with its hymeneal choristers" (p. 165).
   Several critics have suggested that with the introduction of Ike
and his cow the theme of love established through Eula is unhap-
pily wrenched from the mythic to the pitifully grotesque.[19] This
is hardly the case. The generosity of Ike's love is to some extent a
standard against which Eula's impassivity may be measured, and
there are imagistic parallels between the two stories, notably in
the fact that Eula is often described in bovine terms. But Ike's
love affair is not a diminished iteration of Eula's any more than
it is specifically an expansion of Mink's or Houston's. In fact, the
strength and beauty of the idyll are to be found in the very rich-
ness and variety of its connotations. Based in unprofaned love, it
relates to all human relationships and thereby provides one source
of the novel's structural and thematic unity.
   This is particularly true of the events that suggest contrasts
with Flem Snopes. Flem never admits to anything, to the extent

that he does not once speak his own name. Ike guilelessly tries to tell Houston who he is, but mangles his name so badly in the attempt that it bears little relation to Snopes: " 'Ike H-mope,' he said. 'Ike H-mope' " (p. 167). He is hardly even a Snopes in name. Furthermore, he instinctively repudiates the money given him by Houston for saving the cow from the fire. Three times Ike "fumbled at the buttoned pocket" (p. 177) before he is able to extract the coin. In dropping it, "he made no false motion with the hand which held the coin . . . though who to know what motion, infinitesimal and convulsive, of supreme repudiation there might have been, its impulse gone, vanished with the movement" (p. 177). Immediately after the coin vanishes from his hand, Ike steps off the bridge into the ditch below, "though it was doubtless a continuation of the instinct, the inherited constant awareness of gravity, which caused him to look under the bridge for the coin— if he were looking for it as he squatted in the weeds" (p. 178). He squats for a time, "pulling at the weeds" (p. 178), until "watching him you would have said he did not want to find the coin. And then you would have said, known, that he did not intend to find it" (p. 178). This incident carries substantial symbolic meaning for it establishes the fundamental contrast between Flem's valuing of money and Ike's devaluing of it in relation to the cow he has lost. Such implicit contrasts as this are basic to thematic development and structural unity throughout the novel, and in this case, the contrast serves to characterize both Flem and Ike. Flem is recalled in the attitudes of his opposite.

In the reactions of Mrs. Littlejohn and Houston to Ike and his love for the cow, there are further contrasts to Flem. Whereas Flem is Ike's legal guardian and robs him of his ten-dollar inheritance by lending the money at usurious rates of interest, Mrs. Littlejohn is his nominal guardian and keeps for him the money given her by Ratliff after the goat trade. Ignorant of the amount, she gives it to Houston for the cow solely to benefit Ike. " 'What else could he [Ike] do with it?' she said. 'What else did he ever want?' " (p. 195). Houston, too, shows a measure of compassion toward the idiot, which is itself heightened by contrast to the reaction of the violent farmer from whom Ike steals grain. Whereas the farmer beats Ike with a stick, Houston cautions his dog not to harm Ike. "He spoke to the dog. 'Take him [Ike] out of here.

Easy, now' " (p. 167). Enraged at the theft of his grain, the farmer demands a pound fee for the return of the cow. Houston is initially angered at the disappearance of his cow, but he pays the pound fee to reclaim her and offers to give her to Ike without payment. Prevailed upon to accept Ike's inheritance in return for his gift, Houston, like Mrs. Littlejohn, does not count the money.

This is not to say that either Houston or Mrs. Littlejohn sanctions sodomy. Their bond is one of human compassion for a fellow being less fortunate than themselves, a mutual recognition of human frailty and pity for it. Their reactions to Ike contrast with Flem's profiteering exploitation of him, which, in turn, prefigures Ike's ultimate exploitation at the hands of the lesser Snopeses. The generosity by which Houston and Mrs. Littlejohn seek to serve Ike ironically provides for the situation through which his love is most inhumanly profaned. Moving toward Mrs. Littlejohn's barn behind the crowd of men, Ratliff realizes the full implications of what he does not even need to see to know instinctively that it represents a fatal threat to principled existence which must be challenged.

He knew not only what he was going to see but that, like Bookwright, he did not want to see it, yet, unlike Bookwright, he was going to look. He did look, leaning his face in between two other heads; and it was as though it were himself inside the stall with the cow, himself looking out of the blasted tongueless face at the row of faces watching him who had been given the wordless passions but not the specious words. When they looked around at him, he already held the loose plank, holding it as if he were on the point of striking at them with it. But his voice was merely sardonic, mild even, familiar, cursing as Houston had: not in rage and not even in outraged righteousness.

"I notice you come to have your look too," one said.

"Sholy," Ratliff said. "I aint cussing you folks. I'm cussing all of us," lifting the plank and fitting it back into the orifice. "Does he—What's his name? that new one? Lump—does he make you pay again each time, or is it a general club ticket good for every performance?" There was a half-brick on the ground beside the wall. With it he drove the nails back while they watched him, the brick splitting and shaling, crumbling away onto his hands in fine dust—a dry, arid, pallid dust of the color of shabby sin and shame, not splendid, not magnificent like blood, and fatal.

"That's all," he said. "It's over. This here engagement is completed." (p. 196)

All men share in the "wordless passion" represented in Ike's love of his cow; to such an extent, indeed, that the profanation of one man's love, no matter how grotesque, is a profanation of all human love and constitutes self-degradation. For the moral community, founded on love, this is self-destructive.

It is, therefore, through no sense of outraged morality that Ratliff now acts to deprive Ike of his cow. Rather, it is to affirm what is "splendid" in love over the "shabby sin and shame," in which light Ike's love has been placed by the machinations of Snopeses. In this he is no less compassionate than Mrs. Littlejohn. He tells her, "You dont need to tell me he aint got nothing else. I know that. Or that I can sholy leave him have at least this much. I know that too. Or that besides, it aint any of my business. I know that too, just as I know that the reason I aint going to leave him have what he does have is simply because I am strong enough to keep him from it. I am stronger than him. Not righter. Not any better, maybe. But just stronger" (p. 198). Ratliff's strength lies in his capacity to see beyond the immediate fact of Ike's exploitation and to subordinate his compassion for Ike to his commitment to preserve morality. That it is the profferers of temptation rather than the tempted who threaten morality is clearly evident in the fact that Ratliff directs his efforts at I.O. and Lump Snopes rather than at the community. As in the goat trade, Ratliff's intervention takes the form of a barter. Shrewdly pointing out the possible consequences to I.O. of Lump's sideshow, Ratliff forces a situation in which one Snopes is obliged to intercede against another in order to protect his own interests. I.O. is quick to see that his position as schoolmaster is jeopardized by Ike's "stock-diddling" and takes action immediately to put an end to this threat to his personal well-being. In the process he deprives Lump of a lucrative business in ticket sales and cheats the un-Snopes-like Eck out of sixteen dollars and eighty cents, the amount of Ike's inheritance that was paid for the cow. That all of this should be done in the name of morality is a paradox that only intensifies the truly moral dilemma at issue. Justifying to Eck the purchase of Ike's cow, I.O. as-

serts, "It aint the beef and the hide. That's only a circumstance.
It's the moral value we are going to get out of it. . . [the Snopes
name] aint never been aspersed yet by no living man. That's got
to be kept pure as a marble monument for your children to grow
up under" (p. 204). Playing upon the Snopes ruthlessness and
greed, Ratliff exacts some measure of retribution at the same time
that his purposes are so neatly served. His ploy is entirely successful. Through the strength of Ratliff's moral conviction, Ike's love
is ended in order that the love of the moral community may be
affirmed.

In the case of Houston, a more mature but no less dedicated
love is snuffed out with tragic results. When he enters school at
the age of fourteen, Houston is already a man, acquainted with
masculine vices and capable of running his father's farm. Although
he drinks whiskey and has a Negro mistress, "he was not wild, he
was merely unbitted yet; not high-spirited so much as possessed
of that strong lust, not for life, not even for movement, but for
that fetterless immobility called freedom" (p. 205). His freedom
is threatened, however, by Lucy Pate. Against her "steadfast and
undismayable will to alter and improve and remake," Houston
struggles with "furious resistance" (p. 206); his "was a feud, a
gage, wordless, uncapitulating, between that unflagging will not
for love or passion but for the married state, and that furious and
as unbending one for solitariness and freedom" (p. 207). For two
years Houston tries to "efface and exorcise it [Lucy's face] beyond
that of the Negress paramour but it still remained, constant, serene, not reproachful nor even sad nor even angry, but already
forgiving him before forgiveness had been dared or earned; waiting, tranquil, terrifying" (p. 209). At sixteen he flees in desperation to Texas, eventually taking a prostitute to live with him.
Their relationship, though founded upon mutual admiration,
physical satisfaction, and financial feasibility, is loveless, and Houston returns at last to the face which "it had been years now since
he had even remembered that he had forgotten" (p. 211). He
returns, in short, to the human community from which his indomitable masculine independence previously alienated him, prepared after thirteen years of alienation to assume his moral responsibility to love. "He was bitted now, even if it did not show
so much yet. There was still the mark of space and solitude in

his face, but fading a little, rationalised and corrupted even into something consciously alert even if it was not fearful; the beast, prime solitary and sufficient out of the wild fields, drawn to the trap and knowing it to be a trap, not comprehending why it was doomed but knowing it was, and not afraid now—and not quite wild" (p. 214).

It is Houston's tragedy that he cannot totally abdicate the fetterless freedom which had been his but requires about him the symbols of his former state. Although he borrows money, builds a new house, and marries Lucy Pate, he buys a stallion, "as if for a wedding present to her, though he never said so. Or if that blood and bone and muscles represented that polygamous and bitless masculinity which he had relinquished, he never said that. And if there were any among his neighbors and acquaintances—Will Varner or Ratliff perhaps—who discerned that this was the actual transference, the deliberate filling of the vacancy of his abdication, they did not say it either" (p. 214). When the stallion kills Lucy, Houston shoots it, "running first into the stall with the now frenzied animal with nothing but an open pocket knife, until the Negro grappled with him and persuaded him to wait for the pistol to be fetched from the house" (p. 215). Grieving for her "in black, savage, indomitable fidelity" (p. 205), he rids himself of the last vestiges of community membership by selling all but his house, living alone, and avoiding the moonlight, which still represents for him the epitome of the love now lost. " 'I dont understand it,' he would say. 'I dont know why. I wont ever know why. But You cant beat me. I am strong as You are. You cant beat me' " (pp. 216–217). Having accepted love after long resistance to it, he loses it because of his fundamentally selfish unwillingness to be satisfied with just love. By furnishing himself with the stallion, symbol of his pride, he deprives himself of both pride and love and is left to rage against the undefined "You" that he perceives to be tormenting him.

In the ensuing four years, weariness is his self-prescribed penance, and its implicit effect is the abnegation of that fellow-feeling upon which community is founded. Alone at night, drinking whiskey from a stone jug, he is "profane, intolerant, argumentative, with no challenge to be rebutted and no challenger to be vanquished and overcome" (p. 216). Thus, when Mink Snopes at-

tempts the relatively petty deception of wintering his cow on
Houston's land and trying to reclaim it as an accidental stray,
Houston does not possess sufficient flexibility to compromise the
issue. He reacts in the same manner as the outraged farmer who
claimed from him a pound fee for Ike's cow: he demands that
Mink pay pasturage. Instead of attempting a settlement, Houston
produces a gun, places it on a fence post, and dares Mink to race
him to it. When Mink takes the matter to court, Houston is upheld and the cow impounded, thus preparing the way for Mink's
revenge. Lying mortally wounded in the road, Houston is as proud
and intolerant as ever: " 'God damn it, couldnt you even borrow
two shells, you fumbling ragged—' and [he] put the world away"
(p. 217). Only in death is he capable of weeping: "his eyes, still
open to the lost sun, glazed over with a sudden well and run of
moisture which flowed down the alien and unremembering cheeks
too, already drying, with a newness as of actual tears" (p. 217).

In Mink, Ike's idyllic love and Houston's masculine pride are
distorted into an intense self-assertiveness borne of a lifetime of
rage and frustration. As Millgate points out, "each story . . .
[merges] smoothly into its successor: Ike's beloved cow belongs
at first to Houston, Houston himself is murdered by Mink." [20]
Ironically this brutal murder, in the motivation for it and its even-
tual outcome, establishes Mink's fundamental humanity and binds
him to the community of which Ike and Houston are a part.
Earlier in the novel, Ratliff characterizes Mink as "a different
kind of Snopes like a cotton-mouth is a different kind of snake"
(p. 91), and by his cold-blooded murder of the man whom he
tried to cheat he is reminiscent of no one so much as Ab Snopes
of the barn-burning episode. After losing a court case to him, Ab
burned De Spain's barn as an assertion of his twisted notion of
his rights. As Ratliff points out, however, Ab was not always
"soured" and had once taken pride in himself and loved his wife
enough to admit losing a horse trade in order to retrieve for her
a prized milk separator. Mink, too, is asserting his rights as he
interprets them when he murders Houston. Having sued for the
return of his cow and lost, Mink shoots Houston for "the vindica-
tion of his rights and the liquidation of his injuries" (p. 218).
Having shot him, "it was no blind, instinctive, and furious desire
for flight which he had to combat and curb. On the contrary.

What he would have liked to do would be to leave a printed placard on the breast itself: *This is what happens to the men who impound Mink Snopes's cattle,* with his name signed to it" (p. 218). He interprets the fact that he must hide the body as a part of "that conspiracy to frustrate and outrage his rights as a man and his feelings as a sentient creature" (p. 218). As with Ab, human feeling and love has been driven from Mink by an endless succession of tenant cabins and the abject poverty, physical and spiritual, which they represent. Returning home, he mounts to the house "through the yellow and stunted stand of his corn, yellow and stunted because he had had no money to buy fertilizer to put beneath it and owned neither the stock nor the tools to work it properly with and had had no one to help him with what he did own in order to gamble his physical strength and endurance against his body's livelihood not only with ordinary climate but with the incredible spring of which the dry summer was the monstrous abortion, which had rained every day from the middle of May into July, as if the zodiac too had stacked cards against him" (p. 220). Violence is the logical end of unbearable oppression. From Mink's standpoint it can hardly matter that Houston was within his legal rights to impound the cow or that he, Mink, was wrong. As Backman correctly asserts, Mink "pulled the trigger not only against the man who had impounded his yearling but against the whole scheme of his existence." [21]

The ambush of Houston thus becomes, symbolically, the medium by which Mink asserts his right to a place in the moral community. As Brooks states, "Mink has with all his bitterness and viciousness, a sense of honor. It may be little better than a cross-grained pride, but it is at least that. Having really nothing else, Mink has to hold on to this. And the implication is that because it is human it is better than the kind of honor that I. O. Snopes or Flem Snopes displays." [22] Like idiot Ike and proud Houston, Mink too has an inner emotional life, and it exhibits itself in spite of his outwardly stoical reaction to the murder. As a young man he left home romantically in search of the sea with its "drowned intact golden galleons and the unattainable deathless seamaids" (p. 236). Married to the nymphomaniac daughter of a lumber-camp foreman, a woman in whom "he saw not a nympholept but the confident lord of a harem" (p. 237), Mink bases his love affair solely on physical passion and the assertion of his masculinity. Yet he is still tortured years after the marriage by the "loud soundless invisible shades of the nameless and numberless men. . . . the cuckolding shades" (p. 221). Although he cannot hope to escape without money, he spurns the ten dollars that his wife prostitutes herself to get for him, demanding, "Did you sell Will something for it, or did you just take it out of his pants while he was asleep? Or was it Jody?" (p. 240).

In similar fashion Mink refuses to prostitute the self-assertion of personal pride, symbolized in his murder of Houston, by robbing Houston's corpse. Like Ike, he repudiates money. By rejecting Lump's suggestion that they recover Houston's wallet and by resisting Lump's efforts to find the hiding place and thus recover it for himself, Mink reaffirms the fundamental dignity that he found in murdering Houston. He asks simply to be let alone. When Lump insists on exploiting the murder, however, Mink is forced to fight him, knocking him unconscious and uncovering the body a final time to put it forever out of Lump's reach. By so doing he brings about his own capture: "It was as though . . . it was that humanity which had caused him to waste three hours in hope that the cousin would tire and go away instead of striking the other over the head when he ran past the tree where he had lost the axe, which had brought him to this" (p. 250). Sheriff Hampton finds him at dawn, still struggling with Houston's maddened dog.

That Mink has in some measure achieved the dignity which he sought by murdering Houston is evident in the contrasting reactions of Hampton and the deputy. To the deputy, Mink is simply a ruthless killer for whom lynching would be a fitting end. Hampton, however, takes Mink to Jefferson by the long route, against the deputy's inclination, to avoid a lynch threat. He shows concern for Mink's comfort, feeding him on the way and providing him an opportunity to ride part of the way in the shade out of the sun. When Mink attempts suicide by throwing himself under the surrey wheels in an attempt to break his neck, the deputy shouts "Break! God damn it, break! Break!" (p. 257), but Hampton grapples with him, stops the surrey, and revives the prisoner. Arriving in Jefferson, Hampton orders the deputy to "Jump. . . . Lift him out" (p. 257). In all of this Hampton shows a compassion for Mink as a fellow human being that complements Mink's own conception of himself and of his motivation in killing Houston. As a human being capable of pride and honor, he is vulnerable to exploitation and must struggle to defend himself and assert, in some way, his innate dignity. Even when he is imprisoned with a Negro road gang, his unflagging belief in his own rights is undiminished. "Are they going to feed them niggers before they do a white man? he thought, smelling the coffee and the ham" (p. 258).

With Mink in prison the last of the long summer's passion is spent. Fall gives forth one last burst of Indian summer during which "the ardor-wearied earth, ancient Lilith, reigned, throned and crowned amid the old invincible courtesan's formal defunction" (p. 259) before giving way at last to winter. Mink's wife and children come to Jefferson, brought by Ratliff and cared for by him with "not pity: rather, concern" (p. 259), but although they visit Mink regularly, his faith is placed elsewhere, in the blood ties of the clan. He refuses "not only bond (if he could have made one) but counsel. He had stood between two officers—small, his face like a mask of intractability carved in wood, wasted and almost skeleton-thin—before the committing magistrate, and he might not even have been present, hearing or perhaps not hearing himself being arraigned, then at a touch from one of the officers turning back toward the jail, the cell" (p. 259). Seeing "the two small grimed hands, immobile and clasping loosely the bars of the jail window at a height not a great deal above that at which a child would have held them" (p. 259), Ratliff senses wherein Mink's one hope for freedom lies and knows that hope to be vain. "Waiting for Flem Snopes, he thought. For Flem Snopes" (p. 260). As winter sets in Ratliff still insists that Mink's wife and children remain in his care, knowing that Flem will not respond to Mink's need of him. " 'Does he still think—' He stopped himself. He said, 'You aint heard yet when Flem will be back, have you?' She didn't answer. He didn't expect her to. 'You will need to save all you can,' he said" (p. 260).

The loyalty of the wife and Ratliff's concerned, compassionate care for her and her children are in direct contrast to the vain hope for salvation that Mink nourishes and the lack of reaction that his plight elicits from his kinsmen. Earlier in the novel the wife chides her husband for his faith in clan loyalty: Flem, she ways, would "let you rot and die right here and glad of it, and you know it!

Your own kin you're so proud of because he works in a store and wears a necktie all day! Ask him to give you a sack of flour even and see what you get. Ask him! Maybe he'll give you one of his old neckties someday so you can dress like a Snopes too!" (p. 74). Now, certain that no aid will come from the clan, Mink's wife takes a job in the hotel and prostitutes herself to raise money for Mink's defense. She and the children continue to visit him each day, and "that was when it occurred to him [Ratliff] how not once had any of his kin—old Ab or the schoolmaster or the blacksmith or the new clerk—come in to see" Mink (p. 261). When winter reaches its height in the iron cold of December, Ratliff tells himself, "Now they dont even need to have to not come in to see him. . . . For a man to drive them twenty miles in from Frenchman's Bend just on a errand of mercy, even a Snopes dont have to excuse himself from it" (p. 261). Yet Mink still clings to the bars of the jail window.

In March Eula returns with her child, sent home by Flem months too soon to justify the baby's legitimacy to even the most credulous observer. The insensitivity that this attaches to Flem only heightens his already obvious insensitivity to the demands of blood ties. Discussing Mink with the yeomanry of Frenchman's Bend, Ratliff sardonically points out that Mink cannot be waiting for Flem "Because Flem aint coming back here until that trial is over and finished. . . . He aint coming back here where Mink's wife can worry him or folks can talk about him for leaving his cousin in jail. There's some things even a Snopes wont do. I dont know just exactly what they are, but they's some 'somewhere" (pp. 265–266). In contrast to what Mink's wife and Ratliff *have* done in Mink's behalf, Flem's heedless disregard for his kinsman is illustrative of an inhumanity that is the more profound for being premeditated. It constitutes a denial and negation, not only of blood ties and human community, but of those individual rights and that dignity which Mink strove to assert and achieve by murdering Houston.

Despite the profoundly inhuman implications of Flem's unresponsiveness, however, the moral world is yet capable of regeneration and self-affirmation. Significantly, this affirmation takes the form of an assertion of the innate value of clanship and the necessity for generosity and compassion in the moral community.

Ratliff feels impelled to visit the idiot, Ike, and finds him still in Mrs. Littlejohn's barn with "the battered wooden effigy of a cow such as children receive on Christmas" resting on his overalled knees (p. 266). It is a gift from Ike's cousin, the un-Snopes-like Eck, who paid not only the twenty dollars to take the cow from him but an additional twenty-five cents to supply some measure of substitute as well. To Ratliff's question, "You bought him that too?" Eck replies, "Yes. I felt sorry for him. I thought maybe anytime he would happen to start thinking, that ere toy one would give him something to think about" (p. 267).

"The Peasants": "By God, You Cant Beat Him"

COMMENTING early in *The Hamlet* on Flem Snope's initial financial transactions with the Varners and the Negro sawmill workers, Ratliff states: "So he's working the top and the bottom [of the social scale] both at the same time. At that rate it will be a while yet before he has to fall back on you ordinary white folks in the middle" (p. 71). In book four, "The Peasants," the "ordinary white folks" and Ratliff himself are exploited with premeditated cunning as Flem strikes directly at the heart of the moral community: the industrious, often nameless tenant farmers and small land owners who comprise the body of Frenchman's Bend. No longer is he the manipulator of confusing trades or the petty offerer of menial loans at usurious rates of interest. Nor is he satisfied, as in the past, to rely for personal gain on intimidation or chance opportunities. The years of slow and secret acquisition, which culminated in the transaction for Eula, have made him a powerful financial force in the community, the object of fear and wonder. As rapacious and insensitive as before, he is now fully mature in the ways of self-aggrandizement. Selecting the weaknesses of his victims with uncanny precision and exploiting them with inexorable inhumanity, Flem completely captures the imagination of the male population by offering for sale a string of wild ponies, an irresistible symbol of masculine pride and honor. By operating through the agency of the Texan, he avoids legal responsibility for this transaction; moral responsibility he disregards, as usual. Brooks says, "The people of Frenchman's Bend are stirred up to buy what they do not want and cannot afford and will not be able to use. It is Flem, or course, who is the entrepreneur." [23]

Throughout the novel, horses and horse trading are associated with the principle of masculinity. Two notable examples are Ab Snopes's trade with Pat Stamper, into which he enters with "the entire honor and pride of the science and pastime of horse-trading in Yoknapatawpha County depending upon him to vindicate it" (p. 34), and Houston's purchase of the stallion which represents for him "that polygamous and bitless masculinity which he had relinquished" (p. 214). The "peasants" are no less susceptible to the lure of horses, and although Flem's Texas ponies are obviously dangerous, untamed and untamable, they immediately capture the imagination of the men of Frenchman's Bend. The ponies are "wild as deer, deadly as rattlesnakes" (p. 271), and when the Texan releases them into the corral, he vanishes "into a kaleidoscopic maelstrom of long teeth and wild eyes and slashing feet" (p. 274). Yet the watching men are enthralled by the circus scene before them and linger through the fading afternoon and evening in rapt attention.

In concert with their enchanted mood, the land becomes moonridden as evening advances, and the men fall completely under the spell of the fantastic ponies. "The moon was almost full then. When supper was over and they had gathered again along the veranda, the alteration was hardly one of visibility even. It was merely a translation from the lapidary-dimensional of day to the treacherous and silvery receptivity in which the horses huddled in mazy camouflage, or singly or in pairs rushed, fluid, phantom, and unceasing, to huddle again in mirage—like clumps from which came high abrupt squeals and the vicious thudding of hooves" (p. 276). In "the dreaming lambence of the moonlight" the pear tree across the road is "in full and frosty bloom, the twigs and branches springing not outward from the limbs but standing motionless and perpendicular above the horizontal boughs like the separate and upstreaming hair of a drowned woman sleeping upon the uttermost floor of the windless and tideless sea" (p. 277). In this intensely imaginative atmosphere, the men reminisce about such legendary horse traders as Anse McCallum and romanticize his trade for wild ponies until Ratliff brings them up with "a sound, harsh, sardonic, not loud" (p. 277).

Ratliff is laughing, for in their apparently casual conversation he recognizes the degree to which the men are enthralled by the horses and the attempts at self-deception that their memory of Anse's horses represents. His laugh is seconded by the song of a mockingbird. The men sit "stubborn, convinced, and passive, like children who have been chidden" (p. 277). Almost guiltily the talk changes to crops and trees, but Ratliff draws it back to horses with more explicit warnings. " 'And if I was you,' Ratliff said, 'that's just exactly where I would be come sunup tomorrow [in their own pastures]. Which of course you aint going to do. I reckon there aint nothing under the sun or in Frenchman's Bend neither that can keep you folks from giving Flem Snopes and that Texas man your money' " (p. 278). When this warning is ignored and Eck Snopes is unable to offer insights into the ownership of the ponies, Ratliff retires with a final unheeded caution.

> "All right. You folks can buy them critters if you want to. But me, I'd just as soon buy a tiger or a rattlesnake. And if Flem Snopes offered me either one of them, I would be afraid to touch it for fear it would turn out to be a painted dog or a piece of garden hose when I went up to take possession of it. I bid you one and all goodnight." He entered the house. They did not look after him, though after a while they all shifted a little and looked down into the lot, upon the splotchy, sporadic surge and flow of the horses, from among which from time to time came an abrupt squeal, a thudding blow. In the pear tree the mockingbird's idiot reiteration pulsed and purled.
> "Anse McCallum made a good team outen the two of hisn," the first man said. "They was a little light. That was all." (p. 279)

By the simple expedient of choosing ponies to sell, Flem has awakened in his prospective customers the irresistible urge to buy, an urge so powerful that even the obvious viciousness of the horses and Ratliff's evocations of Flem's morals as a trader are not sufficient to deter them.

When the auction begins on the following day, more than fifty men are present to discuss the dangers inherent in dealing with Flem Snopes, to witness the close escape of Eck and his son from

the corral, to comment on the viciousness of the horses, and finally to buy them "for sums ranging from three dollars and a half to
eleven and twelve dollars" (p. 293). Although the tension slowly
mounts among the men, the women remain unaffected. Throughout the auction Mrs. Littlejohn comes and goes with her washing,
in calm and thrifty contrast to the captivated men at the corral
who stand "with, buttoned close in their overalls, the tobacco-
sacks and worn purses, the sparse silver and frayed bills hoarded
a coin at a time in the cracks of chimneys or chinked into the
logs of walls" (p. 286). Ironically, the poorest among them are
more unreasonably affected than the more solvent, and in the case
of Henry Armstid the desire to own a horse results in actual madness. In him are represented the ultimate, pathetic ramifications of
the need for masculine assertiveness, and the results of his mania
are illustrative of the amorality of his tempter. Over the anguished objections of his wife, Armstid pays his family's last five
dollars for one of the ponies, striking his wife when she objects
and daring the other bidders to fight him if they top his bid. By
the end of the day, "the mad look in his eyes had a quality glazed
now and even sightless" (p. 293), and he drives his wife into the
corral to aid in catching the horse he has bought. When she fails
to turn the galloping pony, he strikes her with a coiled plow line.
" 'Why didnt you head him?' he said. 'Why didnt you?' He struck
her again; she did not move, not even to fend the rope with a
raised arm. The men along the fence stood quietly, their faces
lowered as though brooding upon the earth at their feet. Only
Flem Snopes was still watching" (p. 295).

Unmoved earlier by the wife's impassioned pleadings on behalf
of her family, the beating finally moves the Texan to intervene and
put an end to Armstid's mad inhumanity. But when the Texan returns the money to the wife, Flem objects. When Armstid retrieves the money from his wife a second time, he offers it not to
the Texan but to Flem. " 'It's my horse,' he said. 'I bought it. These
fellows saw me. I paid for it. It's my horse. Here.' He turned and
extended the banknote toward Snopes. 'You got something to do
with these horses. I bought one. . . . Ask him.' Snopes took the
banknote. The others stood, gravely inattentive, in relaxed attitudes along the fence" (p. 296). The Texan is fooling no one but
himself when he promises Mrs. Armstid: "Mr. Snopes will have

your money for you tomorrow. Better get him [Armstid] in the wagon and get him on home. He dont own no horse. You can get your money tomorrow from Mr. Snopes" (p. 297). When the Texan includes Armstid's horse in the number yet to be sold, Flem hurries him into the buggy and away, speaking to him "a little shortly, a little quickly" (p. 297). Flem will no more return the five dollars than the Texan will get to Jefferson with all of the profits. Armstid's money is gone and, as Bookwright says of the Texan, "His pockets wont rattle" (p. 299).

As the men prepare to capture the horses they have bought, the land is again illumined with "that other-worldly quality of moonlight, so that when they stood once more looking into the lot, the splotchy bodies of the ponies had a distinctness, almost a brilliance, but without individual shape and without depth—no longer horses, no longer flesh and bone directed by a principle capable of calculated violence, no longer inherent with the capacity to hurt and harm" (p. 299). Taking courage from this transformation, they hardly notice that the mockingbird is again singing in the pear tree or that Ratliff, absent all day, has returned. In the lot, the ponies, "huddled again, were like phantom fish, suspended apparently without legs now in the brilliant treachery of the moon" (p. 300). In this enchanted setting, led by the madman Armstid in "the mazy moonlight" (p. 301), the spellbound men enter the lot to take possession of the ponies they have purchased. "Then an indescribable sound, a movement desperate and despairing, arose among them [the ponies]; for an instant of static horror men and animals faced one another, then the men whirled and ran before a gaudy vomit of long wild faces and splotched chests which overtook and scattered them and flung them sprawling aside and completely obliterated from sight Henry and the little boy, neither of whom had moved though Henry had flung up both arms, still holding his coiled rope, the herd sweeping on across the lot, to crash through the gate which the last man through it had neglected to close" (pp. 301–302). As the horses race through the tangle of wagons in the lane, one detouring through Mrs. Littlejohn's house and frightening Ratliff, only to be turned at last by Mrs. Littlejohn herself, the men in the lot rise to begin the vain chase. Only Henry Armstid is seriously injured; only the child, Wallstreet Snopes, goes completely un-

touched. Confronting the horses again in Mrs. Littlejohn's hall-
way, "the boy did not move, and for the third time the horse
soared above the unwinking eyes and the unbowed and untouched
head" (p. 303). His youthful innocence of horse fever is his shield.
Horse madness is Armstid's downfall. The last horse disappears
"hobgoblin and floating, in the moon," galloping past the still intact wagon where Mrs. Armstid sits and down the road "gashed
pallid and moony between the moony shadows of the bordering
trees" (p. 303). On the bridge Vernon Tull and his family sustain
a final, unwarranted injury, and the horse is gone.

   In the aftermath of this wild melee, there is the incongruity of
pathos and sardonic humor, both of which reflect on Flem Snopes.
Ratliff and his companions, "treading the moon-blanched dust in
the tremulous April night" (p. 306), hear the far-off galloping of
hooves and fading cries of the pursuers, punctuated now by the
screams of Henry Armstid: "the scream sank into a harsh respi-
ration: 'Ah. Ah. Ah' on a rising note about to become screaming
again. 'Come on,' Ratliff said. 'We better get Varner' " (pp. 305–
306). In the moonlit window of Varner's house, Flem's wife Eula
appears, reminiscent of other masculine dreams lost and unattainable, representing "to those below what Brunhilde, what Rhine-
maiden on what spurious river-rock of papier-mâché, what Helen
returned to what topless and shoddy Argos, waiting for no one"
(p. 306). In the lushly blooming pear tree, the mockingbird still
sings, but in the moonlight there is hope for regeneration as well as
spellbinding deceit. " 'A moon like this is good for every growing
thing outen earth,' Varner said" (p. 307). Laughter, the first in
book four, follows the description of moonlit conceptions and is
then stifled by Armstid's renewed screaming: "Ah. Ah. Ah" (p.
307). Varner's subsequent pessimistic comment that "breathing is
a sight-draft dated yesterday" (p. 308) recalls the issuer of sight-
drafts, Flem Snopes, and, in the context of Armstid's pained
cries, fixes Flem as the propagator of that misery.

   Two days later, by the light of morning, Ratliff investigates the
practical consequences of the horse auction, humorously rehears-
ing his own part in the action at Mrs. Littlejohn's, questioning the
loungers at the store, and commenting on the whole with controlled irony. Although he cannot bring Lump Snopes to admit to
Flem's ownership of the horses, he is clearly convinced that Flem

did own them, and he baits the clerk accordingly. None of the horses have been recaptured, and even though Eck has found one of his dead, "that wasnt Flem's, because that horse was give to Eck for nothing" (p. 311). Most of the men are still searching, losing more time from their spring crops, and Ratliff says, "The only new horse-owner in this country that could a been found without bloodhounds since whoever it was left that gate open two nights ago, is Henry Armstid. He's laying right there in Mrs. Littlejohn's bedroom where he can watch the lot so that anytime the one he bought happens to run back into it, all he's got to do is to holler at his wife to run out with the rope and catch it—" (p. 311). Concurrent with the mention of Armstid's name, the men on the gallery are joined by Flem himself. At once the clerk's anger at being baited turns to vengeful humor as he vacates his chair for Flem "with a sort of servile alacrity" (p. 311). " 'You're just in time,' he said. 'Ratliff here seems to be in a considerable sweat about who actually owned them horses. . . . Maybe you could put his mind at rest' " (pp. 311–312). At Flem's characteristically noncommittal answer, "the clerk guffawed, chortling, his features gathering toward the center of his face as though plucked there by a hand. He slapped his leg, cackling. 'You might as well quit,' he said. 'You cant beat him' " (p. 312). When Ratliff renews his discussion of Armstid's injury, the clerk interrupts: "If a man aint got gumption enough to protect himself, it's his own look-out" (p. 312).

In essence this ruthless sentiment is a fundamental of the Snopes credo of acquisition, and Ratliff attacks it with bitter irony. His monologue now is essentially a plea for the restoration of the five dollars Armsid paid for the horse, and as such it comprises a direct attack against Flem Snopes. Beneath the description of the grinding poverty to which the Armstids are reduced, there are numerous barbed references to Flem's ownership of the horses and the Texan's promise that the money would be returned. "And Henry Armstid [Ratliff said], that's all right because from what I hear of the conversation that taken place, Henry had already stopped owning that horse he thought was his before that Texas man left. And as for that broke leg, that wont put him out none because his wife can make his crop" (pp. 312–313). Armstid's young daughter takes an ax to bed with her because the country is "still more or less full of them uncaught horses that never belonged to Flem

Snopes" (p. 314). Such comments arouse in the loungers an undercurrent of compassion. They defend the Armstids; having aid-
ed them in the past, they are willing to aid them again. Lump,
however, stares coldly, "watching Ratliff quite hard now, unwinking" (p. 313). Flem remains impassive: "If Ratliff had looked
at Flem Snopes, he would have seen nothing below the down-
slanted peak of the cap save the steady motion of his jaws. Another sliver was curling with neat deliberation before the moving
knife" (p. 313).

Ratliff's vain appeal is capped by the appearance of Mrs. Armstid, "gaunt in the shapeless gray garment, the stained tennis shoes
hissing faintly on the boards" (p. 315). By appearing, she sacri-
fices whatever vestiges of pride and self-esteem are left to her
after her debasement at the auction, coming hopelessly to beg for
the return of the five dollars promised her by the Texan. As Ratliff related, her decision to ask for the money was not lightly
made but was a product of anguish and fear for her family. Because of this fact Flem's reaction is yet more viciously insensitive.
"Snopes raised his head and turned it slightly again and spat neatly
past the woman, across the gallery and into the road. 'He took all
the money with him when he left,' he said" (p. 315). In the face
of this lie, she is helpless. Although she saw Flem take the money
from her husband, she cannot prove that he has it still or that he
even had claim to it by right of ownership of the horses. As she
turns to go, Flem offers the final insult to her extreme need, "a
little sweetening for the chaps" (p. 317) that is worth, Ratliff
notices, five cents. Spitting past her again, Flem resumes his seat,
whittling. "The clerk in the doorway cackled suddenly, explo-
sively, chortling. He slapped his thigh. 'By God,' he said, 'you
cant beat him' " (p. 317). As a final devaluation of Flem's gift of
"sweetening," St. Elmo Snopes is soon discovered stealing candy
from the same case from which Mrs. Armstid's came. The price to
her was five dollars.

Although the abasement of Mrs. Armstid registers with great
impact on the sensitive Ratliff, there is no need for him to comment further on her desperate situation. He has already made a
strong appeal for her, and no more poignant expression of her
condition could be made than is provided by her lifeless acceptance of Flem's inevitable lie and the mocking token gift.

"You're right kind," she said. She rolled the sack into the apron. . . . She moved again. "I reckon I better get on and help with dinner," she said. She descended the steps, though as soon as she reached the level earth and began to retreat, the gray folds of the garment once more lost all inference and intimation of locomotion, so that she seemed to progress without motion like a figure on a retreating and diminishing float; a gray and blasted tree-trunk moving, somehow intact and upright, upon an un-hurried flood. (p. 317)

The case for the Armstids is, for the moment, closed, and Ratliff, clearly shocked by its implications of amorality, turns in a mood of near desperation to a reestimation of Flem's and his own motives. To Bookwright's earnest opinion that Flem has returned earlier than expected from Texas in order to keep Mink from rotting in jail, Ratliff sarcastically replies, "he wont be in jail long. Court is next month, and after they send him to Parchman, he can stay outdoors again. He will even go back to farming, plowing" (p. 320). Flem returned simply to assure the cancellation of "all them loose-flying notes that turns up here and there every now and then" (p. 320). Having been threatened by Mink with fire and having suffered a financial loss in the goat trade because of Ike's note, which Mink gave to Ratliff, Flem is coldly and efficiently thwarting the possibility of any such threats in the future by making certain that Mink will be imprisoned. Characteristically, his motives are those of ruthless self-interest.

Conversely, Ratliff is motivated by humanity and generosity. He is principled, courageous, and gifted with unusual insight, and his willingness for personal involvement in the problems and fears of his fellow men constitutes an affirmation of morality that in some measure balances and checks the animal acquisitiveness of the Snopeses. It is important to understand, however, that he is by no means the all-compassionate distributor of infinite largess to a community beset by an implacable opponent. The true strength of the moral community lies not in one man's firm example but in the mutually concerned actions of all of its members and their recognition of their own personal responsibility. While Ratliff assumes a moral responsibility for the helpless idiot, Ike Snopes, he thus refuses to be responsible for Henry Armstid, whose dilemma is a product of his own willfulness. He may appeal to Flem for

fair play, but he will go no further despite being deeply affected
by Mrs. Armstid's abasement. When Bookwright asks if he has
given Armstid five dollars as he gave Ike the inheritance, Ratliff
replies:

> "I could have. . . . But I didn't. I might have if I could just
> been sho he would buy something this time that would sho
> enough kill him, like Mrs. Littlejohn said. Besides, I wasn't pro-
> tecting a Snopes [Ike] from Snopeses; I wasn't even protecting
> a people from a Snopes. I was protecting something that wasn't
> even a people, that wasn't nothing but something that dont want
> nothing but to walk and feel the sun and wouldn't know how
> to hurt no man even if it would and wouldn't want to even if
> it could, just like I wouldn't stand by and see you steal a meat-
> bone from a dog. I never made them Snopeses and I never made
> the folks that cant wait to bare their backsides to them. I could
> do more, but I wont. I wont, I tell you!"
> "All right," Bookwright said. "Hook your drag up; it aint
> nothing but a hill. I said it's all right." (p. 321)

Having resolved that there is nothing else that he can do to correct the injuries perpetrated by the horse auction and perhaps
foreseeing the futility of any further attempts for compensation,
Ratliff absents himself from "the two actions of Armstid pl. vs.
Snopes, and Tull pl. vs. Eckrum Snopes" (p. 321). Just as Flem
Snopes ignored his moral responsibility to return Armstid's money when Ratlliff and Mrs. Armstid appealed to him for it, he now
is equally oblivious to legal responsibility. The same irrefutable lie
serves both ends. "Flem Snopes flatly refused to recognize the
existence of the suit against himself, stating once and without heat
and first turning his head slightly aside to spit, 'They wasnt none
of my horses,' then fell to whittling again while the baffled and
helpless bailiff stood before the tilted chair with the papers he was
trying to serve" (p. 321). So exact has he been in his alien cunning
that he is literally beyond the effective scope of the law while
seemingly within it. The fact that the Texan sold the horses, shields
Flem from all responsibility for them, and the only chink in the
armor is the fact that Flem did take the five dollars from Henry
Armstid. This, however, is covered through the agency of his
kinsman, Lump, whose perjury, though obvious, is declared to
be legal because he has sworn to it. Emulating his cousin in dress as

well as behavior, Lump flaunts from the beginning his insensitivity
to legal justice. Wearing one of Flem's old caps, Lump,

> between spells of rapid blinking would sit staring at the Justice
> with the lidless intensity of a rat—and into the lens-distorted
> and irisless old-man's eyes of the Justice there grew an expression
> not only of amazement and bewilderment but, as in Ratliff's
> eyes while he stood on the store gallery four weeks ago, some-
> thing very like terror.
> "This—" he said. "I didn't expect—I didn't look to see—. I'm
> going to pray," he said. "I aint going to pray aloud. But I hope—"
> He looked at them. "I wish. . . Maybe some of you all anyway
> had better do the same." He bowed his head. (pp. 323–324)

Ultimately, the case of Armstid versus Snopes must be dismissed.
Ironically, the simple perfection with which Flem conceived
the horse auction accounts for Eck's immunity to legal action as
well as his own. Unwilling to lie for Flem, Eck is fully prepared
to assume the cost of the damages done to Tull in his own suit. But
he is not permitted to do so by law. The horse that injured Tull
was not purchased but given to Eck, and as the Justice points out,

> In the law, ownership cant be conferred or invested by word-
> of-mouth. It must be established either by recorded or authentic
> document, or by possession or occupation. By . . . [Mrs. Tull's]
> testimony and . . . [Eck's] both, he never gave that Texas man
> anything in exchange for that horse, and by his testimony the
> Texas man never gave him any paper to prove he owned it, and
> by his testimony and by what I know myself from these last
> four weeks, nobody yet has ever laid hand or rope either on
> any one of them. So that horse never came into Eck's possession
> at all. (p. 330)

Moreover, since Armstid versus Snopes failed to establish Flem's
ownership of the horses, the horse that injured Tull still belongs to
the Texan. Nevertheless, having been injured by the horse, "the
injured or damaged party shall find recompense in the body of
the animal" (p. 331). As the injured party, Tull himself owns the
now dead horse! Whereas Flem will not pay Mrs. Armstid but
should, Eck is willing to pay Tull but is not permitted to.
Despite the comic gusto of the situation, however, there remain the terror in the eyes of the old judge and the fact that Flem

has demonstrated his immunity to yet another set of human values. " 'I cant stand no more!' the old Justice cried. 'I wont! This court's adjourned! Adjourned!' " (p. 332). His cry is echoed some days later in another courtroom, in Jefferson, where Mink Snopes, foresaken by his kinsman, has just been sentenced. "He had not only turned his back to the Court to look out into the crowded room, he was speaking himself even before the Judge had ceased, continuing to speak even while the Judge hammered the desk with his gavel and the two officers and three bailiffs converged upon the prisoner as he struggled, flinging them back and for a short time actually successful, staring out into the room. 'Flem Snopes!' Is Flem Snopes in this room? Tell that son of a bitch——' " (p. 333).

By permitting Mink to be sent to prison, Flem bears out Ratliff's dark conjectures on his insensitivity to the demands of blood ties, irrevocably alienating himself from clan as well as community. Mink's strangled threat reinforces Flem's elemental stature as amoral aggressor and is another in an interconnecting series of anguished cries from exploited victims, which began with Flem's first appearance and Jody Varner's stunned "Hell fire. Hell fire. Hell fire" (p. 20). It is now clear that his power lies in what Hayes describes as "undeterred action resulting from unimpaired perception. He is a man always alert to take what he wants as soon as he sees it. Because he has no sense of his own dignity as a human being, only of his status as agent, he takes any step which heads away from the sharecropper's field. He does not have to plan ahead except to store away possible sources of advantage as they occur. When the time comes to use an advantage, a time dictated by circumstance, then he uses it simply and directly, concerned only with efficacy." [24] It is a power that can be stemmed only by those equally ruthless, and none such exist in the moral world of Frenchman's Bend.

Ironically, those who most clearly understand Flem's motives and methods now fall victim to him. Ratliff, in league with Odum Bookwright and the mad Henry Armstid, are gulled into buying the old Frenchman place through the ruse of a salted gold mine. Ratliff's part in this transaction has understandably attracted considerable critical attention and has brought into question the artistic credibility of the ending of the novel.[25] None of the objections, however, takes into sufficient account the imaginative hold that the Old Frenchman place exerts on the community. From the Frenchman, the hamlet takes it name, though there is nothing left of his mansion but ruins, nothing of his legend "but the stubborn tale of the money he buried somewhere about the place when Grant overran the country on his way to Vicksburg" (p. 4). Throughout the novel the ruined mansion is a symbol of proprietorship in the Bend, changing hands at the moment of Will Varner's capitulation to Flem when pride and passion have been exploited. Even Ratliff "had never for one moment believed that it had no value. He might have believed this if anyone else had owned it. But the very fact that Varner had ever come into possession of it and still kept it, apparently making to effort to sell it or do anything else with it, was proof enough for him" (p. 157). When he considers the fact that Varner "relinquished" the mansion to Flem, Ratliff feels "that the price had been necessity and not cash" (p. 157), and he is certain that the deal has a "little piece of knotted-up string in it" (p. 158). The very possibility that Flem would want something that is worthless is absurd.

When Ratliff discovers that Flem is digging at night in the garden of the ruined mansion, he thus considers it to be proof of a belief that he has long held. He responds imaginatively to the suggestion, and his fancy is quickened by Armstid's ardor. When the conservative, skeptical Bookwright is convinced by Uncle Dick Bolivar and his divining rod, Ratliff's hopes are confirmed. This indicates no avaricious flaw in Ratliff's otherwise generous nature. Rather, he is merely overanxious both to convince himself of something in which he wants to believe and to solve a mystery of long standing. In the same way that the would-be horse buyers discussed Anse McCallum's success with wild ponies in order to buoy up their courage, Ratliff rehearses the history of his faith in the existence of buried treasure.

> There's something there. I've always knowed it. Just like Will Varner knows there is something there. If there wasn't, he wouldn't never bought it. And he wouldn't a kept it, selling the balance of it off and still keeping that old house, paying taxes on it when he could a got something for it, setting there in that flour-barrel chair to watch it and claiming he did it because it rested him to set there where somebody had gone to all that work and expense just to build something to sleep and eat and

lay with his wife in. And I knowed it for sho when Flem Snopes
took it. When he had Will Varner just where he wanted him,
and then he sold out to Will by taking that old house and them
ten acres that wouldn't hardly raise goats. And I went with
Henry last night. I saw it too. (p. 335)

There are no moon-caused transformations to distort Ratliff's perception in "the moonless August darkness" (p. 334). So strong is
his conviction in his old dream, so confident is he in the reliability
of his own reasoned explanation of Flem's digging, that the moonlight which enraptured the horse buyers is not necessary. Ratliff
and his companions seek out Flem and buy the Old Frenchman
place.

Significantly, neither Ratliff nor Bookwright succumbs to the
moneylust that drives Henry Armstid. Only once are they affected
by Armstid's madness, scrabbling into the hole with him to fight
for a shovel, but Ratliff is quick to regain control of himself: "He
drew a long shuddering breath. 'God,' he whispered. 'Just look at
what even the money a man aint got yet will do to him' " (p. 343).
Thereafter, Ratliff's and Bookwright's search for the money is
conducted in the rational and mutually considerate fashion of
partners. Only Armstid continues to dig with furious avarice,
"dragging his stiff twice-broken leg painfully beneath him" (p.
358) to regain the sanctuary of his hole. He continues to dig thus
even after his partners have discovered the deception of the planted money. Lacking the redemptive capacity for humor that Ratliff
and Bookwright possess, the twice-cheated Armstid, buyer of an
untamable horse and a worthless gold hoard, passes out of the
human community into total madness. " 'Henry,' Ratliff said. Then
Ratliff leaned down and touched his shoulder. He whirled, the
shovel raised and turned edgewise and glinting a thin line of
steel-colored dawn as the edge of an axe would. 'Get out of my
hole,' he said. 'Get outen it' " (p. 361).

Ratliff's defeat here is a thematic success: it at once places him
in the community of fallible human beings from which Flem is
alienated and emphasizes Flem's unconquerable amorality. Yet
there should be no dissatisfaction with Ratliff as a character and
no uncertainty as to the outcome of Flem's machinations. Often
in the course of the novel Ratliff has miscalculated Flem's canny
ruthlessness and the extent of his inhumanity. Because of his mis-

judgments he has even lost financially, as when he gives up his gains from the goat trade so that Ike may not be further exploited. Always, however, he is able to adjust his perceptions, to reevaluate his judgments of Flem and his clan in the light of his new experience. By this means he enjoys a modicum of success in his dealings with Snopeses. Each new encounter is based on increased knowledge of the opponent, carefully and painstakingly arrived at through the process of discursive reasoning. Thus, when he has been forced to give up his goat-trading profits to save Ike, Ratliff can look back and say, "I just never went far enough" (p. 88), and be prepared to go further the next time. Here, as soon as he discovers that he has been deceived, he does the same thing, patiently and humorously explaining to Bookwright that Flem did not set out purposely to catch them in particular. " 'He didn't [know],' Ratliff said. 'He didn't care. He just come out here every night and dug for a while. He knowed he couldn't possibly dig over two weeks before somebody saw him' " (pp. 360–361). This, as Hayes points out, is Flem's characteristic mode of operation: it is merely simplified and refined to the point of ultimate effectiveness. As the loungers at the store comment later, "Couldn't no other man have done it. Anybody might have fooled Henry Armstid. But couldn't nobody but Flem Snopes have fooled Ratliff" (p. 365).

The final significance of this episode does not lie merely in the fact that the dreams of fair-minded, moral individuals can be easily exploited by an elemental amoral aggressor, although this is certainly one central issue. More important is the fact that such ravages are not totally debilitating, that the moral world is rejuvenatory and self-regenerative. Ratliff's defeat is only financial and, as Millgate states, it is "not accompanied by any defeat in human terms" [26] as is, for example, Armstid's defeat. Ratliff returns to the community from his hole in the garden of the Old Frenchman place no less committed to moral existence than before he entered it, prepared, "to continue, not merely the struggle against Snopesism, but the perpetual affirmation of life." [27]

It is in recognition of this oblique concentration on the moral world and the character of its inhabitants that Beck states, "If Snopesism is object, response to it is subject." [28] The two elements are in constant and mutually revealing juxtaposition from the

moment that Ab Snopes pounds with his crooked foot across the
gallery of the Varner store to the final scene of the novel. Headed
at last for Jefferson, Flem drives past the Old Frenchman place,
three miles out of his way. "He did not pull out of the road into
line. Instead, he drove on past the halted wagons while the heads
of the women holding the nursing children turned to look at him
and the heads of the men along the fence turned to watch him
pass, the faces grave, veiled too, still looking at him when he
stopped the wagon and sat, chewing with that steady and measured thrust and looking over their heads into the garden" (pp.
365–366). Behind them on the hill is Henry Armstid, whose
"gaunt unshaven face . . . was now completely that of a madman"
(p. 366). In this atmosphere of wonder, compassion, and fear,
Flem's reaction is typically without humanity: "Snopes turned his
head and spat over the wagon wheel. He jerked the reins slightly.
'Come up,' he said" (p. 366). He is literally telling himself to
climb up in the world.

II.

The Town

"The Idea of a Tribe of People"

FOLLOWING the publication of *The Hamlet* in 1940, Faulkner turned from the Snopes family to the expansion of themes
begun in his earlier fiction and to the development of new characters and their histories. *Go Down, Moses* (1942) details the history of the descendants, white and black, of Lucius Quintus Ca-
rothers McCaslin and is the cornerstone of the much-discussed
wilderness theme in Faulkner's fiction. *Intruder in the Dust* (1948)
brings forward from the previous novel Lucas Beauchamp and
Gavin Stevens, the country attorney of the story "Go Down, Moses," and introduces Gavin's nephew, Charles Mallison. Stevens
is quite probably a refinement of the verbose and sensitive Oxford-
educated lawyer Horace Benbow of *Sartoris* (1929) and *Sanctuary*
(1931), who also served with the YMCA during the First World
War. He appears again with Charles Mallison in the collection
of stories *Knight's Gambit* (1949) as a Harvard-educated Phi
Beta Kappa who has spent some years at the University of Heidelberg. *Requiem for a Nun* (1951) reintroduces the heroine of
Sanctuary, Temple Drake, now married to Stevens' second nephew, Gowan Stevens, and Gavin is again presented to defend the
murderess, Nancy Manigoe, and serve as the instrument for Temple's confession of her sins. *A Fable* (1954), Faulkner's only major

novel set outside of Yoknapatawpha County, encompasses some
of the major themes implicit in the Yoknapatawpha novels, but
it constitutes a complete departure from the local framework and
interrelated events of what Malcolm Cowley has called Faulkner's
"mythical kingdom . . . complete and living in all its details." [1]
With the publication of *The Town* in 1957, Faulkner returned
again to his "mythical kingdom" and, after seventeen years, to the
Snopes family.

Despite the favorable critical attention given *The Hamlet* before it, *The Town* was not well received by early reviewers. One,
Alfred Kazin, treated it as yet another, and inferior, chapter in
the story of Yoknapatawpha County and described it as "tired,
drummed-up, borrowing, often merely frivolous." [2] He further
charged:

> The book is a string of anecdotes, some of which are worked
> up from old short stories, and it is dramatically so loose that
> it is plain that Faulkner himself has tired of the Yoknapatawpha
> saga. He does something here that he never did in any book
> before—he coyly serves up whole summaries of the saga to
> link this book with the others. In the past, he would offer such
> material not as "information" to the reader but as the compulsive
> repetition of certain themes. And everybody out of his old books
> comes on stage in this one, as in the grand finale of a review.
> It is a striking example of the loose, improvised, sometimes
> gagman quality of the book that the county attorney, Gavin
> Stevens, who figures so importantly in other Faulkner novels,
> here becomes a completely silly character, is constantly out of
> focus, and at times sounds more like a parody of Quentin Comp-
> son, the romantic intellectual in *The Sound and the Fury*, than
> like a sage, wise conscience of the old order that he was in other
> books.[3]

In Kazin's view Faulkner's subject in the Yoknapatawpha novels
and stories had always been "the Southerner's constantly unavail-
ing effort to make sense of history, to come to terms with the un-
explained failure of the past." [4] In terms of this explanation,
The Town was "a bad novel by a great writer . . . [who] has less
and less interest in writing what are called novels at all." [5]

Subsequent documents strongly indicate that, in the case of
The Town at least, Kazin's emphasis is misplaced. *The Town*,

like *The Hamlet,* is subtitled "A Novel of the Snopes Family," and it is clear that Faulkner early planned on treating this clan in more than one volume. In a letter to Cowley in 1945, he stated that such previously published stories as "Mule in the Yard" and "Centaur in Brass," which were not incorporated into *The Hamlet,* "are to fall in a later volume." [6] His interviews at the University of Virginia in 1957, moreover, make clear the distinction he drew between novels about the South and novels set in the South. Answering Kazin's charge that he was weary of Yoknapatawpha County, Faulkner implied that his then most recent novel fell into the latter category.

> I don't think that I am [tired], though of course the last thing any writer will admit to himself is that he has scraped the bottom of the barrel and that he should quit. I don't quite believe that's true yet. But it's probably not tiredness, it's the fact that you shouldn't put off too long writing something which you think is worth writing, and this I have had in mind for thirty years now. So maybe it could be a little stale to me, though I don't think that's true, either. It was not a novel. I think that anything that can't be told in one standardized book is not a novel. That is, it can't follow the fairly rigid rules which—in which a novel has got to be compressed to be a novel. This is really a chronicle that seemed to me amusing enough or true enough to be put down no matter what rules of integrity it had to violate, so in that sense it's not a novel, it's a chronicle, and I don't think that fatigue had anything to do with it—that is, fatigue with the county, the background. It may have been a staleness because I had thought of it, had remembered it, and planned to write it so long before I got to it.[7]

In a later interview he specified his fascination with the Snopes clan and the necessity he felt to chronicle its entire history. "When I first thought of these people and the idea of a tribe of people which would come into an otherwise peaceful little Southern town like ants or like mold on cheese then—I discovered then that to tell the story properly would be too many words to compress into one volume. . . . That I would have to keep on writing about these people until I got it all told." [8] Clearly, Kazin's conception of *The Town* as an inferior chapter in a Yoknapatawpha saga is at odds with the author's conception of it as part of a Snopes saga set in Yoknapatawpha. It can hardly be called "a bad novel" because it does not conform comfortably to the critic's preconceived notion of the author's "subject."

Nor should it be condemned for using characters from other novels and showing them in new lights. Warren Beck, among others, has praised Faulkner for his "populous fictional backgrounds," [9] and Faulkner himself said of his characters that "they have grown older as I have grown older, and probably they have changed a little—my concept of them has changed a little, as they themselves have changed and I changed. . . . they have grown. I know more about people than I knew when I first thought of them, and they have become more definite to me as people." [10] Gavin Stevens in *The Town* thus must be judged on the basis of his reactions to the unique situations in that novel and not for what he has represented previously. If Gavin is here "a completely silly character," it is not because he reacts differently to Flem Snopes than he does in *Intruder in the Dust* to Lucas Beauchamp. The same, of course, is true of the other major characters, Charles Mallison, V. K. Ratliff, Eula Varner Snopes, and Flem himself. With the exception of Mallison and his uncle, who are new to the Snopes saga, these characters also play major roles in *The Hamlet* and undergo some changes as the milieu changes from hamlet to town. While their success as characters in a trilogy may depend in part on the nature of the changes they undergo from novel to novel, their success or failure in *The Town* depends solely on their behavior in the changed state.

In addition to the change in setting from rural Frenchman's Bend to urban Jefferson, Faulkner's narrative strategy in *The Town* is altered. Here character and event are scrutinized by three narrators whose points of reference vary in proportion to their direct involvement with other characters and each other. Vickery says of them, "Essentially they afford a moral perspective on morality. In addition each has an essential function in contributing something of himself to what Gavin calls 'our folklore, or Snopeslore, if you like.' " [11] Ratliff, who plays so significant a role in *The Hamlet*, is here given a bare six chapters, amounting to only twenty-eight pages. Nonetheless, as Vickery points out, he "establishes the continuity of *The Hamlet* and *The Town* by virtue of his presence and his ironic though humane perspective. . . . He makes available those past events in Frenchman's Bend which

will enable Gavin and his nephew Charles Mallison to understand
the phenomenon of Snopesism." [12] More important, perhaps, is
the fact that he is a realist who knows from experience that
Snopesism is a force which cannot be withstood. As James F. Farnham states, "This perception forces him to come to terms with
reality, and he still tries to do whatever he can to thwart Snopesism, knowing that his goal is impossible of fulfillment." [13] In general, his role amounts to instructing Charles Mallison and directing Gavin's introspected theorizing while serving as a foil to his
rash idealism. At the University of Virginia, Faulkner said that
his object in using three narrators was to view Snopesism from
three different sides and that Ratliff's was the point of view "of
a man who practiced virtue from simple instinct . . . for a practical
reason, because it was better. There was less confusion if all people
didn't tell lies to one another, and didn't pretend." [14]

Charles Mallison, by the same account, is "the mirror which
obliterated all except truth, because the mirror didn't know the
other factors existed." [15] His part in the novel comprises ten chapters, better than half the book, and Millgate points out that "it
is he who provides most of the basic narrative of events. Mallison
also recounts the episodes of the brass stolen from the power
station, of the mule loose in Mrs. Hait's yard, and of the arrival
and rapid departure of Byron Snopes's Indian children." [16] In
this, Mallison is something of a comic straight man, the humorous
episodes being given to him because, according to Faulkner, "I
thought it would be more amusing as told through the innocence
of a child that knew what he was seeing but had no particular
judgment about it. That something told by someone that don't
know he is telling something funny is sometimes much more
amusing than when it's told by a professional wit who is hunting
around for laughs." [17] In this, Mallison differs from Ratliff, whose
retelling of past events is often characterized by a calculated expansion of fact for purposes of humor.

For all of Charles's factual reporting and childlike innocence,
however, his role as narrator is complex and integrally related to
the business of the novel. To begin with, Charles identifies himself as a representative of the collective consciousness of Jefferson,
claiming "when I say 'we' and 'we thought' what I mean is Jefferson and what Jefferson thought" (p. 3).[18] As such he supplies

the "Snopes dilemma" with a dimension and scope that transcend and provide commentary on the acutely personal struggle of his uncle. Seen through Charles's eyes, Snopesism implies a universal challenge to moral existence, to which his uncle's and Ratliff's reactions are but individual responses. Charles is thus the vehicle by which Gavin's romantic involvement and Ratliff's realistic aloofness are brought into context, the objective mimetic touchstone against which their perceptions are recurrently tested. In addition, his factuality often implies judgments of the community morality that he claims to represent, and he points up moral hypocrisy with the same innocence that characterizes his humorous accounts. As a child, Charles is subject to neither the quixotic involvement of his uncle nor the hypocrisy of the community that his observations uncover. He is thereby spared both Gavin's anguish and the community's shame. Under Ratliff's tutelage and with these examples before him, he does develop an identity of his own, becoming eventually what Vickery calls "a precocious critic of that society which has repudiated Eula and accepted Flem." [19] Having begun his Snopes-watching at an incredibly early age and having been throughout the novel "the recipient . . . of confidences and reflections from both Gavin and Ratliff," [20] Charles combines at last the sensitive, verbose idealism of the one with the humanely cryptic realism of the other. In the process of his maturation, he is shielded by his childhood from direct involvement in the events he reports without being denied access to them. Too young to challenge Snopesism, too guileless to ignore it, he is a narrator whose value lies in his ability to report with devastating accuracy what he sees. His reports, by their very factuality, project judgments of society and of other narrators that are unrestricted by personality or recognizable bias.

Gavin Stevens matures in insight in much the same way as his nephew, but Gavin's maturation is accomplished by the painful process of trial and error, of confrontation and defeat. Lacking Charles's innocence and Ratliff's realism, Gavin is a romantic theorizer, a speculator on reality who bases his speculations—and his actions—on self-constructed illusions. Combined with this speculative quality is a romantic readiness, what John L. Longley, Jr. characterizes as "the eagerness of commitment to some area of life, some relationship into which he can project himself with all his energy and emotion. . . . This readiness, this unchecked impulsiveness, this romantic fondness for hopeless causes is in one sense a form of weakness. Faced with such romantic idealism, the reader's reaction to Gavin may range from total sympathy to total exasperation." [21] His role in *The Town* is ideally suited to the exercise of this quality. Gavin, Longley says,

> . . . in the nature of his personality and profession is apt to observe or be involved in anything that happens in Yoknapatawpha. His profession is that of attorney; his hobby is observing human beings, their motives and feelings, and speculating on the content of the human heart. . . . His faults are that he sometimes jumps too hastily to conclusions and that he talks too much—the occupational disease of the legal profession. His fatal flaw is an imperfect sense of ironic detachment; he has such a sense, but it seems to operate either too well at the wrong time or not at all. The result is often laceration of heart and spirit.[22]

His maturation is characterized finally by his movement from the excesses of idealism toward the succinctness of perceptive realism. Because his romantic idealism is so deeply ingrained, however, this development is slow and anguished. In fact, the process is not completed until the end of *The Mansion*, when Gavin can say, with Ratliff, "People just do the best they can" (p. 429).

In *The Town* Gavin's journey toward reality is in three distinct stages, each of which follows a pattern of speculative commitment, active confrontation, and painful defeat. The subjects of his speculations are Eula and Linda Snopes, about whom he creates romantic premises. The nature of his commitment to these premises, in Longley's words, is "the quixotic determination to defend whoever and whatever he decides must be defended, whether defending is requested or even desired or not." [23] What he defends them from, although he is by no means the first to realize it, is Snopesism in general and Flem in particular. In *The Town* Flem is a pivotal character just as he was in *The Hamlet*, and his rise through Jefferson society, by its very inhumanity, provides the spur that goads Gavin to action. The fact that Gavin enjoys almost no success in defending his premises is due in part to Flem's inexorableness and in part to Gavin's own generous overestimation of the goodness and decency of his fellow men. Longley asserts that Gavin "never remembers that many people would not be gentle and compassionate even if they could. He wants to believe that people want to be better than they are or seem to be, and on this basis he acts. . . . Throughout his career there is his inability to anticipate the deviousness of Flem's motives and rapacity." [24] Thus for Gavin, defeat is inevitable, and because he is so totally committed to the illusions of reality that he creates, pain and anguish are inevitable as well.

His maturation as a realist is marked by his gradual realization that total fulfillment is impossible, that, as Farnham says, "man's dreams and hopes are destined to at least partial frustration." [25] To recognize this fact and yet continue and even renew the struggle is the essence of moral regeneration. It is this that Ratliff knows at the outset of *The Town;* it is this that he teaches Charles Mallison long before the boy is old enough to test himself against it; and, finally and most important, it is this realization toward which Gavin is drawn in a series of devastating encounters with Snopesism. Three times Gavin steps forward to stand between Flem Snopes and his victims, and each time he is defeated. Yet each defeat is marked by a reassessment of the previous premise, which in turn provides a new premise to be tested by confrontation. In the process, themes that recur in each new encounter provide the novel with a structural as well as thematic unity.

As a young lawyer, newly graduated from Harvard, Gavin is initially attracted to Eula Varner Snopes by her mythic sexuality. Speculating on his attraction to her, he creates the fiction of her chastity and romantically commits himself to its defense. His illusion is shattered by her own practical realism—offering herself to him out of pity to relieve his frustration—and all action is thwarted, calling forth a major revision of Gavin's concept of reality and the premises on which that concept is based.

In formulating his "second premise," Gavin takes into account his interpretation of the role played by Flem Snopes in the failure of the "first premise," and he bases his new version of reality on protecting Linda from him. Gavin is older now, knows from Ratliff more of the particulars of the Snopes history, and has experienced the operation of Snopesism firsthand with Montgomery Ward Snopes in Europe. Flem, furthermore, is steadily rising in the community, and Ratliff's repeated warnings against

him are sufficiently alarming to Gavin to reinforce his commitment to protect Linda. In addition, his initial defeat has not altogether cooled the ardor of his commitment to Linda's mother,
and this too contributes to his illusions about the daughter. Farnham explains that

> Because [Gavin] cannot have Eula, he feels that he has nothing
> in life, no premise on which to base his existence. But at the
> same moment he realizes that he cannot exist without a premise.
> He, therefore, designates as a premise the protection of Linda
> from Flem's influence, for the association as a counselor with
> the daughter is a substitute for association with the mother as a
> lover. . . .
> A phantasy now becomes Stevens's reason to exist in this
> phase of his journey towards reality. He calls it "the second
> premise."[26]

The illusion that Linda can be protected from Flem is shattered
by Eula in its turn. She describes to Gavin the nature of the hold
Flem exerts on Linda and his motives in holding her. By so doing,
she strips Gavin of his "second premise" and prepares the way
for yet another reevaluation of perceptions.

This time, Gavin's speculations are about Flem himself and
cover the entire range of events that have marked his ascent to
power in Jefferson. Each step in the ascent is examined in terms
of motive, as revealed by accomplished end, and apparent method
of accomplishment. In this manner, Gavin gains his highest degree of insight into Snopesism to date. Yet he goes awry at last
by again underestimating the extent of Flem's ruthlessness. Thus,
while his commitment now is to free Linda from Flem's influence, from which he was previously unable to shield her, this, too,
is based on the romantic idealism that has failed him in the past.
Although he has grasped the truth of some of the parts of Linda's
dilemma and has matured in realism accordingly, he is yet lacking the perceptivity to see the parts in the context of the whole.
When he refuses Eula's plea that he marry Linda, he condemns
Eula to saving Linda herself by her own death. As Longley correctly points out, "Eula's suicide can be seen as Gavin's ultimate
failure, since he did not foresee it and was unable to prevent
it." [27] Despite the fact that he seizes almost hysterically on Rat-

liff's explanation, "Maybe she was bored" (p. 358), Gavin's tears
at the end of the novel are in partial recognition of the fact that
had it not been for his own romantic idealism, he might himself
have been "not just strong enough to deserve [Eula's love], earn
it, match it, but even brave enough to accept it" (p. 359). Mourning Eula, he mourns Linda and himself.

The recurrence of this thematic pattern of maturation toward
realism provides a structural framework upon which to base a
closer examination of the novel. As Beck asserts, "the central factor in *The Town* is the looming presence of Gavin Stevens, in the
representative ordeal of his engagement as witness, devotee, inter-
ventionist, and elegist." [28] Through Gavin's unique development,
the nature of Snopesism and the impact of Snopes amorality on
the moral world are revealed.

"Farming Snopeses"

SET IN the context of the brass-stealing episode, Flem
Snopes's arrival in Jefferson occasions considerable humor at his
expense. The comparative sophistication of this urban environment highlights the rural crudeness of his first steps toward self-
betterment, and his wife's almost immediate infidelity with the
wealthy and prominent Manfred de Spain marks him as an unsuspecting cuckold, the private joke of the entire community. This
is the humor of incongruity: the country man parading his power-
plant superintendency, which he attributes to his own cleverness,
before a community to which that superintendency is proof of
his wife's liaison with the mayor. Because it is tempered with
civic pride, the obvious humor of this situation is never reduced
to burlesque. The community is proud not that Manfred de Spain
can confound Flem Snopes but rather that, in Eula Varner
Snopes, De Spain has found a woman equal in brillance to himself. The son of a major in the Confederate cavalry, himself a
West Point graduate scarred in the Spanish-American War, Manfred de Spain as mayor represents the coming of the new age to
Jefferson.

He led the yearly cotillion and was first on the list of the ladies'

german; if café society—not the Social Register nor the Four
Hundred: Café Society—had been invented yet and any of it
had come to Jefferson, he would have led it; born a generation
too soon, he would have been by acclamation ordained a
high priest in that new national religious cult of Cheesecake as
it translated still alive the Harlows and Grables and Monroes
into the hierarchy of American cherubim. (p. 14)

Into his purview comes Eula Varner Snopes, of whom "there was
just too much of what she was for any one human female package
to contain, and hold: to much of white, too much of female, too
much of maybe just glory" (p. 6). Because of the romantic stature
of the lovers, their liaison becomes the pride of the community,
and Flem's threatening stature goes unremarked. As Charles Mallison says, "our whole town was accessory to that cuckolding. . . .
It was not because we were against Mr. Snopes; we had not yet
read the signs and portents which should have warned, alerted,
sprung us into frantic concord to defend our town from him"
(p. 15).

The "signs and portents" to which Charles here refers are provided in part by his own factual reporting, in part by Ratliff.
From the moment Flem appears in the back-alley restaurant,
Charles's description of him marks him as more than simply an
incongruous country man; he is actually predatory: "a squat
uncommunicative man with a neat minute bow tie and opaque
eyes and a sudden little hooked nose like the beak of a small
hawk" (p. 4). Ratliff warns, "Just give him time. Give him six
months and he'll have Grover Cleveland (Grover Cleveland Winbush was the partner) out of the café too" (p. 4). There follows a series of stories, told by Ratliff, about the influx of Snopeses
into Frenchman's Bend, Flem's rise there, his marriage to Eula,
and his sale of the Old Frenchman place to Ratliff in return for
the restaurant. These brief accounts are not, however, detailed,
and they project very little of the terror of Snopesism. It is for
this reason, perhaps, that Gavin is most impressed not by Flem's
rise but by Ratliff's fall in the affair of the salted gold mine. " 'A
salted gold mine,' Uncle Gavin said. 'One of the oldest tricks in
the world, yet you fell for it. Not Henry Armstid: you' " (p. 8).
Ratliff's rejoinder that the trick is "almost as old as that handker-
chief Eula Varner dropped" (p. 8) goes unnoticed. Yet this

comment, like all of Ratliff's succinct insights, constitutes a warning to both Gavin and the community, a warning inevitably heeded too late if at all. Longley says of this early situation in the novel, "At the beginning of *The Town*, only Ratliff, fresh from his major defeat, is in a position to appreciate the danger which threatens. Gavin, from the vantage point of class, education, and profession, is inclined to view the antics of the red-neck *arrivistes* with little more than amusement. After the 'Centaur in Brass' episode, Gavin's amusement changes to alarm, and he realizes that Snopes-watching is a full-time occupation." [29]

The essential irony lies in the fact that Gavin and the community, amused at the naivete of the country man, contribute to his victimization of them by their own naivete. Within six months of "the first Summer of the Snopeses" (p. 4), Grover Cleveland Winbush has been dispossessed of his part ownership in the restaurant, and, following the Frenchman's Bend pattern outlined by Ratliff, a new Snopes has been installed behind the counter. Within two years Flem has moved from his tent to a rented house and is superintendent of the power plant. While this comes as a shock to the community, the rapacity of Flem as agent is hidden by the humor that the community sees in Flem as cuckold. Charles reports, "Our outrage was primarily shock; shock not that Flem had the job, we had not got that far yet, but shock that we had not known until now that the job existed; that there was such a position in Jefferson as superintendent of the power plant. . . . That was the only shock. It wasn't that the country man was Flem Snopes. Because we had all seen Mrs Snopes by now. . . . And we had known the mayor, Major de Spain, longer than that" (pp. 9–10). Only Ratliff is aware of the dark side of Flem's appointment, seeing both motive and method in his apparent ignorance of his wife's infidelity. In answer to Gavin's question, "This town aint that big. Why hasn't Flem caught them?" Ratliff replies, "He dont want to. . . . He dont need to yet" (p. 15).

The ensuing episode, "Centaur in Brass," reveals the deviousness and cruelty of Flem Snopes in a broadly humorous situation where complex manipulation is checked by the simple expedient of cooperation between those being exploited. That Flem is no more than a figurehead in the power plant is immediately obvious from the fact that he has no responsibilities there. The plant is

already staffed with two Negro stokers, Tom Tom Bird and Tomey's Turl Beauchamp, and Mr. Harker, the sawmill engineer who
cares for the boilers. Even Flem's fifty dollar salary is ten dollars
less than Tom Tom's. It is not surprising, then, that he soon begins to look about for ways of supplementing his wage. So ignorant is he of the workings of steam boilers, however, that he
very nearly is responsible for their destruction, stealing the brass
safety valves and replacing them with thousand-pound steel screw
plugs. When his error in judgment results in a personal financial
loss, his manipulations become more subtle. He turns his attention
to scrap metal sorts the iron from the valuable brass scraps, and
forces Tom Tom to become an accessory to the theft of the brass
by exploiting the veteran stoker's fear of losing his job to Turl. Although this diversion is cleverer than the first and, because of the
exploitation of the Negro fireman, more cruel, it also results in
a financial loss to Flem. Mr. Harker jokes about the thefts, Tom
Tom knows that Flem is stealing brass, not iron, and the auditors
discover a deficit in brass scrap amounting to more than two
hundred dollars. Flem pays the bill, "standing there chewing,
with his eyes looking like two gobs of cup grease on a hunk of
raw dough" (p. 22). In an effort to recoup his loss, he engages
Turl as his agent against Tom Tom to reclaim the stolen brass.

This last ploy, however, is also flawed, and while it reinforces
Flem's rapacity and his willingness to use others for his own ends,
it reveals as well the fact that he is not yet secure in the environment of the town. To Mr. Harker's amusement, Flem fails to
recognize the one human element in his scheme that will doom it.

> So, as Mr Harker said, it was not Turl's fault so much as
> Snopes's mistake. "Which was," Mr Harker said, "when Mr
> Snopes forgot to remember in time about that young light-
> colored new wife of Tom Tom's. To think how he picked
> Turl out of all the Negroes in Jefferson, that's prowled at
> least once—or tried to—every gal within ten miles of town, to go
> out there to Tom Tom's house knowing all the time how Tom
> Tom is right here under Mr Snopes's eye wrestling coal until
> six oclock a m and then with two miles to walk down the rail-
> road home, and expect Turl to spend his time out there . . . hunt-
> ing anything that aint hid in Tom Tom's bed. And when I think
> about Tom Tom in here wrastling them boilers in that-ere same
> amical cuckolry like what your uncle says Miz Snopes and

Mayor de Spain walks around in, stealing brass so he can keep
Turl from getting his job away from him, and all the time
Turl is out yonder tending by daylight to Tom Tom's night
homework, sometimes I think I will jest die. (p. 24)

By the time Flem has discovered his oversight, it is already too
late. Tom Tom, too, is suspicious and takes steps to protect the
sanctity of his home. The centaurlike scene in the moonlight,
from which the episode takes its title, ends in a solemn conference
that spells the end of Flem's plot to profit financially from his
power plant superintendency. With high comic irony, the brass
is deposited in the water tank where Flem originally claimed that
he wanted it.

More than thwarting Flem, however, Tom Tom's concern for
his wife's fidelity, the humane cooperation of the two Negroes,
and Charles's final interpretation of the whole episode provide a
chilling comment on Flem's inhumanity. The contrast between
the behavior of the Negro fireman and the white superintendent in
regard to their wives is immediately obvious, and Tom Tom's
concern only serves to darken Flem's apparent unconcern. The
theme begun here, moreover, is iterated later in Gavin's defense
of Eula and in Maurice Priest's defense of Mrs. Priest. The federation of Tom Tom and Turl also highlights Flem's inhumanity
by contrasting to his solitary self-interestedness. Their mutual
concern is described by Gavin as "a sanctuary, a rationality of
perspective, which animals, humans too, not merely reach but
earn by passing through unbearable emotional states like furious
rage or furious fear, the two of them sitting there not only in
Uncle Gavin's amicable cuckoldry but in mutual and complete
federation too: Tom Tom's home violated not by Tomey's
Turl but by Flem Snopes; Turl's life and limbs put into frantic
jeopardy not by Tom Tom but by Flem Snopes" (pp. 27–28).
Whereas Flem has with secrecy attempted to use them, pitting
one against the other for his own profit, Tom Tom and Turl
unite openly to confound him.

The aspect of this episode that casts Flem Snopes in the most
threatening light, however, is Charles's commentary on the significance of the water tank in which the Negroes deposit the
stolen brass. Charles says that Flem, having resigned as superin-

tendent, can "sit all day now on the gallery of his little back-street rented house and look at the shape of the tank standing against the sky above the Jefferson roof-line—looking at his own monument, some might have thought. Except that it was not a monument: it was a footprint. A monument only says *At least I got this far* while a footprint says *This is where I was when I moved again*" (p. 29). Were the tank a "monument," it would be a monument to Flem's failure, limiting the sphere of his rapacity and signifying, by its permanence, an end of his machinations. But Flem's monument is reserved for his success at the end of the novel, and his rapacity is to encompass all of Jefferson, as signified by the fact that his "footprint" stands out against the entire Jefferson "roof-line." The water tank as "footprint" testifies that he is already moving ahead, that his initial defeat has by no means put a stop to his self-interested designs. In a concluding comment on this first episode in Flem's rise, Ratliff points out this fact and suggests the means by which that rise will be accomplished.

> "Not even now?" Uncle Gavin said to Ratliff.
> "Not even now," Ratliff said. "Not catching his wife with Manfred de Spain yet is like that twenty-dollar gold piece pinned to your undershirt on your first maiden trip to what you hope is going to be a Memphis whorehouse. He dont need to unpin it yet." (p. 29)

Flem may have lost his superintendency, but he still has the asset that secured him the position. Eula is still his wife.

As Gavin soon realizes, Flem has other assets as well. As Snopeses proliferate in Jefferson, Gavin's moral response to Flem's exploitation of his wife is quickly clouded by his public response, as county attorney, to the Snopes immigration. His curiosity about Flem, whetted by the fact that the former power plant superintendent has been living in a rented house for two years with no visible means of support, turns to alarm when Ratliff informs him that Flem is preying upon his imported cousins.

> "He's farming," Ratliff said. "Farming?" I said (all right, cried if you like). "Farming what? Sitting there on that gallery from sunup to sundown watching that water tank?"

Farming Snopeses, Ratliff said. Farming Snopeses: the whole
rigid hierarchy moving intact upward one step as he vacated
ahead of it. (p. 31)

Significantly, the first Snopes imported is only a nominal Snopes,
and in his un-Snopes-like behavior Flem's amorality is again de-
lineated by contrast. Whereas Flem exploited the Negro firemen,
Eck literally broke his neck to save a Negro sawmill worker, demonstrating thereby the courage of concern for his fellow man
which is so obviously lacking in Flem. Gavin says that Eck's
mother "must have, as the old bucolic poet said, cast a leglin
girth herself before she married whatever Snopes was Eck's titu-
lar father" (p. 31). Gavin is not surprised when Eck, installed by
Flem in the back-alley restaurant, is with equal celerity removed.
He describes him as

> . . . having less business here than even in the saw mill since at
> the saw mill all he could do was break his own bones where
> here he was a threat to his whole family's long tradition of slow
> and invincible rapacity because of that same incredible and in-
> nocent assumption that all people practise courage and honesty
> for the simple reason that if they didn't everybody would be
> frightened and confused; saying one day, not even privately
> but out loud where half a dozen strangers not even kin by mar-
> riage to Snopeses heard him: "Aint we supposed to be selling
> beef in these here hamburgers? I dont know jest what this
> is yet but it aint no beef." (p. 33)

Removed by Flem, Eck is given the job of night watchman at
the oil tank, not, as Gavin supposes, by Manfred de Spain through
Flem's agency but by the Masonic lodge of which Eck is a brother.
The fraternal concern of the Masons emphasizes Flem's lack of
sensitivity to the blood ties of clan and adds yet another dimension to his growing amorality.

Alarmed by the contrast that he now sees between Flem's totally self-interested rapacity and Eck's generous honesty, Gavin
romantically theorizes that one more generation of Snopeses might
breed a monster in whom rapacity would be combined with the
outward manifestations of courage and honor. With ingenuous
irony he speculates that Eck's son, Wallstreet Panic Snopes, is
the logical candidate to grow into such a creature. Wall, however,

fiercely resists his Snopes heritage and rises as a successful busi-
nessman through true honor and courage. The monster Gavin
foresees in his portrait of the "horse boy," Wall, is Flem himself,
who as offerer of the spotted horses, might also be called "horse
boy."

> Horse boy, dog boy, cat boy, monkey boy, elephant boy:
> anything but Snopes boy. And then suppose, just suppose;
> suppose and tremble: one generation more removed from Eck
> Snopes and his innocence; one generation more until that in-
> nocent and outrageous belief that courage and honor are practi-
> cal has had time to fade and cool so that merely the habit of
> courage and honor remain; add to that then that generation's
> natural heritage of cold rapacity as instinctive as breathing,
> and tremble at that prospect: the habit of courage and honor
> compounded by rapacity or rapacity raised to the absolute
> *nth* by courage and honor: not horse boy but a lion or tiger
> boy: Genghis Khan or Tamerlane or Attila in the defenseless
> midst of indefensible Jefferson. (p. 35)

Ratliff's chorusing answer to this monologue, "you're wrong,"
provides a rhetorical check to Gavin's theorizing and foreshadows
the ironic developments to follows.

With Eck and his family banished early from the Snopes hierarchy, other Snopeses continue the migration into Jefferson, their
histories told by Ratliff as Gavin's alarm steadily increases. Eck
is replaced in the restaurant by I.O. Snopes, "the blacksmith-cum-
schoolmaster-cum-bigamist, or multiplied by bigamy—a thin un-
dersize voluble weasel-faced man talking constantly in a steady
stream of worn saws and proverbs usually having no connection
with one another nor application to anything else, who even with
the hammer would not have weighed as much as the anvil he
abrogated and dispossessed" (p. 36). Characteristically, animal
images abound. The "weasel-faced" I.O. brings with him his first
wife and his son, Montgomery Ward Snopes, who take over
the boarding house, "the place changed from a boarding house to
a warren, with nailed to one of the front veranda posts a pine
board lettered terrifically by hand: SNOPES HOTEL" (p. 40).
Next to come is "the actual Snopes schoolmaster" (p. 40) with
his two sons, Byron and Virgil, all three of whom are related to
the previous Snopeses primarily by species: "they none of them

seemed to bear any specific kinship to one another; they were just Snopeses, like colonies of rats or termites are just rats and termites" (p. 40.) The schoolmaster remains only until "a posse of enraged fathers caught him and a fourteen-year-old girl in an empty cotton house and tarred and feathered him out of the country" (p. 41), but his sons remain. When Byron becomes a clerk in the Sartoris bank, Gavin believes that the position is "an humble cane out of that same quiver which had contained that power plant superintendency" (p. 43), and describes Byron's inquiry into the principles of banking as obscene curiosity: "he had not entered crawling into the glare of a mystery so much as, without attracting any attention to himself, he was trying to lift a corner of its skirt" (p. 43).

As Flem's minions make inroads into social institutions at the highest as well as the lowest levels, Gavin's alarm reaches a pitch of frustration and outrage that greatly exceeds mere curiosity. In this state he again speculates on the future of Jefferson, ignorant, as before, of the ironies he foreshadows. With Byron Snopes in the Sartoris bank, Colonel Sartoris will be

> dis-stabled of his byre and rick in his turn as Ratliff and Grover Cleveland Winbush had been dis-restauranted in theirs. We not to know how of course since that was none of our business; indeed, who to say but there was not one among us but did not want to know: who, already realising that we would never defend Jefferson from Snopeses, let us then give, relinquish Jefferson to Snopeses, banker mayor alderman church and all, so that, in defending themselves from Snopeses, Snopeses must of necessity defend and shield us, their vassals and chattels, too. (pp. 43–44)

Ironically, in attempting to defend Jefferson against Flem, Gavin will assist in Flem's rise. And Flem will be engaged before long in clearing Jefferson of his Snopes cousins in the name of "civic virtue." Although Gavin's tone here is exasperated and his speculations seemingly fanciful, he is in reality close to foretelling the developments of the future. Ratliff, the realist, is telling him that his speculations are well within the realm of possibility when he says, " 'At first you laughed at them [Snopeses] too. . . . Or maybe I'm wrong, and this here is still laughing?'—looking at me,

watching me, too damned shrewd, too damned intelligent. . . .
'Get out of my office, Ratliff,' I said" (p. 44).

Thus far, Gavin's role in the novel is that of a public-spirited
observer, amused and exasperated by what he sees and theorizing
about it, without, however, becoming involved himself. That
this detachment is to be short-lived is suggested by his early reaction to Eula Varner Snopes and the part she plays in Flem's
machinations. Manfred, he says, has given Flem his opportunities
for advancement, but it is Eula on whom the situation actually
turns. He calls her "that damned incredible woman, that Frenchman's Bend Helen, Semiramis—no: not Helen nor Semiramis: Lilith: the one before Eve herself whom Earth's creator had perforce
in desperate and amazed alarm in person to efface, remove, ob-
literate, that Adam might create a progeny to populate it" (p.
44). It is no surprise that with the same "desperate and amazed
alarm" he attributes to Earth's creator, Gavin finds himself involved with his own Lilith in the person of Eula. Vickery sees
Gavin's involvement as being expressive of a second basic aspect
of his character, making of him "at once a participant in the action and a narrator of a story that happens to include himself.
Moreover, in his reactions to Flem and Eula he is both an individual and a public figure: defender of the old established order by
virtue of his family background and champion of civic morality
by virtue of his office. This dual role is reflected in his character
which combines elements of the poet and the lawyer, the romantic and the conventional moralist, the rebel and the conformist.
Inevitably the one conflicts with the other, complicating motives and thwarting action." [30] While Gavin Stevens, county
attorney, can damn Eula for the role she is playing in Flem's advancement, Gavin Stevens the individual can only love her. Furthermore, Gavin is a romantic idealist, and his love for her takes
the form almost of idolatry. Farnham says of him, "Stevens is
unusual among the people of Yoknapatawpha County because of
the nature of his education and because of the sensitivity of his
mind. His realization of the meaning of Eula Varner as a female
is unique, for his appreciation goes beyond the desire for physical
union. . . . Stevens takes upon himself the role of Eula's protector.
He is her priest and worshipper." [31]

In this context Manfred de Spain becomes, in Gavin's eyes,

Eula's violator, posing a threat to her chastity from which she must be defended. It is significant that, once involved with Eula, Gavin forfeits the objectivity which permitted him to see Flem Snopes's agency behind the comparable contest between Tom Tom Bird and Tomey's Turl Beauchamp. Despite Ratliff's repeated statements of Flem's agency in the exploitation of Eula, Gavin romantically focuses on the manifestation of that exploitation in the person of De Spain.

> "You're going to save her," Mother said, not looking at Uncle Gavin now: just watching the sock she was darning.
> "Yes!" Uncle Gavin said, fast, quick: no in-breathe this time, so quick he almost said the rest of it before he could stop himself, so that all Mother had to do was say it for him:
> "—from Manfred de Spain."
> "You [Gowan] cant help it either, can you?" she said. "You've got to be a man to, haven't you?" She just talked to Uncle Gavin then: "Just what is it about this that you cant stand? That Mrs Snopes may not be chaste, or that it looks like she picked Manfred de Spain out to be unchaste with?"
> "Yes!" Uncle Gavin said. "I mean no! It's all lies—gossip. It's all—"
> "Yes," Mother said. "You're right. It's probably all just that. Saturday's not a very good afternoon to get in the barbershop, but you might think about it when you pass."
> "Thanks," Uncle Gavin said. "But if I'm to go on this crusade with any hope of success, the least I can do is look wild and shaggy enough to be believed." (p. 49)

As Farnham points out, Gavin "is in the paradoxical situation of defending Eula's chastity, which he knows does not exist, from a man in whose role of lover he himself longs to be." [32] Aside from Ratliff, whose advice Gavin ignores, only his twin sister, Maggie Mallison, is romantic enough to know his thoughts yet practical enough to know that "women are not interested in morals" (p. 48). From the vantage point of the uninvolved observer she sees that Flem is at the crux of this conflict. She tells Gowan, "You don't marry Semiramis: you just commit some form of suicide for her. Only gentlemen with as little to lose as Mr Flem Snopes can risk marrying Semiramis" (p. 50).

The conflict between Gavin and Manfred de Spain is characterized by a comic ferocity in which Gavin's desperate attempts to establish his self-created illusion as a reality are recurrently thwarted by De Spain's taunts. Gavin attempts to demonstrate Eula's respectability by having his sister call on her, praising the ladies of the Byron Society and the Cotillion Club who follow Maggie's example, and arranging for the Snopeses to be invited to the Cotillion Ball. By so doing he unwittingly gives Flem an assist in his social ascent. Throughout his attempts at imposing outward respectability on Eula, however, Gavin is subjected to severe embarrassments at the hands of his brother-in-law and his rival. When the Cotillion invitations are issued, Maggie's husband says, "Well by godfrey, that puts you one up on Manfred de Spain, dont it? He's a lone orphan; he hasn't got a wife or a twin sister who was one of the original founders of Jefferson literary and snobbery clubs; all he can do to Flem Snopes's wife is—" (p. 56). Later he asserts that Gavin is really harmless, incapable of protecting Eula's honor even if it existed: "it aint that he [Gavin] dont want to make trouble: he just dont know how. Oh, I dont mean he wont try. He'll do the best he knows. But he just dont know how to make the kind of trouble that a man like Manfred de Spain will take seriously" (p. 58). When Manfred enters the conflict himself, taunting Gavin with the cutout on his roadster, the senior Mallison's perception of Gavin's helplessness is borne out. To Jefferson, De Spain's roadster symbolizes everything that its owner stands for: "that vehicle alien and debonair, as invincibly and irrevocably polygamous and bachelor as De Spain himself" (p. 14). To Gavin, the sound of the cutout represents a direct challenge that he meets with the sophomoric trick of planting a sharpened rake head in the road to stop it. Although the "ripping . . . and jeering" (p. 62) are indeed silenced, they are replaced by De Spain's own laughter in the Mallison living room as he waits for his tire to be repaired. Mr. Mallison explains that Gavin has asked to be excused from the toddy drinking with De Spain because "he seems to have heartburn these days" (p. 68). By defending the honor of the "country man's" wife, Gavin himself has become the object of the community's collective amusement, another unsophisticated cuckold against whom the people of the town are allied as Manfred's confederates.

This role reversal is continued in the exaggerated comedy of the "Rouncewell panic" episode. By sending a corsage to Eula, Gavin

assumes the prerogative of the husband. When Maggie strenuous-
ly objects, he is forced to send corsages to all the women of Jefferson, thereby forcing not only their husbands but Manfred himself to follow suit. Significantly, it is not Flem who receives the
cuckold's corsage from De Spain, but Gavin himself.

> It was the rake-head, with two flowers like a bouquet, all bound
> together with a band or strip of something that Gowan knew
> was thin rubber but it was another year or two until he was
> a good deal bigger and older that he knew what the thing was;
> and at the same time he realized what it was, he said he knew
> it had already been used; and at the same time at least how Uncle
> Gavin was supposed to believe it had been used, which was the
> reason Mr De Spain sent it to him: that whether Uncle Gavin
> was right or not about how it had been used, he would never
> be sure and so forever afterward would have no peace about
> it. (pp. 71–72)

The events of the Cotillion Ball, witnessed by Gowan and narrated by Charles Mallison, elevate the Gavin-Manfred rivalry to
a more universal plane where simple amusement is replaced by
fear and even terror. Whereas previously Eula's mythic qualities
are merely described, those qualities are here dramatized by the
impact that she has on Manfred, Gavin, and the men of Jefferson.
Begun as a dirty joke to taunt Gavin, Manfred's dance with Eula
ends as a commentary on elemental human emotion represented
in Eula's "splendid unshame," a commentary that not only shakes
Manfred's artificial pride in himself as cuckolder but also reveals
the hypocrisy of his allies, the people of the town. Charles recalls
that

> when I was old enough, fourteen or fifteen or sixteen, I knew
> what Gowan had seen without knowing what he was seeing:
> that second when Mr de Spain felt astonishment, amazement
> and unbelief and terror too at himself because of what he found
> himself doing without even knowing he was going to—dancing
> like that with Mrs Snopes to take revenge on Uncle Gavin for
> having frightened him, Mr de Spain, enough to make him play
> the sophomore tricks like the cut-out and the rake-head and
> the used rubber thing in a corsage; frightened at himself at
> finding out that he couldn't possibly be only what he had thought
> for all those years he was, if he could find himself in a condition

capable of playing tricks like that; while Mrs Snopes was dancing
that way, letting Mr de Spain get her into dancing that way in
public, simply because she was alive and not ashamed of it like
maybe right now or even for the last two weeks Mr de Spain
and Uncle Gavin had been ashamed; was what she was and
looked the way she looked and wasn't ashamed of it and not
afraid or ashamed of being glad of it, nor even of doing this
to prove it, since this appeared to be the only way of proving it,
not being afraid or ashamed, that the little puny people fallen
back speechless and aghast in a shocked circle around them,
could understand; all the other little doomed mean cowardly
married and unmarried husbands looking aghast and outraged
in order to keep one another from seeing that what they really
wanted to do was cry, weep because they were not that brave,
each one knowing that even if there was no other man on earth,
let alone in that ball room, they still could not have survived,
let alone matched or coped with, that splendor, that splendid
unshame. (pp. 74–75)

In this heady atmosphere Gavin's intervention signifies more
than the mere revenge of the nominal cuckold. It amounts to an
affirmation of moral existence, undertaken, it is true, from the
point of view of the romantic idealist, but no less sincere for that.
Unlike Manfred de Spain, Gavin never takes time to be frightened
by Eula's mythic proportions. In Eula's purity, which momentarily frightens De Spain, Gavin sees only the symbolic purity of
all women threatened now by the way De Spain is dancing. Thus
Charles Mallison can say of him, "Uncle Gavin wasn't trying
any more to destroy or even hurt Mr de Spain because he had
already found out by that time that he couldn't. Because now
Uncle Gavin was himself again. What he was doing was simply
defending forever with his blood the principle that chastity and
virtue in women shall be defended whether they exist or not"
(p. 76). Significantly, the rose he receives for his efforts comes
not from Eula but from his sister, Maggie. It represents not the
passionate reward to a lover but the platonic reward to an idealist,
and Gavin, when Maggie tells him that Eula sent it, is wise enough
to say, "You lie. . . . You did it" (p. 76).

In addition to dramatizing the differences between Manfred,
Gavin, and "the married and unmarried husbands" of the town,
the events of the Cotillion Ball serve to further the sense of Flem
Snopes's inexorable rapacity and ruthlessness. In the two years

since his first "footprint" was left on Jefferson, Flem has remained
outwardly inert, farming Snopeses at the lowest level of society
in back-alley restaurants and dilapidated boarding houses. As Gavin watches the influx of Snopeses, his amusement turns slowly to
alarm, and with Byron in the bank he even speculates that a
Snopes may someday take over the high office of county attorney.
Yet, ironically, it is Gavin himself who, by inviting Eula to the
Christmas Cotillion sponsored by the socially elite of Jefferson,
affords Flem the opportunity to rise still further. As always, Flem
exploits to the fullest his opportunities for personal advancement.
Charles Mallison says of his appearance at the ball, "Mr Snopes
was there too, in a rented dress suit, and Jefferson probably thought
at first that that rented dress suit was just the second footprint
made on it, until they had time to realise that it wasn't anymore
just a footprint than that water tank was a monument: it was a
red flag. No: it was that sign at the railroad crossing that says
Look Out for the Locomotive" (p. 73). Living in a rented house,
dressed in a rented suit, Flem is slowly acquiring the forms of
social acceptability, the "habits of courage and honor," at which,
in combination with rapacity, Gavin shuddered in his speculations
about Wall Snopes. He even has a nominal cuckold whose defense of his wife's supposed chastity relieves him of the necessity
of ritually defending her himself; as Charles comments, "It should
have been Mr Snopes of course because he was the husband, the
squire, the protector in the formal ritual. But it was Uncle Gavin
and he wasn't any husband or squire or knight or defender or
protector either except simply and quickly his own" (p. 75).
Comparing Flem's rise in Jefferson to a trip to a "Memphis whorehouse," Ratliff has earlier told Gavin that Flem does not need to
unpin the "twenty-dollar gold piece" that Eula's infidelity represents to him. While Maggie Mallison's comment after the fight
that the people of Jefferson act "like a god damn whorehouse"
(p. 77) indicates that Flem has arrived, there is still no necessity
for him to unpin the "gold piece" by publicly exposing the lovers.
In addition to assisting in the creation and upholding of Flem's
illusion of respectability, Gavin has provided for its continuance.

In the events of the Cotillion Ball, then, the rapacity of Flem's
motives and the ruthlessness of his methods are both revealed. In
contrast to Gavin's active, principled intervention on behalf of

moral existence, Flem's passive insensitivity to any issue except his own self-aggrandizement points up his fundamental lack of morality. His motive is personal wealth; his method is the exploitation of Eula's mythic sexuality, which has the power to frighten even the self-assured Manfred de Spain and reduce the entire community to "little puny people . . . doomed mean cowardly" (p. 75). In this state the town itself is as much in Flem's thrall as Eula and as liable to exploitation. As long as the townspeople remain the "allies" and "confederates" of the lovers, they are susceptible to the same injuries, the same anguish and loss incurred by those in whom they take a civic pride. Speaking with no little foreboding of a future time, Charles Mallison says: "And after a while more still and she was dead and Mr de Spain had left town wearing public mourning for her as if she had been his wife and Jefferson finally quit talking about her, my bet is there was more than me in Jefferson that even just remembering her could feel it still and grieve" (p. 74). In the humorous episode in which Grenier Weddel attempts to emulate as a lover the more splendid Manfred de Spain, the resultant injuries, like Gavin's, are described as marking Flem Snopes's rise: "Mr Snopes left more footprints than . . . [Gavin's bloody nose] on Jefferson that night; he left another bloody nose and two black eyes" (p. 77). Commenting on the significance of such "footprints," Longley says, "Flem is exceptional in that he turns human impulse and emotion to his own profit and moves utterly unconcerned over the human wreckage that occurs." [33]

Yet another aspect of Flem's character is revealed by Ratliff's account of Mink Snopes's imprisonment and trial. As has already been suggested by his farming of Snopeses and Eck's dismissal as restaurant manager, Flem lacks even the fundamental human commitment to the blood ties of clan loyalty. This aspect of his character is reinforced by his failure to come to Mink's assistance. Ratliff characterizes Mink as "the only out-and-out mean Snopes we ever experienced. . . . we had never run into one before that was just mean without no profit consideration or hope atall" (p. 79). Because there is no "profit consideration" in Mink's killing Houston, there is no benefit to Flem in saving Mink, and while Ratliff and Mink himself clearly believe that Flem could save him, he does not. His method here is simply to ignore the situation.

In the face of Mink's growing sense of "the injustice and the betrayal," Ratliff sees clearly that "Flem by now must a heard about the killing and was deliberately keeping away from Frenchman's Bend or maybe all Mississippi so he wouldn't have to help him, get him out of it" (p. 80).

The attitude that Flem assumes toward civic law in his cousin's murder trial is the same attitude that governs his reactions toward Gavin's suit against the power plant bonding company. He simply absents himself from the proceedings, thereby stifling inquiry into the missing brass. To Gavin Stevens, intent upon defending Eula's chastity, Flem's absence is inconsequential. Gavin has not yet abandoned his original premise that it is Manfred de Spain who is the threat, and he attacks him now through Flem, whom, for the purpose of his suit, he considers to be Manfred's agent because he is Manfred's employee. Although Gavin acts in his role as public figure, his action is motivated by his response as an individual to Eula. Ratliff says of this confusion of motives and misdirection of action, "Now he had to do something, he didn't care what" (p. 82). He adds that Gavin conducts his suit openly rather than approaching Manfred privately because "he didn't want nothing from De Spain because the only thing De Spain had that he wanted, Lawyer didn't know his-self that was what he wanted until his paw told him that last afternoon" (p. 83). In this state of confusion, Gavin's attempt at positive action dwindles to mere talk. He insists on filing the suit despite all reasonable arguments to the contrary. The bonding company lawyer points out the irony: "If you find brass in the tank, there wont be no crime because the brass already belongs to the city. . . . I mean if the brass aint missing there aint no crime because it wasn't never stole" (p. 85).

Essentially, Gavin is as guilty of malfeasance of office in his suit against De Spain as he feels De Spain himself was in hiring Flem. He is using his own public office to further his individual concerns. If the irony of this situation is lost on him, however, it is not lost on Manfred, Judge Stevens, Judge Dukenfield, or the town. Ratliff says that Gavin continues the suit "because he didn't know either what he wanted. And even when next day his paw told him what his behavior looked like he wanted and for a minute Lawyer even agreed, that still wasn't it" (p. 86). Judge Dukenfield adjourns the preliminary hearing with the humorous comment, "I dont believe either plaintiff or defendant will need more counsel than are represented tonight but they are welcome to bring juniors if they like—or should we say seconds?" (p. 87). As the hearing adjourns, the townspeople leave the courtroom "still laughing and talking and joking back and forth, still not taking no sides but jest mainly enjoying it" (p. 87). Pondering the implications of his behavior, Gavin retires to his office, "setting alone—provided it was him of course and providing he was alone—how does the feller say it? inviting his soul?" (p. 87).

Gavin's "inviting his soul" prefaces the interview between him and Eula and constitutes a brief but scathing self-scrutiny in which he sees at last the correlation between his bond company suit and his "playing with tacks in the street like a vicious boy" (p. 89). He compares his behavior in both cases to that of a "child striking matches in a hay-stack yet at the same time trembling with terror lest he does see holocaust" (pp. 89–90). Moreover, he perceives that he has spent "two hundred nights of fevered projection of my brother's mantle to defend and save her honor from its ravisher" (p. 91). The holocaust that he has anticipated and dreaded is union with Eula: "I to be swept up as into storm or hurricane or tornado itself and tossed and wrung and wrenched and consumed, the light last final spent insentient husk to float slowing and weightless, for a moment longer during the long vacant rest of life, and then no more" (p. 91). With the prospect of such a union immediately before him, his idealization of her reaches fantastic heights. Hearing her footstep on the stair, he thinks, "How can you move and make that little noise, with only the sound of trivial human feet: who should have moved like Wagner: not with but *in* the sonorous sweep of thunder or brass music, even the very limbs moving in tune with the striding other in a sound of tuned wind and storm and mighty harps" (p. 89). Crossing to the door he feels terror at his own "courage, desperation, despair—call it whatever you like and whatever it was and wherever I found it" (p. 90).

This romantic terror turns immediately to amazed disbelief when Eula enters the office not as the mythic goddess of Gavin's imagination but simply as a woman. His shocked reaction that *"she cant possibly be this small, this little"* (p. 90) is followed in

turn by the flowing away of his desire for her. He had expected
union in a consuming tempest; "only it didn't happen, no con-
sumption to wrench, wring and consume me down to the ultimate last proud indestructible grateful husk, but rather simply to
destroy me as the embalmer destroys with very intactness what
was still life, was still life even though it was only the living
worm's" (p. 91). To his amazement Eula moves about the office
with the curiosity of a normal woman, pulling down the blinds.
No Wagnerian thunder rolls forth; her speech is practical and
straight to the point. With clinical self-assurance she proposes,
"Do it here. In your office. You can lock the door and I dont
imagine there'll be anybody high enough up this late at night
to see in the window" (p. 91).

    This behavior not only shocks Gavin but frightens him, and he
immediately begins to grasp for motives that will justify her proposal in terms of his ideal of her as essentially chaste. He is horri-
fied to discover, however, that her own stated motive in coming
is as simple and practical as her behavior: " 'Because you are
unhappy,' she said. 'I dont like unhappy people. They're a nui-
sance. Especially when it can—' " (p. 93). It is inconceivable to
him that she should apparently value so lightly that for which he
has so long suffered. Her realistic concern with his merely physical needs is simply incommensurate with his romantic concern
for her respectability, and he declines to accept her on the terms
of her practical philosophy that "you just are, and you need, and
you must, and so you do" (p. 94). As he correctly says, "If I had
just had sense enough to say *I am, I want, I will and so here goes*
—If I had just done that, it might have been me instead of Manfred? But dont you see? Cant you see? I wouldn't have been me
then?" (p. 94). Gavin is still the romantic, and while he might
have been willing to continue his romantic rivalry with Manfred,
"cuckolding him on his mistress" (p. 94), he is not willing to
compromise his idealism by reducing himself to the practical level
on which Manfred has cuckolded Flem. Manfred he now knows
is simply amused by him: he says, "Manfred wouldn't really mind
because just I cant hurt him, harm him, do any harm; not Manfred,
not just me, no matter what I do. That he would really just as
soon resign as not and the only reason he doesn't is just to show

me I cant make him" (p. 93). Therefore, he theorizes that Eula must have come to protect Flem, and gallant Gavin is no more prepared to cuckold an impotent man than he is to involve himself in Snopesism. " 'No,' I said, cried. I might—would—have struck her with my out-flung arm, but there was room: out of the trap now and even around her until I could reach the door knob and open it. Oh yes, I knew now. 'I might buy Manfred from you but I wont buy Flem,' I said. 'Because it is Flem, isn't it? Isn't it?' " (p. 95).

From his new perspective he sees that it is futile to prosecute Manfred and that, by declining to enter into a rivalry with the husband, he cannot prosecute Flem. His continuing confusion between his public and private motives thus thwarts any action. He tells Eula, "Dont worry about your husband. . . . Just say I represent Jefferson and so Flem Snopes is my burden too. You see, the least I can do is to match you: to value him as highly as your coming here proves you do" (pp. 95–96). The next day Judge Stevens declares, "The plaintiff in this suit has of this date withdrawn his charge and his bill of particulars. The suit—if it was a suit—no longer exists. The litigants—plaintiff, defendant and prisoner—if there was a prisoner—are discharged" (p. 98).

If Gavin's suit against Manfred is foolish it is also chivalrous, deeply principled in its motivation, and generously concerned in its execution. Beck says that Gavin's chivalry

> . . . is fundamental, in that he is protagonist of the ethic which is most explicit in putting women and children first but which applies in defense of all common human rights and of any decency, civility, and gentility conservative of such rights. Gavin's quixotism is not an aberration but simply an extravagance, a generous expenditure in the direction of the humane, setting the perhaps possible above the probable, and if it is cavalier, it is gallantly so, sensing honor vitally as something beyond position and assumption, to be lived up to in progressive conduct. Such a pursuit, as Gavin finds repeatedly, must face up to the always difficult transit from theory to practice, and must go the tortuous second mile in the spirit of the law, beyond its masking letter. And for Gavin Stevens too, as for others, the issue is to be joined at last on personal and private grounds, in the solitary

subjective struggle against despair, to maintain firmness of mind
while avoiding hardness of heart.[34]

It is obvious from Gavin's tears that this struggle is intense and the
price exacted high. He has upheld his principles with courage, but
he has forfeited thereby his opportunity to possess Eula. In Manfred's taunting laughter, moreover, he sees that the struggle is not
yet over. To his father's question, "Then what is it you do want?
For him not to be alive? Is that it?" he can only reply, "What must
I do now, Papa? Papa, what can I do now?" (p. 99). Manfred can
respond to Eula on the merely physical level, as Ratliff says, need-
ing only "for both of them to agree on when and where next and
jest how long away it would have to be" (p. 99). Gavin, however,
"never understood her and never would: that he never had jest
Manfred de Spain to have to cope with, he was faced with a simple
natural force repeating itself under the name of De Spain or Mc-
Carron or whatever into ever gap or vacancy in her breathing as
long as she breathed; and that wouldn't never none of them be
him" (pp. 100–101). Only Flem Snopes, the impotent husband,
can understand Eula. Because he does not respond to her physically, his perception of her is never clouded.

Gavin's decision to leave Jefferson for the University of Heidelberg is completely commensurate with his decision to forfeit Eula.
Having been sorely challenged in defense of his romantic ideals,
he is in a sense cloistering himself away from temptation by entering a university, representative of intellectual rather than physical
activity. Ratliff points out with genuine sympathy that Gavin has
suffered a defeat, but it is a defeat of which he can be justly proud:
"Because there was more folks among the Helens and Juliets and
Isoldes and Guineveres than jest the Launcelots and Tristrams and
Romeos and Parises. There was them others that never got their
names in the poetry books, the next-best ones that sweated and
panted too. And being the next-best to Paris is jest a next-best too,
but it aint no bad next-best to be. Not ever body had Helen, but
then not ever body lost her neither" (p. 101). Furthermore, Gavin's defeat as an individual aspirant for possession of Eula does
not signify that he has given up his other struggles, specifically
against Snopesism. Just before he leaves, in fact, he charges Ratliff
with continuing the fray in his name.

"I was hoping to see you before I left, to pass the torch on into your active hand. You'll have to hold the fort now. You'll have to tote the load."

"What fort?" I says ."What load?"

"Jefferson," he says. "Snopeses. Think you can handle them till I get back?"

"Not me nor a hundred of me," I says. "The only thing to do is get completely shut of them, abolish them." (p. 102)

Although Ratliff is willing to resist Snopesism in any way that he can, he is realistic enough to know that such resistance will not be completely successful until Snopesism has been abolished. This is yet to be proven to Gavin, whose major interest is in his romantic vision of great forces contending together. To him the battle itself is an imperative if the end is to be of value.

The time that Gavin spends at the University of Heidelberg does nothing to quell his idealism, and when the First World War opens he very nearly sides with the German cause, realizing only at the last minute that the Germany of 1914 "was no longer the Germany of Goethe and Bach and Beethoven and Schiller" (p. 103). His opportunity for Snopes-watching is also continued when to avoid the draft Montgomery Ward Snopes enlists in the YMCA and is sent overseas. Before long, however, Montgomery turns the YMCA canteen, whose managerial control Gavin had given him, into a house of prostitution, and Gavin, who had unknowingly assisted in this exploitation by taking Montgomery to France, writes to Ratliff, "*Dont mention that name to me again. I wont discuss it. I will not*" (p. 107). Even in France Gavin cannot escape Snopesism, and Ratliff says of Montgomery Ward, "He was the hair-shirt of . . . [Gavin's] lost love and devotion, whether he knowed it or not or cared or not" (p. 114). A second Snopes draft-dodger, Byron Snopes, feigns a heart ailment in order to avoid going abroad and having to give up his lucrative sideline of stealing from the Sartoris bank. This leads Ratliff, who has been left to do the "holding and toting" by himself, to comment that "the reason Snopeses were successful was that they had all federated unanimously to remove being a Snopes from just a zoological category into a condition composed of success by means of the single rule and regulation and sacred oath of never to tell anybody how" (p. 107). In contrast to Montgomery Ward and Byron,

Eck Snopes, who is legitimately ineligible for military service, ironically is blown up at home. Eck is buried by his brother Masons who found him a job when his cousin Flem fired him from the restaurant, but his death is totally ignored by the Snopes clan. Characteristically, it is Ratliff who delivers his elegy. "Eck wasn't a Snopes. That's why he had to die. Like there wasn't no true authentic room for Snopeses in the world and they made theirselves one by that pure and simple mutual federation, and the first time one slips or falters or fails in being Snopes, it dont even need the rest of the pack like wolves to finish him: simple environment jest watched its chance and taken it" (p. 107).

In this atmosphere of creeping Snopesism, Gavin returns from the war in time to witness the ironic fulfillment of his earlier romantic projections. With the death of Colonel Sartoris, Manfred de Spain is voted the new president of the Sartoris bank by the major stockholders. One of them is Flem Snopes, who "had been buying up the stock in lots anywhere from one to ten shares for several years" (p. 118). When Byron Snopes's thefts are discovered by an audit of the books, Manfred mysteriously acquires sufficient funds to cover the loss himself, and Ratliff says "it was two or three days before anybody seemed to notice how at the same time they announced that Mr Flem Snopes was now the new vice president" (p. 120). This appointment is the first step toward the realization of Gavin's previous half-serious statement "let us then give, relinquish Jefferson to Snopeses, banker mayor alderman church and all" (p. 44).

At the same time that Flem enters the bank as vice-president, two other Snopeses begin their rise in the community. Cloaking his activities in the same cloth of respectability worn by Flem, Montgomery Ward Snopes opens his photographic studio, Atelier Monty. In contrast to the suspect nature of Montgomery's business, Wallstreet Panic Snopes purchases a grocery store and works diligently at acquiring an education. Montgomery is the son of a true Snopes, "the first of what Ratliff called 'them big gray-colored chaps of I.O.'s'" (p. 104); Wall is the son of Eck, whom Gavin "refused to believe . . . was ever a Snopes" (p. 127). Whereas it was Wall at whom Gavin trembled in his speculations on the "horse-boy," it is Montgomery Ward who poses the actual threat to Jefferson by selling "female excitement" (p. 126) in the back room of his studio. Wall, ironically, develops into one of Jefferson's most upstanding citizens. It is therefore not Wall but Montgomery Ward from whom, in Gavin's previous speculations, Snopeses "in defending themselves from Snopeses . . . must of necessity defend and shield us, their vassals and chattels, too" (p. 44). Although the form that this defending and shielding will ultimately take is not yet clear to Gavin, he can be certain that there will be no hesitancy to "defend and shield" when the need arises. The fundamental Snopesian insensitivity to clan ties has already been demonstrated in the dilemmas of Eck and Mink. It is reiterated in Ab's treatment at the hands of his grandsons, Vardaman and Bilbo. Ab's "Snopes industry" is his watermelon patch, which he cultivates not for financial profit but "as a bait for the pleasure or sport or contest or maybe just getting that mad, of catching boys robbing it; planting and cultivating and growing watermelons just so he could sit ambushed with a loaded shotgun behind a morning-glory vine on his back gallery until he could hear sounds from the melon patch and then shooting at it" (p. 130). Vardaman's and Bilbo's "Snopes industry" is baiting Ab with shouts of "chaps in the melon patch!" (p. 131) and then "dodging and running and still laughing while the old man scrabbled up his piled rocks to throw at them" (p. 130). It is this open insensitivity even to other members of the clan that Ratliff is later to characterize as "Snopes out-and-out unvarnished behavior" (p. 370).

To Gavin, who "has been watching Snopeses for going on ten years now . . . [and who] even taken one all the way to France with him to keep his-self abreast" (p. 112), such obvious Snopes traits are of little interest except for the edification of new initiates to Snopes-watching such as Charles Mallison. Gavin's concern is for the larger, more devious aspects of the visitation to which he is witness, the subtle nuances of amorality that provide fuel for his burgeoning speculations on the nature of reality. In his romantic attempts to affirm the moral nature of reality as he defines it, he has witnessed the collapse of his first premise: that Eula is chaste and that her chastity must be defended. Despite his defeat, he still clings to his belief in the innate rightness of principled existence, and his opposition to the amoral forces that he perceives to be at work in Jefferson in the persons of Snopeses remains firm. In combination with his romantic idealism, this commitment makes inevitable his further personal interventions against the aggressor. Such intervention requires only a cause to be defended, a premise on which to base action. When Charles Mallison describes Linda Snopes as walking "exactly like a pointer dog walks just before it freezes onto the birds," Gavin replies, "I know what you mean. . . . I know exactly what you mean" (p. 131). His involvement with Linda is immediate, and it only remains to find a premise that suits her.

"He Only Knew He Wanted, Had to Have"

SPEAKING of Faulkner's narrative mode in the Snopes trilogy, Beck explains that for all of its complications and retellings, its involuted yet fluent variations, it is nonetheless "steadily cumulative." [35] Indeed, because the fiction is committed to complexity, the narrative mode is most expeditious. Beck says:

> Nor is this complexity a sheer subjective brooding either in the *personae* or by their creator; character and circumstance interplay dramatically, much complication is produced by aggression and corrective intervention. . . . The method dramatizes a tentative approach toward relative certainties which do not preclude but rather make way for continued reestimation. It accepts as a chief constant a recurrence in modifying context, where increasingly known familiar elements fall into successively new combinations and a return to the same finds identity of another aspect.[36]

The use of this mode is perhaps nowhere more explicit than in Gavin's attachment to Eula's daughter, Linda, and the events ensuing from that attachment. Whereas his commitment to Eula was founded upon lust tempered by his romantic idealization of her, his commitment to her daughter is founded on the memory of that lust and the realization that it will never be assuaged or effaced. Gavin, however, also realizes that he is saddened not by the absence in Linda of her mother's sexuality but by the fact that he was unable to match Eula's vitality. Having felt the force of this natural impulse, Gavin justifies her failure to reproduce herself in

Linda in terms of natural law. He says, "Because even Nature, loving concupiscent uproar and excitement as even Nature loves it, insists that it at least be reproductive of fresh fodder for the uproar and the excitement. Which would take time, the time necessary to produce that new crop of fodder, since she—Eula Varner—had exhausted, consumed, burned up that one of hers" (p. 133). By an ironic juxtaposition Gavin rationalizes that it is not he but Eula who is thereby doomed: "doomed never to efface the anguish and the hunger from Motion even by her own act of quitting Motion and so fill with her own absence from it the aching void where once had glared that incandescent shape" (p. 133).

Despite the fact that Eula is lost to Gavin forever by being thus doomed, Gavin himself can still, in Beck's words, assert "the continuity of being and the conservation of the matter of experience." [37] He rejects the poet's lament "that Fancy passed me by And nothing will remain": it "is a damned lie since, praise, O gods! Nothing cannot remain anywhere since nothing is vacuum and vacuum is paradox and unbearable and we will have none of it even if we would, the damned-fool poet's Nothing steadily and perennially full of perennially new and perennially renewed anguishes for me to measure my stature against whenever I need reassure myself that I also am Motion" (p. 135). Gavin has committed himself to his self-imposed illusion that he was Eula's lover, but his desire for her is destroyed when her real nature proves incommensurate with his idealized perception of her. Nonetheless, the memory of that desire remains, and it is out of that memory that Gavin creates a second illusion; he reasons that having been Eula's lover he is thereby the father of her child. According to Longley, "he gives up the woman [Eula] but retains the dream. All of his subsequent behavior—what Ratliff calls simply 'not losing Helen'—can be explained in terms of this dream. . . . This is the basis . . . of his private myth concerning Linda. Linda is not, could not be, the child of Flem. Since Eula is not Gavin's wife in fact but should have been, then Linda is not his child but ought to be, hence she is." [38] Ever the irrepressible fabulist, Gavin goes a step further in the development of his new illusion by imagining himself to be Linda's actual father, Hoake McCarron:

So that girl-child was not Flem Snopes's at all, but mine; my

child and my grandchild both, since the McCarron boy who
begot her (oh yes, I can even believe Ratliff when it suits me)
in that lost time, was Gavin Stevens in that lost time; and, since
remaining must remain or quit being remaining, Gavin Stevens
is fixed by his own child forever at that one age in that one
moment. So since the son is father to the man, the McCarron
fixed forever and timeless in that dead youth as Gavin Stevens
is of necessity now the son of Gavin Stevens's age, and Mc-
Carron's child is Gavin Stevens's grandchild. (pp. 135–136)

As Farnham states, by becoming McCarron, "Stevens has . . . created a private reality based on self-imposed illusion. . . . Fortunate-
ly for Stevens, he is sadly aware of his own delusion, and he is able
to continue his existence." [39]

This romantic transference of identity is rooted in richer earth
than mere vicarious self-fulfillment, however. Gavin's initial interest in Linda is a raison d'être in which his antagonism toward
Snopesism finds an outlet in the protection of a nominal member
of the tribe. He says, "To save Jefferson from a Snopes is a duty;
to save a Snopes from a Snopes is a privilege" (p. 184). Like all of
Gavin's romantic declarations, the phrasing of this commitment is
a long time in coming and develops through a series of interrelated
theories and perceptions. Behind each of them Flem Snopes lurks
as a felt presence against which Gavin instinctively reacts. Gavin
has said that Eula is not herself a Snopes. "Eula Snopes it could
never be simply because it must not simply because I would de-
cline to have it so" (p. 132). Furthermore, he knows that Flem is
impotent because "I had—had had to—watched them in bed together" (p. 132). Finally, he thinks, "not for the first time . . . how
apparently all Snopeses are male, as if the mere and simple incident of woman's divinity precluded Snopesishness and made it
paradox" (p. 136). In this context, Linda bears the same relationship to Flem as daughter that Eula bears to him as wife. She is thus
in danger of the same exploitation suffered by her mother. Seen
in the modified context of the Linda-Flem relationship, Gavin's
decision to protect her constitutes a recurrence of his previous
commitment to protect Eula. He calls it "the second premise" (p.
135).

As quixotic and romantic as his means of arriving at this premise
may be, there is little doubt that it is based at last on principled

opposition to Snopesism in general and Flem in particular. As Beck points out, "Snopesism most acutely affronts and unavoidably challenges Gavin by its victimizing of Eula and its threats to Linda; the magnanimity of Gavin's concern for both Eula and Linda, resting in moral conviction, is the opposite pole to Snopes meanness. On this contrast the trilogy is structurally poised; in these terms Gavin's quixotism, extreme as it is, seems the minimum ameliorative measure and thus the only honorable position this side of compromise." [40] Gavin's fantasies concerning Eula and Linda thus serve a twofold function. They provide Gavin, first, with a reason to challenge Snopesism and, second, with a medium through which to do so. By associating himself with Eula and Linda in the respective roles of lover and father, he assumes the responsibility for their protection; by attempting to protect them, he places himself in direct conflict with the forces he despises. Neither the foolishness of his behavior toward them nor the ineffectiveness of his speculations and interventions on their behalf obscures his deeply principled antagonism to amorality. Flem Snopes represents a force destructive of everything that Gavin values and believes; and, as such, he is the central figure at whom Gavin's moral assertions, however fumbling, are directed.

This is made abundantly clear by the fact that Gavin never tires of watching Flem and speculating on the significance of his machinations. Throughout the development of Gavin's "second premise," Flem remains in the background, a vague but menacing component of Gavin's slowly evolving ruminations. Flem's centrality is reasserted, however, when Gavin returns immediately to "Snopes-watching" after deciding that Linda must be protected. Typically, Gavin's endeavors in this line turn upon theory and counter theory, which in turn are chorused by Ratliff's corrective negations. Flem is the focus of their attention, "the first actual living vice president of a bank we had ever seen to notice" (p. 137), and Gavin comments with surprise "that he was trying to be what he—a Snopes or anyway a Flem Snopes—thought a bank vice president was or should be" (p. 137). In answer to Gavin's theory that Flem is "preparing himself to show his nephew or cousin Byron how to really loot a bank" (p. 138), Ratliff replies, "No, no. . . . You boys have got Flem Snopes wrong. He's got too much respect and reverence not jest for money, but for sharpness too, to outrage and debase one of them by jest crude robbing and stealing the other one" (p. 138). When Gavin speculates that Flem has moved his money from his own bank to the Bank of Jefferson in order to avoid stealing from himself, Ratliff's answer is the same: "No no, I tell you! . . . I tell you, you got Flem all wrong" (p. 142). Flem has "active reverence" for money, and having worked so tirelessly and so ruthlessly to become vice president of the bank, "the last thing he would ever do is hurt [it]. . . . because any bank whether it's hisn or not stands for money, and the last thing he would ever do is to insult and degrade money by mishandling it" (p. 142).

Gavin's penchant for grasping at the first theory that comes to mind is here balanced by Ratliff's patient analysis of action in terms of his progressively clearer perception of Flem's character. His analogy describing Flem's secrecy expresses the crux of the "Snopes dilemma" and of his realistic way of dealing with it.

> Confound it, the trouble is we dont never know beforehand, to anticipate him. It's like a rabbit or maybe a bigger varmit, one with more poison or anyhow more teeth, in a patch or a brake: you can watch the bushes shaking but you cant see what it is or which-a-way it's going until it breaks out. But you can see it then, and usually it's in time. Of course you got to move fast when he does break out, and he's got the advantage of you because he's already moving because he knows where he's going, and you aint moving yet because you dont. But it's usually in time. (p. 143)

Whereas Gavin has an explanation for every movement he perceives in the "bushes," Ratliff follows the pattern of movement in order to intercept Flem when he "breaks out." Unlike Charles Mallison, whose chronicling of Flem's "footprints" makes him a passive observer of accomplished facts, Ratliff takes an active and effective part in the opposition to Snopesism. Although he must often admit that he does not know how Flem plans to accomplish his ends, his realistic assessments of what he does know guarantee him at least a modicum of success.

This is the case when, to Gavin's astonishment, Ratliff intercedes on behalf of Wallstreet Panic and his wife. By investing in Wall's grocery store, Ratliff reasserts the business shrewdness that characterizes his dealings in sewing machines. At the same time, he outflanks Flem by saving Wall the necessity of borrowing from him and assists Wall's wife in her crusade to "beat Snopes from the inside" (pp. 149–150). Essentially, Ratliff beats Flem at his own game of investment, depriving him of yet another Snopes "that a earnest hardworking feller might make a forced share-crop on" (p. 150). Lacking a sense for business, Gavin never conceives of such practical solutions to Snopesism. He is amazed by Ratliff's actions, because "we—or that is, I—thought that it was his [Eck's] father-in-law who had found the money to save him, until now. 'Well, I'll be damned,' I said. 'So it was you'" (p. 149). By allying himself with Wall and his wife, Ratliff has created the same spirit of generous cooperation that gained Tom Tom Bird and Tomey's Turl Beauchamp success in the "Centaur in Brass" episode.

The Wall-Ratliff alliance serves further to emphasize Gavin's isolation from the realists who oppose Snopesism. Ratliff replies to his continued queries about Flem's banking manipulations not as an individual observer but as the spokesman for the newly formed partnership between himself and Wall. "'Oh,' he said, 'is that what you're worried about? Why, we aint sho yet. All we're doing now is watching the bushes shake'" (p. 150). Gavin is too impatient for immediate answers, however, too lacking in basic shrewdness to understand Ratliff. He says, "Between the voice and the face there were always two Ratliffs: the second one offering you a fair and open chance to divine what the first one really meant by what it was saying, provided you were smart enough. But this time that second Ratliff was trying to tell me something which for whatever reason the other could not say in words" (p. 150). When Gavin is finally told that Flem's manipulations are designed to make him president of the Sartoris bank, he is too idealistic to believe it. To become president, Flem would need Eula's assistance against Manfred de Spain, and Gavin cannot envision her giving such assistance. He declines to have it so. "'To be president of it himself,' I said. 'No!' I said. 'It cant be! It must not be!' But he [Ratliff] was just watching me. 'Nonsense,' I said" (p. 151). Unable to see beyond Flem's desire for money, Gavin is simply unequipped to analyze his behavior in any terms except the acquisition of personal wealth. "'Rapacity,' I said. 'Greed. Money. What else does he need? want? What else has ever driven him?'" (p. 152).

His question goes unanswered: "But he [Ratliff] just looked at me, and now I could actually watch that urgency fade until only the familiar face remained, bland, smooth, impenetrable and courteous" (p. 152). To blindly naive idealism such as Gavin's, there is no answer except in the trial and error of experience. What Ratliff has shrewdly accomplished through realistic attention to action in progress, Gavin must come to through his own anguish: "Because he missed it. He missed it completely" (p. 153).

What Gavin has missed is the overall image that Flem Snopes now projects and that his machinations in the community progressively produce. Fascinated by the immediate manifestations of Flem's machinations, Gavin constructs complex theories to explain them in terms of his perception of Flem as a force threatening moral order. He does so, however, without reference to the end to which Flem's action ultimately leads. By so doing he loses the perspective to see that Flem is steadily creating the illusion of belonging to the very moral order that Gavin perceives him to imperil. From the time when Flem first affected homemade bolt-cloth shirts and a black bow tie, he has studiously copied the outward appearance of the members of the community. His rented house, his tuxedo, which Charles Mallison calls "a red flag" (p. 73) and his menacing black hat, "of the broad black felt kind which country preachers and politicians wore" (p. 138), are the most recent signs of this parroting. They represent the attempts of an alien nature to insinuate itself into the moral community. Because this movement into the ordered sphere of the community is unaccompanied by any corresponding moral development and is, in fact, accomplished by methods totally antithetical to such principles, the illusion of belonging is fragile. Once created, it must of necessity be continually nourished and protected.

It is for this reason that Flem intercedes to replace the pornographic postcards in evidence against Montgomery Ward Snopes with moonshine whiskey. Moonshining is a crime punishable, in Judge Long's court, by a five-year prison sentence. Yet it is socially acceptable in the community. Selling tickets to view pornography is not a civil offense, but it is socially outrageous, and Flem cannot afford the scandal of being related to a pornographer. In attempting to avoid such a scandal, he capitalizes on his self-created image as the vice-president of the Sartoris Bank and "a up-and-coming feller in the Baptist church" (p. 172). Cloaking his self-interested motives in civic concern, he tells Gavin that he too wants Mongomery Ward to go to prison, "But not this way. I'm thinking of Jefferson" (p. 168). This statement brings to ironic fulfillment Gavin's earlier half-amused prophecy that Jefferson would be relinquished to Snopeses, "banker mayor alderman church and all, so that, in defending themselves from Snopeses, Snopeses must of necessity defend and shield us, their vassals and chattels, too" (p. 44). Realizing, however, that "he and Mr Snopes were looking at exactly the same thing: it just wasn't with the same eye" (p. 166), Gavin refuses to be defended by Flem, whose eyes "were not really looking at you at all, like a pond of stagnant water is not looking at you" (p. 166). He righteously replies, "Then it's just too bad for Jefferson" (p. 168).

The suit that Gavin determines to press against Montgomery Ward parallels the one against Manfred de Spain that was dropped. In both cases Gavin's decision to bring charges is based on his refusal to compromise with Flem Snopes, and in both he is guilty of using his public office for personal ends. He is motivated to file suit against Manfred by jealousy, against Montgomery Ward by moral outrage, which began when Montgomery turned the YMCA canteen into a house of prostitution. Furthermore, both defendants are technically innocent: it was Flem, not Manfred, who stole the city's brass, and Montgomery Ward has broken no civil laws. Indeed, Gavin has him arrested for violation of the antiquated statute against operating a motor vehicle within city limits, and he plans to have him committed to the penitentiary by relying on Judge Long's extreme Puritan sensibility. As was the case with the suit against Manfred, however, the confusion of public and private roles negates positive action. Despite the fact that Gavin refuses Flem, there are others in Jefferson who are open to appeal on less subjective grounds. Sheriff Hub Hampton readily responds to Flem's appeal that Jefferson be kept clean and permits him to replace the pornographic album with moonshine whiskey. " 'Damn it' he said, 'it's Jefferson. We live here. Jefferson's got to come first, even before the pleasure of crucifying that damned—' " (p. 174). Ironically, it was Gavin who unknowingly suggested this ploy to Flem with his talk of Wilbur Provine's still and the sentence given Provine by Judge Long. Just as Gavin

spared Flem by dropping the suit against De Spain, so here he unknowingly assists him in protecting himself.

What makes possible such unlikely assistance, of course, is Gavin's wrongheadedness in regard to Flem's motives and his lack of
objectivity in interpreting the events he witnesses. Longley points
out that "for the first time in his [Flem's] life, his public reputation is a matter of tangible value to him," [41] but Gavin cannot
see beyond Flem's amoral methods of capitalizing on that reputation. Whereas Ratliff can put himself in Flem's place and correctly speculate that "we're vice president of a bank now and we
cant afford to have it knowed even a unsavory nephew was running a peep show of French postcards" (p. 172), Gavin and
Charles Mallison assume that Flem will ignore Montgomery Ward
as he ignored Mink: Charles says, Flem "had already got shut of
one Snopes through a murder charge so why should he balk at
getting rid of another one with just a dirty postcard" (p. 166).
When Flem does balk and successfully manipulates Montgomery
Ward to his own ends, Gavin is amazed and finds serious fault
with the incorruptible Hub Hampton. Yet Hampton's compliance with Flem's suggestion is dramatic proof in itself that Flem's
image is effective. Flem himself states as much when, returning
the key to Montgomery Ward's studio, he parrots Hampton's reasons for giving him the key: " 'I'm interested in Jefferson,' Mr
Snopes said, reaching for the door and opening it. 'We got to live
here' " (p. 176). Even Ratliff's explicit statement of the nature of
what he ironically calls "civic pride" is not sufficient to enlighten
Gavin.

> When you jest want money, all you need to do to satisfy your-
> self is count it and put it where cant nobody get it, and forget
> about it. But this-here new thing he has done found out it's
> nice to have, is different. It's like keeping warm in winter or
> cool in summer, or peace or being free or contentment. You
> cant jest count it and lock it up somewhere safe and forget about
> it until you feel like looking at it again. You got to work at it
> steady, never to forget about it. It's got to be out in the open,
> where folks can see it, or there aint no such thing. (p. 175)

As Gavin watches, mystified, the urgency again fades from Ratliff's face: "And still he [Gavin] missed it, even set—sitting right

there in his own office and actively watching Flem rid Jefferson of Montgomery Ward. And still I couldn't tell him" (p. 177).

The fact that Gavin's subjective idealism blinds him to Flem's developing respectability and renders him incapable of successfully opposing him has a direct bearing on his relationship with Linda. Ignorant of Flem's public image, Gavin reacts to Flem's fundamental malevolence when he romantically commits himself to the proposition that "that girl-child was not Flem Snopes's at all, but mine" (p. 135). He does so, however, without reference to the fact that Linda herself considers Flem to be her father. When Gavin assumes the role of paternal surrogate, intent upon what Maggie Mallison calls "forming her mind" (p. 179), Linda therefore interprets his attentions as the advances of a lover. This, in turn, makes it impossible for him to protect her from Flem as a father. At sixteen Linda is fascinated by Gavin, but she is not a little frightened at the prospect of being courted by a thirty-five-year-old bachelor. The rest of Jefferson is amused and somewhat saddened by what seems to be his adolescent foolishness. Mr. Mallison says, "Maybe he's concentrating on just forming her form first you might say, without bothering too much yet about her mind" (p. 180), and Charles Mallison comments, "I reckon Jefferson was too small for a thirty-five-year-old bachelor, even a Harvard M.A. and a Ph.D. from Heidelberg and his hair already beginning to turn white even at just twenty-five, to eat ice cream and read poetry with a sixteen-year-old high-school girl" (p. 180).

Given the narrative similarities between Gavin's interest in Linda and his earlier interest in Eula, which Mr. Mallison characterizes as "heartburn" (p. 68), there is every reason for Jefferson to misconstrue Gavin's behavior. The events which culminate in Gavin's fight with Matt Levitt so closely parallel those of the previous episode that his protestations that he merely wants to save her from Flem are completely ignored. When Matt Levitt's "yellow cut-down racer" (p. 183) drives past the Mallison home where Linda is having Sunday dinner, Charles Mallison says, "Suddenly it was like I had smelled something, caught a whiff of something for a second that even if I located it again I still wouldn't know whether I had ever smelled it before or not" (p. 184). Vickery sees in this recurrence of incidents and events from one episode to the next the quality of legend or folklore: "De

Spain's use of a cutout on his car to annoy Gavin recalls McCarron's splendid horse and buggy and anticipates Matt Levitt's use of his gaudy racing car to express his displeasure with Linda." [42] Like McCarron and De Spain, Matt Levitt is also a fighter, having won the Golden Gloves in Ohio. Mr. Mallison believes Matt to be Gavin's rival and sees a relationship between him and De Spain: " 'By Cicero, Gavin,' Father said. 'You're losing ground. Last time you at least picked out a Spanish-American War hero with an E.M.F. sportster. Now the best you can do is a Golden Gloves amateur with a homemade racer. Watch yourself, bud, or next time you'll have a boy scout defying you to mortal combat with a bicycle' " (p. 187).

In Gavin's reaction to these recurring elements, however, there are redeeming factors that signal his true purpose in regard to Linda. He, at least, does not regard Matt Levitt as a rival, because he does not view himself as Linda's lover. Romantic though his perception of his relationship to Linda may be, it is not clouded by the physical passion that Eula inspired in him. It is thus Matt, not Gavin, who issues the challenge to fight, and although he bloodies Gavin's face as did De Spain before him, it is Matt who is rebuffed by Linda. Gavin reacts to this beating and to Linda's accompanying hysteria in a manner commensurate with his paternal concern for her. Even his proposal to her is no more than a rhetorical question, expressive of his paternal concern, that is quickly qualified when it elicits her resigned but desperate assent. He rephrases his original question, "Do you want to marry me?" (p. 192) as "Do you want to get married?" (p. 192), and Linda gratefully accepts him as a counselor.

> "You mean I dont have to?" she said.
> "Of course not," I said. "Never if you like."
> "I dont want to marry anybody!" she said, cried; she was clinging to me again, her face buried again in the damp mixture of blood and tears which seemed now to compose the front of my shirt and tie. "Not anybody!" she said. "You're all I have, all I can trust. I love you! I love you!" (p. 193)

Despite the misinterpretation of his behavior to which his blindness to Flem's image leaves him open, Gavin is faithful to his own generous concept of the necessity of protecting Linda. Maggie

Mallison realizes this when she permits him to send Linda a fitted travelling case as a graduation present, but she is realistic enough to try to protect him from further abuses. In order that the case cannot be interpreted as the gift of a lover, she signs the accompanying card *"Mr and Mrs Charles Mallison, Charles Mallison, Jr, Mr Gavin Stevens"* (p. 200). Charles Mallison says,

> Then we were outside again, our three reflections jumbled into one walking now across the plate glass; Mother had Uncle Gavin's arm again.
> "All four of our names," Uncle Gavin said. "At least her father wont know a white-headed bachelor sent his seventeen-year-old daughter a fitted traveling case."
> "Yes," Mother said. "One of them wont know it." (p. 201)

Maggie's action provides Gavin with relative anonymity, symbolized by the jumbling of the reflections in the plate glass window, and places him in the protection of the rules of social decorum. Her method is both practical and effective: Linda alone will know that the gift is from Gavin.

Gavin, however, is concerned not with his own reputation but with Linda's. Although he realizes that his foolish behavior has endangered Linda's reputation and that Levitt's fist "marked her too even if it didn't leave a visible cut" (p. 203), he is still faced with the problem of resolving the apparent difference between principle and reality, of finding a way to fulfill his commitment to Linda without damaging her "good name." He phrases this problem thus:

> You see? That was it: the very words *reputation* and *good name*. Merely to say them, speak them aloud, give their existence vocal recognition, would irrevocably soil and besmirch them, would destroy the immunity of the very things they represented, leaving them not just vulnerable but already doomed; from the inviolable and proud integrity of principles they would become, reduce to, the ephemeral and already doomed and damned fragility of human conditions; innocence and virginity become symbol and postulant of loss and grief, evermore to be mourned, existing only in the past tense *was* and *now is not, no more no more*. (p. 202)

The resolution of this problem, which to Maggie Mallison is a simple matter of practicality, is to Gavin a complex ordeal of anguished posturings. He is as indecisive as Maggie is self-assured, playing the role of objective unconcern to which he is not committed and in which he is obviously uncomfortable. When Linda visits him in his office after Matt Levitt's departure, he behaves like a flustered Prufrock: he has time "to discard a thousand frantic indecisions" (p. 205) only to find that he has committed all of the errors against which he warns himself. "So I did all three: waited in the office too long, so that I had to follow down the stairs too fast, and then along the street beside her not far enough either to be unnoticed or forgotten" (p. 205). Again, he waits "the interminable time until a few minutes after half past three filled with a thousand indecisions which each fierce succeeding harassment would revise" (p. 206) in order to arrive late for his rendezvous with Linda. In both cases his carefully planned casualness gives quite another impression: Linda interprets his embarrassment and his purposeful lateness to be signs that he is still courting her. When he makes a second appointment to meet her in the drugstore, it is she who keeps him waiting, which even Charles Mallison interprets as part of the formal ritual of lovers. He says, "The record. The victrola. This is the same tune it was playing before, aint it? Just backwards this time" (p. 215). The last vestiges of anonymity are destroyed when Linda does appear for their meeting. She is dressed to please an older man, an admirer, "wearing not the blouse and skirt or print cotton dress above the flat-heeled shoes of school; but dressed, I mean 'dressed,' in a hat and high heels and silk stockings and makeup who needed none and already I could smell the scent" (p. 216). Clearly, she interprets his secret gift and the college catalogues he has sent as evidence of his sustained interest in her, but his secrecy and embarrassment indicate to her that his interest is amorous. Ironically, his behavior furthers the very impression he is trying to repress.

Millgate attributes Gavin's inability to bring about the results that he intends to "the internal conflict within Stevens himself between, on the one hand, the principles inculcated into him by his background and his education, and, on the other, the often contradictory demands of actual living. Trapped and immobilized by these opposing pressures, Stevens is reduced to ineffec-

tuality." [43] This radical failure to produce positive results links
Gavin's concerned relationship with Linda to his antagonistic
opposition to Flem. Concomitant with the appearance of Linda
"decked and scented to go wherever a young woman would be
going at four oclock on a May afternoon" (p. 216), she tells Gavin that she cannot leave Jefferson and does not wish to. Her mode
of dress renders futile his extravagant attempts to protect her
reputation; her decision to remain in Jefferson blocks his plan to
protect her from Flem's influence by sending her to an Eastern
college. Together, these setbacks constitute a serious threat to the
accomplishment of Gavin's "second premise" and elicit from him
further theories upon which to base successive action. As usual,
his theorizing is based on circumstantial evidence. Assuming
that her mother is behind Linda's dressing up to meet him, Gavin posits a direct relationship between the girl's fancy clothes and
her statements. He ultimately sets the blame for both on Eula:
"Because now I knew why the clothes, the scent, the makeup
which belonged on her no more than the hat did. It was desperation, not to defend the ingratitude but at least to palliate the
rudeness of it: the mother who said *Certainly, meet him by all
means. Tell him I am quite competent to plan my daughter's
education, and we'll both thank him to keep his nose out of it*"
(p. 218). Lacking, "that capacity for sympathetic imaginative
identification which alone could enable him to approach the
truth," [44] Gavin never notices that, like the rest of Jefferson, Linda too considers Flem to be her father and is influenced by his
wishes. Thus, the same abstracting imagination that thwarts his
attempts to form Linda's mind by making him seem foolish is
responsible for directing him to the wrong parent to argue for
sending Linda away. He is too impatient for answers to listen to
Ratliff's desperate attempts to correct him: " 'What?' he [Rat-
liff] said. 'You're going to see Eula because Eula wont let her
leave Jefferson to go to school? You're wrong. . . . But wait, I tell
you! Wait!' he said. 'Because you're wrong—' " (p. 219).

Gavin's misconception of Linda's relationship to Flem is reflected in his perception of Flem's material possessions, and
Eula's revelation of his mistakes regarding the latter provide the
setting in which his theories about the former are destroyed.
Speaking earlier in the novel of Flem's house, Charles Mallison

says, "When Mr Snopes first came to Jefferson he rented the house. Then he must have bought it because since he became vice president of the bank they had begun to fix it up" (pp. 188–189). Inured to his own perception of Flem as a transient alien, Gavin ignores any suggestion in him of permanence and stability. He describes himself as "passing through the little rented (still looking rented even though the owner or somebody had painted it) gate up the short rented walk toward the little rented veranda" (p. 219). He condescendingly notes that the coffee service is "not silver but the stuff the advertisements dont tell you is better than silver but simply newer" (p. 220) and describes the furnishings as being a copy of "the photograph from say *Town and Country* labelled *American Interior*, reproduced in color in a wholesale furniture catalogue, with the added legend: *This is neither a Copy nor a Reproduction. It is our own Model scaled to your individual Requirements*" (p. 221). Ironically, this legend is perfectly descriptive of Flem's furniture: Eula tells Gavin, "It had to be exactly what it was, for exactly what he was" (p. 222). Since Flem himself is a copy of what he envisions a vice-president of a bank to be, his "individual Requirements" in furniture call for a copy of the "American Interior." Lacking any taste himself and motivated solely by appetite, Flem must rely on the salesman to choose his furniture for him. Eula says, "Yes. We went to Memphis. He knew exactly what he wanted. No, that's wrong. He didn't know yet. He only knew he wanted, had to have" (p. 221). When she tells Gavin that Flem also owns the house, Gavin is bewildered at the inconsistencies between reality and his perception of it: " 'I dont want coffee,' I said, sitting there saying *Flem Snopes Flem Snopes* until I said, cried: 'I dont want anything! I'm afraid!' " (p. 223).

If these revelations produce fear, however, it turns to desperation and something akin to horror when Eula reveals that it is not she but Flem who will not permit Linda to leave Jefferson. With a flood of recognition, Gavin realizes that Flem is using Linda to feed his appetite and fulfill his self-created image, which requires "a vice president's wife and child along with the rest of the vice president's furniture in the vice president's house" (p. 224). Flem is driven by "that furniture catalogue picture after all, scaled in cheap color from the Charleston or

Richmond or Long Island or Boston photograph, down to that one which Flem Snopes holds imperative that the people of Yoknapatawpha County must have of him" (p. 224). Since Flem holds both Linda and Eula by maintaining the illusion that he is the girl's father, he cannot risk Linda's discovering the truth. If she were ever enlightened, she would scandalize his reputation by leaving him. This, in turn, would set Eula free, causing him further scandal and losing him the opportunity to gain control of Eula's inheritance from Will Varner. Although Gavin romantically overestimates the extent to which Linda's bastardy is known outside of Jefferson, he is correct in his analysis of the danger to Flem represented in Linda's going away to school. He says, "Now he is vice president of a bank and now a meddling outsider is persuading the child to go away to school, to spend at least the three months until the Christmas holidays among people none of whose fathers owe him money and so must keep their mouths shut, any one of whom might reveal the fact which at all costs he must now keep secret" (p. 225).

Although these insights signify that Gavin has taken a major step toward understanding Flem's motives, he is still far too much the romantic idealist to accept Eula's practical solution to Linda's dilemma. In order to break Flem's hold on Linda, Gavin proposes to tell her himself who she is. Here, as before, he shows his lack of "sympathetic imaginative identification," which Millgate says is responsible for his ineffectualness: he accepts the fact that Linda thinks Flem is her father, but he ignores the corollary that children love their fathers. With narrow pomposity he asks Eula, "What more could she want than to believe me, believe anyone, a chance to believe anyone compassionate enough to assure her she's not his child?" (pp. 225–226). In the ensuing byplay the diametric opposition of idealist and realist is dramatically demonstrated by Gavin's inability to accept the practical logic of Eula's suggestion for freeing Linda from Flem. She tells him that "women aren't interested in poets' dreams. They are interested in facts. It doesn't even matter whether the facts are true or not, as long as they match the other facts without leaving a rough seam" (p. 226). Linda believes that Gavin loves her, and Eula urges him to free her from Flem by marrying her. To his objections that marriage would only tie her to Jefferson all the

more, Eula replies, "The marriage is the only fact. The rest of it
is still the poet's romantic dream. Marry her. She'll have you.
Right now, in the middle of all this, she wont know how to say
No. Marry her" (p. 227). As with Flem in the Montgomery
Ward episode, Gavin and Eula are looking at the same thing
with different eyes. Here as there, Gavin refuses to compromise
his principles with practicality and is rendered ineffectual in
what he hopes to accomplish.

As a final irony, Gavin actually furthers Flem's purposes by insisting on the maintainance of his own romantic ideals. Millgate
points out, in fact, that throughout the novel "whenever Stevens
achieves some form of positive action he does precisely what will
assist Flem Snopes." [45] In this case, he achieves partial knowledge of Flem's motives, but he does not connect opposition to
those motives with the solution suggested by Eula. It is not until
Ratliff tells him that Flem has a financial interest in having Linda remain single that he understands why Eula suggested he marry the girl. Even when Ratliff tells him this, however, Gavin does
not understand the full impact of his own failure. Rather, he attributes his misunderstanding to his not having listened to the
right women, to which Ratliff replies, "Or the wrong ones neither. . . . You never listened to nobody because by that time you
were already talking again" (p. 229). Not only has Gavin refused
to marry Linda himself, but his behavior toward her has driven
away her only other suitor, Matt Levitt. In effect, he is responsible for keeping both Linda and Eula in bondage to Flem, thereby assuring the maintainance of Flem's facade of respectability
and protecting his interest in Eula's estate. To this extent he fulfills the role in which he saw himself with bitter irony while
forming Linda's mind: "family friend to Flem Snopes who had
no more friends than Blackbeard or Pistol" (p. 205).

This "friendship" recurs in the modified context of the "Mule
in the Yard" episode, in which high humor provides the vehicle
for Gavin's continued assistance in Flem's steadily darkening designs. Like its predecessor, "Centaur in Brass," "Mule in the
Yard" has a definite structural and thematic function. Robert
Penn Warren asserts that "humor in Faulkner's work is never
exploited for its own sake. It is regularly used as an index, as a
lead, to other effects," [46] and Steven Marcus notes that the hu-

morous episodes in *The Town* mark one of the "main subdivi-
sion[s] of the narrative." [47] Against the frantic comic backdrop
of I.O. Snopes's contest with Old Het and Mrs. Hait, Flem's cold
manipulations to rid Jefferson of yet another unrespectable
Snopes and Gavin's helpless participation as his "witness" culminate at last in Ratliff's grim and foreboding summary of the
whole. As Millgate points out, "Centaur in Brass," "Mule in the
Yard," and the episode of the "Snopes Indians" are integral to
the narrative, iterating major themes and marking the progress
of the archetypal Snopes:

> When Faulkner incorporates [the] short-story material into
> *The Town*, he distributes the relatively self-contained comic
> episodes in such a way that they operate within the book's
> aesthetic pattern as discrete, static elements set off against the
> flow of the narrative which contains them, while in social and
> thematic terms they serve as reminders of what Snopesism
> means in practice and are ironically counterpointed against
> the irrelevance and ineffectuality of Gavin Stevens's anti-Snopes
> crusade. Because they are so discrete and self-contained, and
> because we may be aware of their previous independent exist-
> ence as short stories, these episodes perhaps retain something
> of the character of set-pieces; yet they have structural and con-
> textual functions beyond those of the simple comic interlude,
> and each of them is linked with the main action of the novel,
> marking another step in the career of Flem Snopes.[48]

Told with factual accuracy by Charles Mallison and devoid of in-
terpretive comment, "Mule in the Yard" is characterized by the
humor of understatement. Its impact is the greater when Flem
emerges with cold, calculating efficiency to rid himself of I.O.
Snopes, setting the stage for Ratliff's analytical interpretation of
the depth of Flem's meanness and the consequences of his amorality.

While Gavin is a party to the events by virtue of the public
office he holds, he is nonetheless incapable of influencing the
course of the action, thus remaining a helpless bystander as
Flem's intrigues unwind. He is hired by Old Het as Mrs. Hait's
lawyer but is never called upon to render her assistance. Flem
employs him as a "witness," but he gives no testimony. Although
I.O. Snopes gives ample testimony of Flem's part in dunning the

railroad, Gavin is not asked to judge the legality of the hoax. In
short, he is rendered helpless as a lawyer by the absence of traditional legal forms and the inapplicability of civil law to the proceedings in progress. I.O., Flem, and Mrs. Hait are traders in the
finest tradition, and the principles and ideals of civil law on
which Gavin bases his action as county attorney do not apply to
their dealings. Despite the fact that Gavin does and says nothing,
his presence is required to intimidate I.O. and to give the impression that Flem and Mrs. Hait have the law on their side.
When Flem asks him how much he owes him for this service,
Gavin is unable to set a price: "Uncle Gavin said he started to say
one dollar, so that Mr Flem would say One dollar? Is that all?
And then Uncle Gavin could say Yes, or your knife or pencil or
just anything so that when I wake up tomorrow I'll know I didn't
dream this" (p. 254). He has permitted Flem to use his own respectable reputation for the furtherance of his purposes, and for
such a service there literally is no price.

Interpreting this episode to Charles Mallison, Ratliff delves
below the surface of the humor to point out the implications of
Flem's ruthlessness and Gavin's vulnerability to harm in opposing him. He tells Charles that there has been enough laughing,
"because as soon as you set down to laugh at it, you find it aint
funny a-tall" (p. 257). Flem's ouster of I.O. Snopes represents
further evidence that he has discovered the tangible value of his
reputation, and having made this discovery, he is more dangerous
than ever.

> "That's right," Ratliff said. "When it's jest money and power
> a man wants, there is usually some place where he will stop;
> there's always one thing at least that ever—every man wont do
> for jest money. But when it's respectability he finds out he wants
> and has got to have, there aint nothing he wont do to get it and
> then keep it. And when it's almost too late when he finds out
> that's what he's got to have, and that even after he gets it he
> cant jest lock it up and set—sit down on top of it and quit, but
> instead he has got to keep on working with ever—every breath
> to keep it, there aint nothing he will stop at, aint nobody or
> nothing within his scope and reach that may not anguish and
> grieve and suffer." (p. 259)

It is Flem's need for respectability that Gavin has missed and

about which Ratliff cannot tell him. He explains to Charles his
reasons for not telling Gavin in the same terms that Eula used
to dissuade Gavin from telling Linda about her parentage: "Because he wouldn't believe me. This here is the kind of a thing
you—a man has got to know his—himself. He has got to learn it
out of his own hard dread and skeer. . . . you can even insulate
against having to believe it by resisting or maybe even getting even
with that-ere scoundrel that meddled in and told you" (p. 258).

Eula's and Ratliff's similar practicality, together with the fact
that they both perceive Flem's fear of Linda's marrying, allies
them as realistic and potentially effective opponents of Snopesism. Gavin, however, is linked with Linda, who assists Flem by
following his wishes as Gavin does by misinterpreting his intentions. This association brings to mind Gavin's original commitment to Linda at the same time as it marks the close of the second
phase of his maturation toward realistic opposition to Snopesism.
By specifying the mistakes that Gavin has made about Flem in his
relationship with Linda, moreover, Ratliff not only darkens Flem's
character substantially but also looks forward to more threatening events to come. Linda is to leave Jefferson for the state university after all, and, should she marry there, Flem will have lost
everything for which he has worked. As Ratliff says, "So Flem's
got to strike now, and quick. He's not only got to be president of
that bank to at least keep that much of a holt on that Varner
money by at least being president of where Uncle Billy keeps it
at, he's got to make his lick before the message comes that Linda's
done got married or he'll lose the weight of Uncle Billy's voting
stock" (p. 261). Linda's marriage would free Eula from Flem and
sever his relationship to Uncle Billy as son-in-law. Gavin's attempts to protect Linda from Flem and fulfill his commitment to
the "second premise" merely compound her danger by making
Flem desperate. Thwarted at every turn by his own romantic perception of reality, Gavin's generous commitment to Linda is no
more effective than that which he made to Eula. In the steadily
modifying context of recurrent challenges, however, Gavin's failures are characterized by an unflagging faith in the principles of
moral existence, which reveals by contrast the amoral nature of
his opponent.

"A Virtuous Wife Is a Crown to
Her Husband"

THE EVENTS ensuing from the collapse of Gavin's "second premise" are often cited to demonstrate two major failures of *The Town*: the weakness of Gavin as a narrator and the humanization of Flem Snopes. Since Flem's impact on the moral world is revealed largely through the consciousness of Gavin Stevens, these supposed defects are to some extent mutually dependent. Irving Howe deplores Gavin's theorizing as "the frantic verbal outpourings of . . . the District Attorney with a degree from Heidelberg and a passion for rant, who serves so disastrously as Faulkner's 'alter ego' " [49] and blames Gavin for Flem's "softening."

> Through both *The Town* and *The Mansion* Flem Snopes drives steadily toward economic domination in Jefferson. The meaning of this is fully indicated, but Flem himself, as a character in a novel, is not nearly so vivid in these books as he was in *The Hamlet*. Partly this seems due to a flagging of creative energies, partly to a propensity for avoiding the direct and dramatic. The action of *The Town* and, to a large extent, *The Mansion* is usually strained through the blurred and blurring consciousness of Gavin Stevens, surely the greatest wind-bag in American literature, and Charles Mallison, who shows promise of becoming the runner-up.[50]

Howe objects to Flem's becoming "still another item in the omnivorous musings of Gavin Stevens," which verge "at times on a sociological and psychological explanation for his [Flem's] behavior, which Flem would be the first to scorn." [51] He concludes: "That Flem Snopes, of all the marvelous monsters in American literature, should end up seeming shadowy and vague—who could have anticipated this?" [52]

Answers to these and similar charges are found in the several critical interpretations that see Gavin as a character whose uniquely romantic makeup is central to the developing opposition between morality and amorality. Longley asserts that "Mr. Faulkner . . . is deliciously, ironically aware of the foolishness of Gavin, and no one is more keenly aware of it than Gavin himself. But he chooses to persist, and it is very difficult to understand

how anyone could fail to sympathize with his motives." [53]
Taking exception to Howe's statement that Gavin serves as the
"alter ego" of the author, Brooks suggests the means by which
Flem's amorality is revealed:

> What is likely to prove the worst stumbling block to the
> reader of the novel is the possibility—especially if he has read
> much Faulkner criticism—that he may take Gavin to be Faulk-
> ner's mouthpiece. His previous reading of *Knight's Gambit*—or
> even of *Light in August,* if his reading was not very careful—
> could dispose him toward this view. But if he makes this mistake,
> he is very likely to miss the tone and even the basic meaning
> of the novel. For if any one thing about this novel soon becomes
> clear, it is that Gavin, and not for the first time in Faulkner's
> fiction, is treated as a figure of fun—almost as the butt of the
> author's jokes.[54]

Committed to his own romantically generous view of reality, Gavin is so often and so disastrously wrong in his speculations about
Flem that Flem's amorality is revealed by contrast. Although
Howe may "yearn to see [Flem] in diabolic motion, free and on
his own, without the explanatory or intervening remarks of anyone, let alone Gavin Stevens," [55] Faulkner's fictional technique in
The Town has a more subtle complexity. Poised in constant opposition to Gavin Stevens, whom Beck calls a "man of feeling as
well as aristocrat of the moral world," [56] the grotesque Flem is
seen in the light of ultimate contrast, fully the archetype of amorality.

Indeed, this method of characterization is hardly new to *The
Town,* for Flem is seldom, if ever, seen "free and on his own"
as Howe would have him. The simplicity of his elemental amorality can be revealed only in the context of the complexity of the
moral universe. It is for this reason that, as Flem assumes the outward manifestations of respectability, Faulkner relies more and
more on Gavin's hypersensitivity to moral challenges to reveal
Flem's unchanged nature. Although he remains in the background
of the action, parroting the forms of civic and moral responsibility,
the cumulative effect of the pattern of appraisal and reappraisal
by the three narrators is to project his centrality as amoral aggressor. As Beck correctly states, "Recurrently appearing throughout,
he [Flem] is also felt as an almost ubiquitous presence, by his

impingements upon the affairs and the apprehensions of others.
. . . Flem is . . . an ultimate and invariable point of reference, the
one whom all the others watch, the figure who haunts all other
minds yet whose mind is never seen into, the object to which the
variously subjective modes of the trilogy are related." [57] However
respectable he may seem to the rest of Jefferson, however civic-
minded he may appear to be as he rids the town of his less pol-
ished relatives, Flem is never free of Gavin's intense scrutiny, in
the light of which his amorality is defined.

This is not to say that Gavin's perceptions of Flem are always,
or indeed ever, entirely accurate or that they need to be in order
to reveal Flem's amoral nature. On the contrary, as Ratliff says,
Gavin is constantly making the mistake of either overestimating
or underestimating Flem (p. 175). Although Gavin projects his
theories with considerable self-assurance, there is a quality of uncertainty about them, demonstrated by the fact that they are constantly being corrected by Ratliff, among others. This unreliability
in Gavin as a narrator, which Beck attributes to his "fundamental
magnanimity," [58] serves only to strengthen the contrast between
him and Flem. The errors that Gavin makes in analyzing Flem's
motives and methods darken Flem's character when they are revealed and, at the same time, are expressive of Gavin's magnanimity. While unrealiability makes Gavin appear foolish, it represents faithfully, in Beck's words, "a typical error of the generous
mind, the attribution of its own sensibilities and even its scruples
to others. This can become, as it does with Stevens, the humane
man's most dangerous vulnerability; yet its alternative, a complete defensive cynicism, must be worse, according to Faulkner's
treatment of the question." [59]

This aspect of Gavin's character is nowhere plainer than in
chapter seventeen of *The Town*. Gavin's speculations on Flem as
a victim of his environment and time are based only on the most
circumstantial evidence and demonstrate the extent to which his
perception of reality is colored by his generous moral idealism. Earlier in the novel, speaking of his loss of Eula, Gavin expresses the
fear that "maybe Nothing will last, that maybe Nothing will last
forever" and then rejects the possibility in what constitutes an affirmation of the principles of moral existence: "Nothing cannot
remain anywhere since nothing is vacuum and vacuum is paradox

and unbearable and we will have none of it even if we would" (p. 135). After the collapse of his "second premise," Gavin is again faced with the possibility of the existence of such a vacuum in the form of Flem's increasingly obvious lack of morality. Since amorality would constitute the same unbearable paradox in the moral world as does a vacuum in the natural world, Gavin rejects it also. He justifies Flem's behavior in terms of normal human responses to social abuse, maintaining his idealistic perception of reality by generously attributing to Flem his own "sensibilities and . . . scruples." Although this judgment is highly unrealistic, it too is an affirmation of morality, thus emphasizing the amorality of Flem Snopes through the ironic contrast of Flem's actions and Gavin's perception of them. In terms of the full development of this contrast and the resulting dramatic tension, in which morality and its opposite are seen to be mutually revealing, Gavin's perceptual errors become necessities. His unreliability as a commentator on Snopesism characterizes him as a moral "aristocrat" and supplies the recurrent ironies by which Flem's amorality is defined.

This method of characterization by contrast is both subtle and complex and may lead to misreadings.[60] Noting the initial persuasiveness of Gavin's arguments, Millgate warns that "only the closest reading of *The Town* reveals the full dangers of a literal dependence upon Stevens's excited, melodramatic, and, as often as not, entirely erroneous versions of events. Stevens's tendency is to see himself, Flem, Eula, and Linda as if they were all figures in a pattern, characters of myth, fable, or morality play." [61] It is Gavin Stevens, not Faulkner, who invests Flem with the qualities of "humility" (p. 263), "sacrifice" (p. 263), "regret" (p. 264), and "innocence" (p. 265), traits so totally lacking in Flem that their attribution to him invokes their antitheses. These are characteristics of Gavin himself, and, by attributing them to Flem, Gavin essentially projects himself into what he perceives to be Flem's milieu. By such means Gavin lives figuratively through the same set of circumstances in which Flem is involved literally, and the contrast between their motives and passions is perfectly dramatic.

Quite justifiably, this contrast centers upon the separate ways in which Gavin and Flem value honor. As Beck says, "Gavin, with the generous apprehensions of an honorable and imaginative man, . . . supposes Flem wants revenge on De Spain, instead of what material advantage he can take." [62] While defending his initial premise that Eula was chaste, Gavin felt the weight of the cuckold's horns himself and took various measures to avenge himself on De Spain, sabotaging his car, fighting him, and pressing suit against him for malfeasance of office. He even declined to accept the "material advantage" of physical union with Eula. In his present speculations he applies his own former motives and passions to Flem in order to explain the latter's behavior. In this light, Flem becomes "the innocent cuckolded husband" (p. 270) who "from that very first day . . . realised that he himself had nothing and would never have more than nothing unless he wrested it himself from his environment and time, and that the only weapon he would ever have to do it with would be just money" (p. 263). In order to get money, Flem sacrificed "his inalienable right and hope" as a man "to father another man's bastard on the wife who would not even repay him with the passion of gratitude, let alone the passion of passion since he was obviously incapable of that passion, but merely with her dowry" (p. 263). Lacking the education that Gavin values so highly, Flem is handicapped in the pursuit of self-betterment by "the humility of not knowing, of never having had any chance to learn the rules and methods of the deadly game in which he had gauged his life" (p. 266). In banking his money he is forced to rely on "that simple trust of one human being in another, since there was no alternative between that baseless trust and a vulnerable coffee can buried under a bush in the back yard" (p. 275). At the same time, he is harassed by Manfred de Spain, the "hereditary predator" (p. 266) and aristocrat of the old order who exercises upon him "his natural and normal *droit de seigneur*" (p. 273).

By such characterizations Gavin's speculations assume the heroic-romantic proportions of myth or fable. In terms of this fable, Flem's acquisition of money and position becomes the modus operandi for the righteous cuckold's "vengeance and revenge on the man who had not merely violated his home but outraged it—the home which in all good faith he had tried to establish around a woman already irrevocably soiled and damaged in the world's . . . sight, and so give her bastard infant a name" (p. 270). In reality, however, it was Gavin himself who assumed responsibility for defending Eula's name and being father to her child, just as it was he who sought revenge on Manfred. His fable is so completely expressive of his own personality and so antithetical to Flem's that he even rejects Flem's actual method of ousting Manfred from the bank in favor of one more in line with his own sensibilities. Because it would be too "simple" (pp. 293, 294) for Flem to approach Mrs. Varner with evidence of Eula's adultery, Gavin imagines Flem confronting Will Varner himself and through a complicated set of circumstances sacrificing his claim to Eula's inheritance in order to have revenge on De Spain. He says, "You will have to imagine this" (p. 291). Since Flem and Will are ancient enemies, there would be no little heroism in Flem's daring to face him, and the confrontation satisfies Gavin's penchant for romance. He speculates that Flem "had to go, walk himself into that den and reach his own hand and jerk the unsuspecting beard and then stand while the uproar beat and thundered about his head" (p. 294). This would be the only honorable way to enlist Varner as his agent, the only way to wreak fully satisfying revenge on Manfred. But it is Gavin's way, not Flem's. " 'No no,' Ratliff said. 'He [Flem] never seen Will. I know. I taken him out there. I had a machine to deliver to Miz Ledbetter at Rockyford and he suh-jested would I mind going by Frenchman's Bend while he spoke to Miz Varner a minute and we did, he was in the house about a minute and come back out and we went on and et dinner with Miz Ledbetter and set up the machine and come on back to town' " (p. 295). Juxtaposed against the commonplace and practical events that Ratliff relates, Gavin's climactic and sensitively drawn portrait of romantic confrontations utterly dissolves. Unencumbered by moral concerns, Flem is the epitome of simplicity and the antithesis of Gavin himself, of whom, Ratliff says, "if it aint complicated up enough it aint right and so even if it works, you dont believe it" (p. 296). By direct contrast to Gavin's generous perception of him, Flem is revealed in the dark light of his vicious amorality.

Although he points out that Gavin's speculations are wrong, Ratliff protests that he himself does not know what Flem could have given Mrs. Varner "that was important enough to make Uncle Billy light out for town at two oclock in the morning" (p. 299). He is shrewd enough, however, to know that "it had something to do with folks, people, and the only people connected with Jefferson that would make Uncle Billy do something he hadn't suspected until this moment he would do are Eula and Linda" (pp. 299–300). To prove her gratitude to Flem for permitting her to go away to school, Linda has written a will leaving her inheritance from Eula to him. Since Will Varner's will divides his own holdings equally between Jody and Eula, Linda's will provides Flem with a claim to literally half of the Varner estate. This includes Varner's controlling interest in the Sartoris bank. Flem shows Linda's will to Mrs. Varner instead of to Will himself because she best suits his purpose. Ratliff says, "Uncle Billy jest hated him [Flem] because Flem beat him fair and square, at Uncle Billy's own figger, out of that Old Frenchman place, while Miz Varner hated him like he was a Holy Roller or even a Baptist because he had not only condoned sin by marrying her daughter after somebody else had knocked her up, he had even made sin pay by getting the start from it that wound him up vice president of a bank" (p. 297). Flem is, in fact, a Baptist deacon, and to Mrs. Varner, Linda's will is yet another instance of Flem's making a profit from his original condonation of sin. Flem leaves it to her to tell her husband about the will, trusting that her aroused Puritan righteousness will heighten Varner's outrage at again being duped. When Varner arrives in Jefferson, Flem directs the old man's anger against Manfred by the simple expedient of telling Varner that Manfred is Eula's lover. He thereby forces Varner to join with him in ousting De Spain from the bank presidency. With De Spain removed, Flem uses his half interest in Varner's estate to vote himself president, replacing Manfred and duping Varner yet again.

As a self-contained expression of Flem's calculating ruthlessness, this transaction establishes his economic domination of Yoknapatawpha County. In its impact on the community, however, there is a larger imperative suggestive of moral as well as economic oppression. In Charles Mallison's words, Jefferson was "founded by Aryan Baptists and Methodists, for Aryan Baptists and Methodists" (p. 306):

> ... ours [was] a town established and decreed by people neither Catholics nor Protestants nor even atheists but incorrigible nonconformists, nonconformists not just to everybody else but to each other in mutual accord; a nonconformism defended and

preserved by descendants whose ancestors hadn't quitted home
and security for a wilderness in which to find freedom of thought
as they claimed and oh yes, believed, but to find freedom in
which to be incorrigible and unreconstructible Baptists and
Methodists; not to escape from tyranny as they claimed and
believed, but to establish one. (p. 307)

This is the "tyranny" of the Puritan ethic, the tenets of which
Flem invokes, in the guise of a righteous husband, to secure Will
Varner's support in banishing Manfred. By openly charging the
lovers with adultery, however, Flem exploits not just Varner but
the entire community, which shares Varner's ingrained theological heritage. What Charles Mallison described early in the novel
as the natural love of "two people in each of whom the other had
found his single ordained fate; each to have found out of all the
earth that one match for his mettle" (p. 15), he now calls "not
just sin but mortal sin" (p. 307). What was formerly the town's
"pride that Jefferson would supply their battleground" (p. 15)
he now perceives as "our own baseness in helping to keep it [the
love affair] hidden all this long time" (p. 308). By imposing on
this mythic love affair the restrictions of the Puritan ethic, Flem
has altered the standard by which Jefferson judges natural love,
making sinners of the lovers and hypocrites of the town. This dis-
tortion of point of view threatens the moral structure of the community and demonstrates the extent to which morality is vulnerable to the machinations of amorality. The illusion that morality
is synonymous with the tenets of an austere theology results at
last in Charles Mallison's equation of "righteousness and simple
justice" with the "saw of retribution" that seeks the "nail" of sin
in Jefferson's "moral tree" (p. 307).

Critics in general are inclined to view the existence of this
double standard as Faulkner's bitter comment on the illness of
modern society and to see Flem, as Andrew Lytle does, as the
hero of a godless community of self-deluding moralizers.[63] In a
similar vein, Joseph Gold, contending that Flem's rise fulfills "the
dreams and hopes of all those around him," [64] attributes his success to Jefferson's moral cowardice. The people of Jefferson, Gold
says, "want only to cover up and hide from sight the evil in their
midst. To fight Snopesism would involve examining and then
changing themselves first, and rather than make the effort, under-

go the strain, they will absorb Snopeses and Snopesism, demanding only that it conform to their own pattern of evil and appear respectable." [65] Such comments suggest Jefferson's submission to Flem, whereas, in fact, the town justifiably submits to its theological heritage, which Flem manipulates for his own ends. As Vickery points out, the danger to the moral community lies in the fact that, "in repudiation of Eula as a sinner, Jefferson also repudiates its own roots in the physical and emotional world which is the source of its strength." [66] What has scarcely been noticed, however, is the tone of uncertainty that underlies Charles Mallison's account of Jefferson's theological posture and provides hope of moral regeneration. He says that "the very fabric of Baptist and Methodist life is delusion, nothing" (p. 308), and he is so far from being himself irretrievably in the grip of the Puritan ethic that he can still note and appreciate that Eula moves "like water moves somehow" (p. 310). The natural love that mocked the doctrinal definition of decency has, like "the pear tree in the side yard," "bloomed and gone," and the mockingbird sings now in the "pink dogwood" (p. 310) that bears no fruit. Yet, wearied of the sterile Puritan interpretation of sexual love as sin, Charles Mallison says of the mockingbird that "he had sung all night long all week [in the dogwood tree] until you would begin to wonder why in the world he didn't go somewhere else" (p. 310).

In effect, Charles Mallison is drawn between the opposing poles of his individual human capacity and admiration for love and the abstract dictates of an inherited commitment to decency. The very fact that this conflict exists is evidence that there has been no repudiation of "the physical and moral world." Rather, the tension created by this juxtaposition of alternatives is what vitalizes morality and lends it its regenerative vitality. The absence of such tension is what characterizes amorality, which in Flem's case is demonstrated by his unresponsiveness to love, religion, or the human values that both project. Flem condones Eula's love affair with De Spain as an investment and assumes the facade of righteousness in order to take his profit. In Mr. Garraway, the hermit of Seminary Hill who passes judgment on Eula and Manfred from the point of view of Protestant theology, this moral tension has stultified, and his moral vision is severely restricted. He is an "inflexible unreconstructible Puritan" (p. 312) who views the world "with an old man's dim cloudy eyes magnified and enormous behind the thick lenses of his iron-framed spectacles" (p. 313). Like his religion, Mr. Garraway's store and even some of its produce were inherited from his father; like his moral stature, his store is "small [and] dingy" (p. 312) and stocked with "the tainted meat or rancid lard or weevilled flour or meal he would not have permitted a white man—a Protestant gentile white man of course—to eat at all" (p. 315). Like Mrs. Varner, Mr. Garraway is as incensed at Flem's eighteen-year condonation of sin as he is at the sinners. Of Flem he says, "I knew the husband! He deserved it [cuckolding]!" (p. 313). Nonetheless, the sinners must be banished: " 'She must go,' he said. 'They must both go—she and De Spain too' " (p. 314).

Unlike Mr. Garraway, Gavin the lawyer is possessed of moral vision sufficient in scope to permit him to examine alternatives for moral judgment, but he places them in an idealized perspective. Because of his sophisticated education, he is to a large extent free of the domination of the Puritan ethic, and he can question it as Mr. Garraway cannot. Why, he asks, must the lovers be banished? "Why only now? It was one thing as long as the husband accepted it; it became another when somebody—how did you put it?—catches them, blows the gaff? They become merely sinners then, criminals then, lepers then? Nothing for constancy, nothing for fidelity, nothing for devotion, unpoliced devotion, eighteen years of devotion?" (p. 314). Symbolically, Gavin leaves Mr. Garraway and goes to a higher ridge, "beyond Seminary Hill," from which he can view the road "leading from Jefferson to the world" (p. 315). From this vantage point he imagines himself to be highly objective, as "detached as God himself" (p. 316); and, with Yoknapatawpha County spread before him like the "miniature of man's passions and hopes and disasters" (p. 316), he relates to each other the opposing standards for judgment that so trouble Charles Mallison. Adopting Mallison's symbol for doctrinal morality, Gavin sees the blooming dogwood as "one faint diffusion" that remains "even though the last of west is no longer green and all of firmament is now one unlidded studded slow-wheeling arc and the last of earth-pooled visibility has drained away" (p. 317). Yet the dogwood has no light of its own but takes light from "the spring darkness, the unsleeping darkness

which, although it is of the dark itself, declines the dark since dark
is of the little death called sleeping" (p. 317). In the "spring darkness" the dogwood's diffusion is "faint as whispers: the faint and
shapeless lambence of blooming dogwood returning loaned light
to light as the phantoms of candles would" (p. 317). Theological
morality, which is clearly suggested by the candle image, is an
abstract "phantom," bodiless and lightless except insofar as it borrows "loaned light" from concrete human love. The "spring darkness," which supplies light to the dogwood, represents life itself,
"peopled and myriad, two and two seeking never at all solitude
but simply privacy, the privacy decreed and created for them by
the spring darkness, the spring weather, the spring which an
American poet, a fine one, a woman and so she knows, called girls'
weather and boys' luck" (p. 317). Human life lights the candle
of theology, and human life depends upon love. Therefore, the
morality of love, based on "constancy . . . fidelity . . . [and] devotion," must take primacy over doctrinal morality.

   This is a humanism of the heart, which, despite Hyatt Waggoner's objection that "Stevens is more than ever a mask for Faulkner
at this point," [67] is typical of Gavin's moral stance in his opposition to Snopesian amorality. Moreover, the narrative method of
interior monologue, used to elucidate and reconfirm this humanism, fits the pattern by which, in Beck's words, the narrators'
"seriously motivated inquiries simplify issues sufficiently to allow
direct intervention." [68] If it is true, as Brooks contends, that "the
pressure of small-town respectability and a Puritan ethic sharpens
. . . the sense of Eula's romantic desirability," [69] then it is clearly
justifiable that Gavin should affirm the primacy of natural human love with reference to her and that he should do so at a time
when what Brooks refers to as the "taboos, obstacles, and hin-
drances" [70] of the Puritan ethic are most intensely felt. This affirmation constitutes an unraveling of the distortions that Flem
produces when he assumes the Puritan righteousness of Jefferson's
founders, and it provides the characteristic theoretical foundation
on which all of Gavin's interviews with Eula are based. Indeed,
his speculations on the morality of love are prompted by her
note asking him to meet her and are punctuated throughout by
his asides regarding the way in which he will be able to assist
her. Both structurally and thematically, his poetically conceived,

deeply committed reaffirmation of the love ethic is integrally related to Flem's exploitation of the outward forms of love and doctrinal decency. In contrast to Gavin's generous humanism, Flem's calculating manipulation of Eula, Manfred, Linda, Will Varner, and the Jefferson community as a whole, reveals his amorality.

The specific steps that Flem takes to gain the bank presidency have been discussed earlier, and, by the time of Gavin's final interview with Eula, the success of his ruthless venture is assured. What remains in question is the way in which his method of ousting Manfred will ultimately affect Eula and Linda. By giving up his bank for Eula, Manfred affirms the value of love over social respectability. Because they are bound together by love, Eula can do no less for her lover than he has done for her. She must leave Flem, whom she married to gain social respectability, in order to justify Manfred's sacrifice. There is a practical imperative, as well. As she points out to Gavin, "If I dont go with him [Manfred], he'll have to fight. He may go down fighting and wreck everything and everybody else, but he'll have to fight. Because he's a man. I mean, he's a man first. I mean, he's got to be a man first. He can swap Flem Snopes his bank for Flem Snopes's wife, but he cant just stand there and let Flem Snopes take the bank away from him" (p. 331). By setting in motion the set of circumstances that dispossesses Manfred of his bank, therefore, Flem forces Eula to abandon him. This threatens the public revelation of her adultery and has dangerous implications for Linda's reputation. By capitalizing on Linda's desire to go away to school, for which Gavin is responsible, Flem has insinuated himself into her affection. Linda tells her lawyer, Mr. Stone, that she must will to Flem her inheritance from her mother "because my father has been good to me and I love and admire and respect him" (p. 328). If she were to go away with Manfred and Eula, Linda would be abandoning the father she loves and, in effect, condoning her mother's adultery. By remaining in Jefferson, however, she would face the censure of being the daughter of an adulteress. Since Flem's insensitive use of her will, which symbolizes her love for him, clearly indicates that he does not love her, Linda would be left defenseless. Concerned, as always, for Linda's welfare, Gavin says to Eula, "Dont you see? Either way, she is lost? Either to go with you, if that were possible, while you desert her father for another man; or stay here in all the stink without you to protect her from it and learn at last that he is not her father at all and so she has nobody, nobody?" (p. 330). Eula's answer is typically practical: "That's why I sent the note. Marry her" (p. 330).

Ironically, Eula's plea for practical assistance comes at a time when Gavin is most idealistic. His commitment is to his theory of love; hers, to her responsibility as a lover. Her protection of Linda's reputation is part of that responsibility because Linda is the child of Eula's love for McCarron, and her present danger is a result of Eula's love for Manfred. Married to Gavin, Linda would enjoy the sanctuary from public opinion provided by his name as well as the support of his honest concern for her. Gavin, however, is not a lover but a theorizer; and, although he perceives Linda's danger and feels compelled to protect her, the means for that protection are as unrealistic as his imagined relationship with her through McCarron. Committed, as he is, to his idealized love ethic, he insists that marriage is not merely a form for convenience of reputation but that it must be founded on mutual love. He carries this theory to such an extreme, in fact, that Eula warns him at one point in their interview not to pity Flem for his impotence, his inability to love. When she suggests that he marry Linda, he declines on the grounds that he is "not too old so much as simply discrepant; that having been her husband once, I would never relinquish even her widowhood to another" (p. 332). Although he does finally swear an oath to Eula, he nonetheless makes it a condition that Linda must at least want him if not return his love in fact. He tells Eula that he will marry Linda "After you're gone, if or when I become convinced that conditions are going to become such that something will have to be done, and nothing else but marrying me can help her, and she will have me, but have me, take me. Not just give up, surrender" (pp. 332–333).

While this attitude is decidedly noble insofar as it affirms Linda's inherent right to enjoy "girls' weather and boys' luck," his refusal to marry her is tragically unrealistic in that it ignores her equally valid right to respectability in the eyes of the deeply Puritan community. Love, like amorality, must have a medium in which to flourish, and just as Gavin was unable to grasp

Ratliff's point that the success of Flem's schemes depended upon his acquiring respectability, so he misses Eula's point that the hope which he cherishes for Linda depends upon the same. He says of Ratliff, "Between the voice and the face there were always two Ratliffs: the second one offering you a fair and open chance to divine what the first one really meant by what it was saying, provided you were smart enough" (p. 150). But Gavin can only "watch that urgency fade until only the familiar face remained, bland, smooth, impenetrable and courteous" (p. 152). As inscrutable to Gavin as Ratliff's face are Eula's eyes, "all one inextricable mixture of wistaria cornflowers larkspur bluebells weeds and all, all the lost girls' weather and boys' luck" (p. 332); and, when he denies her urgent plea that he marry Linda, he watches her disappear "through the gate and up the walk, losing dimension now, onto or rather into the shadow of the little gallery and losing even substance now" (p. 334). He concludes that perhaps "what is going to happen to one tomorrow already gleams faintly visible now if the watcher were only wise enough to discern it or maybe just brave enough" (p. 334). Gavin is neither "smart enough" to perceive Flem's need for respectability nor "wise enough . . . or maybe just brave enough" to recognize that, in Brooks words, "the sanctions against those who defy the community mores are still powerful enough to render respectability something above mere conformity." [71] Ratliff's sadly sympathetic comment that "he [Gavin] missed it completely" (p. 153) is replaced, at the end of Gavin's interview with Eula, by the "constant racket" of the mockingbird singing in the dogwood tree (p. 334).

As before, the dogwood tree symbolizes for Gavin the traditional demands of doctrinal morality. The mockingbird's song reminds him that, no matter how much he may approve the morality of love, he is incapable of loving in accordance with its dictates. He is an "old man, already white-headed" (p. 317), "discrepant" (p. 332), and therefore respectable in the opinion of the Puritan community whether he wishes to be or not. When Eula first requested that he meet her, he had asked himself, *"Why cant you let me alone? What more can you want of me than I have already failed to do?"* (p. 313). He finds the answer in traditional Puritan respectability, which accrues to him by virtue of his incapacity to live as she does in "the ectoplasm of devotion too thin to be crowned by scorn, warned by hatred, annealed by grief" (p. 335).

> The spring night, cooler now, as if for a little while, until tomorrow's dusk and the new beginning, somewhere had suspired into sleep at last the amazed hushed burning of hope and dream two-and-two engendered. It would even be quite cold by dawn, daybreak. But even then not cold enough to chill, make hush for sleep the damned mockingbird for three nights now keeping his constant racket in Maggie's pink dogwood just under my bedroom window. So the trick of course would be to divide not him but his racket, the having to listen to him: one Gavin Stevens to cross his dark gallery too and into the house and up the stairs to cover his head in the bedclothes, losing in his turn a dimension of Gavin Stevens, an ectoplasm of Gavin Stevens impervious to cold and hearing too to bear its half of both, bear its half or all of any other burdens anyone wanted to shed and shuck, having only this moment assumed that one of a young abandoned girl's responsibility. (pp. 334–335)

Still the idealist, Gavin wrongly assumes that Eula has accepted his terms for protecting Linda and that his oath has assured the fulfillment of Eula's love by removing the last obstacle in the way of her desire to "unpin, shed, cast off the last clumsy and anguished dimension, and so be free" (p. 335). This freedom from the restrictive confines of the community's definition of respectability he associates with freedom from Flem, whom Eula married to gain respectability for herself and Linda and to whom both love and respectability have a tangible value. So long as it is respectably hidden from public sight, Eula's love affair with De Spain represents to Flem "the twenty-dollar gold piece pinned to the undershirt of the country boy on his first trip to Memphis" (p. 335). By revealing their love in a scandalous light, Flem unpins the gold piece and gains the bank presidency. Gavin reasons that Eula's freedom is proof of this fact. He mistakenly credits Flem with having freed Eula from matrimony just as he himself frees her from responsibility for Linda's reputation.

Throughout *The Town* the theme of the moral idealist's inability to act positively in the real world provides the vehicle by which Flem's amorality is revealed. In his attempts to protect Eula and Linda, Gavin continually subjects them to greater adversity, ironically aiding the very force that he means to oppose. The generous humanity of his romantic commitments, together with the ineffectuality of his actions, consistently reveals by contrast Flem's insensitivity to all but personal appetite and his devastating effectiveness in appeasing it. In Gavin's final interview with Eula and the events that follow it to the end of the novel, this theme is brought to its tragic climax. By affirming his theory of natural love and denying the significance of community sanction to it, Gavin ironically contributes to the termination of the love on which his theory is based and assures the continuance of the community's sanction of Flem. His refusal to compromise Linda's right to love by marrying her forces Eula, in Charles Mallison's words, "to choose death in order to leave her child a mere suicide for a mother instead of a whore" (p. 340). Eula's suicide not only fulfills her responsibility to Linda by protecting the girl from the castigation of the community but also fulfills her obligation to Manfred in that she literally does leave Flem. With the lover dead for whom he would have fought, Manfred leaves Jefferson quietly, affording Flem the opportunity to occupy his house as well as his bank. To Flem, Eula's death represents the extinction of the last threat to his respectability, the "jumping" of what Ratliff earlier described to Charles Mallison as "one more uncivic ditch . . . like Montgomery Ward's photygraph studio and I.O.'s railroad mules" (p. 257). Far from freeing Eula, as Gavin imagined, by unpinning the twenty-dollar gold piece, Flem has rid Jefferson of its Snopes adulteress as surely as he rid the town of its Snopes pornographer and its Snopes insurance con man. Gavin's implication in Eula's suicide here involves him in the same unintentional support of Flem's respectability as did his previous arrest of Montgomery Ward and his legal presence in the intimidation of I.O.

Moreover, by his instrumentality in convincing Linda that Flem is her father, Gavin shields Flem from the possibility that he will be implicated publicly in Eula's suicide. As Millgate points out, "he [Gavin] could do no other than assure Linda that Flem was her father in view of what he had promised Eula in that final interview, and in view, indeed, of the reasons for which Eula had chosen suicide." [72] By this assurance Gavin allays "the only remaining threat" to Flem, which Ratliff describes as "what might

happen if that-ere young gal that believed all right so far that he
[Flem] was her paw, might stumble onto something that would
tell her different. That she might find out by accident that the
man that was leastways mixed up somehow in her mother's suicide, whether he actively caused it or not, wasn't even her father,
since if somebody's going to be responsible why your maw killed
herself, at least let it be somebody kin to you and not jest a out-
right stranger" (p. 348). Content to believe that Flem is her
father, Linda will remain silent no matter what her suspicions
may be and fulfill the demands of propriety by attending the un-
veiling of the monument to her mother.

Whereas Flem's first monument, the water tower, symbolizes his
initial failure in Jefferson, the monument to Eula is symbolic of
his ultimate success. Gavin's part in the erection of Eula's monument is necessitated by his commitment to her, which began with
his determination to protect her chastity and culminated with his
affirmation of the morality of her love. As he attempted the former
by inviting Eula and Flem to the Cotillion Ball, where Flem discovered the value of respectability, he attempts the latter by im-
mortalizing her in a monument, which attests to Flem's acquisition of respectability. The carving of Eula's face, which Gavin
selects for the monument, is truly mythic, a "marble medallion
face . . . that never looked like Eula a-tall you thought at first,
never looked like nobody nowhere you thought at first, until you
were wrong because it never looked like all women because what
it looked like was one woman that ever man that was lucky enough
to have been a man would say, 'Yes, that's her. I knowed her five
years ago or ten years ago or fifty years ago and you would a
thought that by now I would a earned the right not to have to
remember her anymore'" (pp. 354-355). Nevertheless, Ratliff
says, "it was Flem's monument; dont make no mistake about
that" (p. 349). By copying others he has gained respectability, and
while he is not expert, as Gavin is, in the aesthetics of Italian
marbles and would not recognize the face of love, he has come a
long way since he had to rely on a Memphis furniture dealer to
choose his furniture and treat him honestly. Ratliff says of the
monument, "It was Flem that paid for it, first thought of it,
planned and designed it, picked out what size and what was to be
wrote on it—the face and the letters—and never once mentioned

price. Dont make no mistake about that. It was Flem. Because this too was a part of what he had come to Jefferson for and went through all he went through afterward to get it" (p. 349).

Because it is Flem's, and because Gavin contributes to it, the monument is ultimately expressive of the moral contrast between them. Gavin's contribution is the open, idealized face of moral love; Flem's the ironic inscription of amoral practicality: "A Virtuous Wife Is a Crown to Her Husband Her Children Rise and Call Her Blessed" (p. 355). To Flem, Eula's virtuousness lay in the fact that she was discreet and that she died "a mere suicide . . . instead of a whore." The crown with which she presented Flem was the presidency of a bank and a monument to attest to the inviolacy of his reputation. Her children "rise and call her blessed," as Linda does, because she got more from life than a husband such as Flem. Linda says, "When I thought he [Flem] wasn't my father, I hated her and Manfred both. . . . But now that I know he is my father, it's all right. I'm glad. I want her to have loved, to have been happy" (p. 346). Gavin reaffirms his vision of Eula as a love goddess beyond social or doctrinal reproach by sending Linda to Greenwich Villiage, "a place with a few unimportant boundaries but no limitations where young people of any age go to seek dreams" (p. 350). Flem reconfirms his amorality by spitting on Eula's grave before dismissing Linda: "He leant a little and spit out the window and then set back in the seat. 'Now you can go,' he says" (p. 355). Mourning the "waste" that Eula's death represents, Gavin seizes almost hysterically on Ratliff's explanation that "maybe she was bored" (p. 358). His tears at the end of the novel are in recognition of his own folly, of the fact that, had it not been for his romantic idealism, he might himself have been "not just strong enough to deserve [Eula's love], earn it, match it, but even brave enough to accept it" (p. 359). As Millgate correctly points out, "Although remaining incapable of a full involvement in the life around him, Stevens nevertheless gains dignity from the totality of his commitment to some of the most permanent and positive of man's ideals." [73] By contrast to him, Flem is drained of all humanity, all capacity for commitment or emotion beyond his own self-aggrandizement. To him, Eula was a twenty-dollar gold piece that earned eighteen years of interest. And Flem, as Ratliff says many times, does not waste money. The principle that motivates his exploitation of Jefferson is no less vicious than that which motivates Byron Snopes's "Snopes Indians." They are the extrinsic manifestation of the Snopes principle, representing as Ratliff says, "The last and final end of Snopes out-and-out unvarnished behavior in Jefferson" (p. 370). Flem sends them back to Texas, for now, literally, Snopesism wears a decent coat of varnish.

III.

The Mansion

"Mink": "The Ancient Immutable Laws of Simple Blood Kinship"

The Mansion, published in 1959, is the final novel of the Snopes trilogy, which, at the University of Virginia two years earlier, Faulkner claimed to "have had in mind for thirty years now." [1] As such, it is necessarily subject to the demands placed upon it by both *The Hamlet* and *The Town*; yet Faulkner has met these prerequisites without sacrificing the organic integrity of *The Mansion* itself. Not only do the stories of Mink and Linda span almost the entire action of the trilogy, but, as Elizabeth Kerr points out, they are also convergent. Kerr says, "*The Mansion* has two converging lines of action: the story of Mink, beginning in 1908, and the story of Flem, Linda, and Gavin, beginning in 1937 with the return of Linda to Jefferson. Thus *The Mansion* overlaps both *The Hamlet* and *The Town*." [2] This overlapping goes well beyond the mere linear development of plot and action and is a source of unity for both the novel and the trilogy as a whole. Based in the converging stories, the narrative circles back upon past injuries and partial victories, representing the culmination of themes developed throughout the continually altering perspectives which metamorphose character, action, and episode into what Vickery calls "patterns of circularity, repetition, and recurrence." [3] Such patterns reconstitute previous themes in terms of present imperatives, providing depth and amplitude to the trilogy without detriment to the internal unity of *The Mansion* itself.

The pattern is nowhere plainer than in the treatment of Flem Snopes. In *The Hamlet* and *The Town*, his implacable rapacity is revealed largely in terms of the devastation of human hopes and dreams that marks his passing. The scope of his machinations, which in *The Hamlet* are personal and extend to all individuals in the community of Frenchman's Bend, narrows somewhat in *The Town* with the refinement of his goals and the increasing subtlety of his methods. Arrived in Jefferson, he works toward acquisition of the symbol of economic dominance, the bank, by directly exploiting its representatives. While this method has indirect consequences for the community, the sense of personal anguish and defeat is confined to a relatively few individuals. In *The Mansion* Flem's goals are achieved; and "though his omnivorous greed is in no way diminished, yet it is rendered in some sense trivial because its deprived of further goals." [4] This is not to suggest, however, that Flem Snopes is any less central to *The Mansion* than to the novels preceding it. It is simply that present needs demand modification of presentation. In accordance with the steady narrowing down of sensibilities through which Flem's amorality is presented from *The Hamlet* to *The Town*, he is revealed now almost exclusively in terms of reactions to the past injuries of Mink Snopes and Linda Snopes Kohl. His violations of blood kinship and family become the metaphor by which his exploitation of all human principles is expressed. As Longley correctly says, "The whole great pattern of rise and fall, injustice and punishment, exploitation and retribution, is being reabsorbed into the Snopes family, being taken over by people who are themselves named Snopes." [5] Motive, established by the repetition of reaction to past event, is justified as attitude by the isolation from society of the main respondents. Culminating at the moment of Flem's death, the acutely personal nature of Mink's self-righteous obsession with revenge and the almost philosophical remoteness of deaf Linda's commitment to oppose inhumanity in all of its forms define Flem's archetypal amorality with new intensity and vastly increase the scope of its significance.

The opening section of *The Mansion*, entitled "Mink," rehearses the events of 1908 leading to the murder of Jack Houston and brings the narrative forward to 1946 through the thirty-eight years of Mink's imprisonment. In the repetition and extension of events originally narrated in *The Hamlet,* however, there are subtle alterations in tone, point of view, and incident which call forth a reestimation of Ratliff's pronouncement, in *The Town,* that Mink was "the only out-and-out mean Snopes we ever experienced" (p. 79). Pointing to the fact that Mink is the only Snopes possessed of a sense of honor, Brooks states that "Faulkner has not only altered perspective [in *The Mansion*] but added details calculated to allow us to see the situation from Mink's point of view: that of a deprived man, conscious of his weakness, conscious of his poverty, and fiercely resenting any insult to his dignity." [6] Another aspect of Mink's character is illuminated by Beck's assertion that the sections of *The Mansion* devoted to Mink are colored throughout by "Mink's grim sense of provocation and his unrelenting purpose." [7] This change of focus constitutes an expansion of the suggestions in *The Hamlet* that Mink's "meanness" is in some degree justified as an assertion of his innate value as a human being and as a defense of his identity. Whereas, in the earlier novel, Mink's violence is treated as the logical end of unbearable oppression, in *The Mansion* it is shown to be commensurate with his primitive cosmology. As Beck says, "Mink's 'meanness,' seen into more closely, and literally reviewed in fuller relations, is seen beyond." [8] In his expanded portrait in *The Mansion,* Mink's motives and actions are firmly based in the principled and deeply felt belief that existence is fundamentally a test of man's will to endure and that it is retributive.

One characteristic of this belief is Mink's alienation from all civil institutions and social rituals. Not only is he set apart by his debilitating poverty, but his isolation extends to all aspects of his life. He views himself as "not being a rich man like Houston but only an independent one, asking no favors of any man, paying his own way" (p. 8). He has no faith in the God commonly associated with religious ceremony and views churches as "places which a man with a hole in his gut and a rut in his britches that he couldn't satisfy at home, used, by calling himself a preacher of God, to get conveniently together the biggest possible number of women that he could tempt with the reward of the one in return for the job of the other—the job of filling his hole in payment for getting theirs plugged the first time the husband went to the field and she could slip off to the bushes where the preacher was waiting" (p. 5). In place of faith in God, Mink substitutes what Theodore Greene calls "a perverted variant of a faith in a primitive Jahweh, jealous and unredemptive but righteous." [9] Mink defines the object of his faith as *"them—they—it,* whichever and whatever you wanted to call it, who represented a simple fundamental justice and equity in human affairs, or else a man might just as well quit; the *they, them, it,* call them what you like, which simply would not, could not harass and harry a man forever without someday, at some moment, letting him get his own just and equal licks back in return" (p. 6). In the predestinarian universe that Mink envisions, man's only hope lies in his ability to endure until the time arrives for his personal retribution.

This sense of metaphysical justice finds its temporal equivalent in the preordained laws of clanship. To Mink civil law is of no moment, being merely an expedient for retaining material possessions. But Mink's poverty is such that, as Brooks explains, "he possesses only two things of value: his identity and the savage pride with which he defends that identity." [10] Since his identity is defined not in terms of society, from which his poverty isolates him, but in terms of his membership in a family, to which he is bound by blood, his refuge is not in civil but in clan law. An injury to one member is, in effect, an injury to the entire clan, and the avenger of that injury is entitled to the protection of his fellows. When Mink is forced to murder Houston, therefore, he looks for aid to his cousin, Flem, "the only person who had the power to save him and would have had to save him whether he wanted to or not because of the ancient immutable laws of simple blood kinship" (p. 5). Flem's power to save Mink stems from his association with Will Varner, his business associate and father-in-law, who is not only the major economic force in the community but also the justice of the peace. Flem is "the one Snopes of them all who had risen, broken free, and either been born with or had learned, taught himself, the knack or the luck to cope with, hold his own, handle the They and Them which he, Mink, apparently did not have the knack or the luck to do" (p. 35). In Mink's eyes, Flem's obligation to save him from trial for murder is compounded, moreover, by the fact that it is Flem's absence from Frenchman's Bend, that is responsible for the set of circumstances which leads Mink to murder Houston. With characteristic simplistic logic, Mink thinks that *"if Flem had been here he could a stopped all this on that first day before it ever got started. Working for Varner like he done, being in with Houston and Quick and all the rest of them. He could do it now if I could jest a waited. Only it wasn't me that couldn't wait. It was Houston his-self that wouldn't give me time"* (p. 37). Flem is involved in the cycle of retribution from the outset, for his absence from Frenchman's Bend in Mink's time of need is a violation of the metaphysical laws of retribution, which he, alone of all Snopeses, can manipulate. His premeditated absence from the murder trial is a violation of the temporal laws of clanship and makes him liable to the same revenge that Mink wreaks upon Houston. Thus, through thematic regeneration and expansion, the trilogy clearly projects the self-destructive consequences of Flem's archetypal amorality.

The emphasis upon Flem's power in the eyes of his clansmen and his failure to use that power for their protection is further expressive of the purposeful nature of his amorality and demonstrates, by his absence at critical junctures in the narrative, the method by which the amorality is most often defined. Stressing Flem's unswerving and steadfast amorality, Beck points out his centrality to the trilogy:

> Flem seems the ultimate of the amoral, so much so that he can scarcely be accounted cruel, being merely insensitive, literally ruthless. It is thereby that he becomes a pivotal point in the trilogy's structure and theme. Recurrently appearing throughout, he is also felt as an almost ubiquitous presence, by his impingements upon the affairs and the apprehensions of others. Unique and just this side the incredible in his absoluteness, he is also paradoxically the very archetype of his tribe and kind, the monolithic image beside whom all other Snopeses are lesser creatures on the scale of Snopesism. Their elements assembled in him are as if chemically modified in another compound, transmuted into the completely inhuman, utterly stable beyond influence or appeal. Flem thus is an ultimate and invariable point of reference, the one whom all the others watch, the figure who haunts all other minds yet whose mind is never seen into, the object to which the variously subjective modes of the trilogy are related. This disposition is indeed one of the central factors in a splendid narrative strategy. It is also suggestive of a dark

minor theme, that beyond immorality is a worse end toward
which it drifts, amorality. Flem's relative poise in *The Mansion*
is to be seen then as arrival unchallenged at this unamenable
end.[11]

In *The Mansion*, as in *The Town* and *The Hamlet* before it,
Flem's amorality is revealed largely by contrast to the morality of
those who watch him and whose minds he haunts. With the establishment of Mink's revenges as more than mere "meanness," his
revenge upon Flem takes the character of justice that is predestined for crimes transcending the merely personal.

As has been noted earlier, Mink's obsession with revenge upon
Flem is deeply rooted in the events surrounding the murder of
Jack Houston. Vickery comments that the recounting of the murder "serves a purpose other than reminding new or forgetful read-
ers of past events. In essence, it reinforces the thematic continuity
of the trilogy by establishing a parallel between the passionate ar-
rogance of Houston and the cold ruthlessness of Flem Snopes.
Both deny to Mink even a minimal recognition of his humanity
and thereby diminish their own. . . . the pattern of action recalled
in 'Mink' is imposed on the 'Flem' section of *The Mansion*." [12]
To Mink, the wealthy Houston embodies the principle of economic domination by which Mink, as a tenant farmer, is kept in
virtual servitude to a landlord. The contrast between them is expressed largely in terms of their possession of livestock, which itself reflects their basic natures. Houston is "the arrogant intoler-
able man" who owns "the bad-eyed horse and the dog that bared
its teeth and raised its hackles any time anybody went near it"
(p. 7). Mink "had no horse to ride when he had to go for a tin of
snuff or a bottle of quinine or a piece of meat" (p. 8). The quarrel
between them is initiated when Houston rides Mink down in the
road. Although at the time Mink has no serious thought of retali-
ation, in the course of the next year he is beset by a series of
hardships, the reparation for which he undertakes as retribution
for Houston's having insulted him. When his only "milk cow,"
mated to the "scrub bull belonging to a Negro" (p. 8), fails to
calve, Mink is forced to winter her and then "to keep the barren
and worthless cow up under fence while she exhausted his own
meager pasture . . . to feed her out of his meager crib during the
rest of that summer and fall, since the local agreement was that all

stock would be kept up until all crops were out of the field" (p. 9). Releasing her in November, he finds her missing and locates her at last "in Houston's pasture with his beef herd" (p. 9). Dwelling upon the fact that Houston is "not only rich enough to be able to breed and raise beef cattle, but rich enough to keep a Negro to do nothing else save feed and tend them" (p. 9), Mink recalls that the same Negro cares for "that blooded stallion too, and even that damn hound running beside the horse he [Houston] thundered up and down the road on" (p. 11). With this association in mind, Mink seeks to repair his own straitened circumstances by repaying Houston for the earlier insult. He leaves his cow in Houston's field for the winter to be fed and bred to Houston's pedigreed bulls.

While the rationale behind such behavior can hardly be deemed logical in any traditional sense, from Mink's point of view it constitutes a primitive justice. Houston's barn is warmer than Mink's cabin, his Negro servant better dressed than Mink's family, his cattle better fed than Mink himself. In terms of the injustice of the situation, Mink's behavior is a form of revenge against the entire scheme of his life. He curses the barn, the Negro, and the cattle, but he curses "above all the unaware white man through or because of whose wealth such a condition could obtain, cursing the fact that his very revenge and vengeance—what he himself believed to be simple justice and inalienable rights—could not be done at one stroke but instead must depend on the slow incrementation of feed converted to weight, plus the uncontrollable, even unpredictable, love mood of the cow and the long subsequent nine months of gestation; cursing his own condition that the only justice available to him must be this prolonged and passive one" (p. 12). But even this "revenge and vengeance" is not totally effective, this "justice" not complete, for he knows he will be forced to buy back the cow from Houston with money "with which he, Mink, could have bought a gallon of whiskey for Christmas, plus a dollar or two of the gewgaw finery his wife and his two daughters were forever whining at him for" (pp. 12–13). In addition to foregoing these simple pleasures, moreover "he would have to go fawning and even cringing a little when he went to recover his cow" (p. 13). While he knows this to be necessitated by the circumstances of his life in relation to society and while he is willing to do what he must, he endures the test at no sacrifice to his iden-

tity as a man: "his pride was that he was not reconciled. Not he to
be that meager and niggling and puny as meekly to accept something just because he didn't see yet how he could help it" (p. 13).
Not deigning to deal with Houston's Negro servant, Mink insists on
conducting his business directly with Houston, as an equal.

The circumstances resulting from the interview serve to intensify the sense of Mink's isolation from society by contrasting his
belief in "*them*," who represent "a simple fundamental justice and
equity in human affairs" (p. 6), with the civil laws that govern his
relationship with Houston. Houston refuses to return the cow for
the eight dollars that Mink offers him and threatens Mink with a
pistol. When Houston suggests that they duel for the pistol, Mink
refuses, lending some credence to his later claim that he did not
wish to kill Houston but was forced to it by Houston himself. Certain that he is being further tried by "*them*," who are "still test-
ing, trying him to see just how much he could bear and would
stand" (p. 16), Mink takes his case to the justice of the peace, submitting himself without hope of restitution to the ritual of membership in society. When Varner supports Houston in the suit,
Mink "was not really surprised at what happened" (p. 16). Lacking the eighteen dollars and seventy-five cents to reclaim his cow,
he is obliged to work out the price by digging post holes at fifty
cents a day for "thirty-seven days and from light till noon on the
next one" (p. 17). His cow, now bred and freshened for milking,
is to remain with Houston, who insists on keeping her because "if
she's here Snopes can see her every day and keep his spirits up
about what he's really working for" (p. 18).

Mink accepts these conditions not because they are legally binding in terms of civil law but rather because they represent to him
yet another test of his will to endure. He had thought that finding
his cow in Houston's field was a sign that his preordained time for
retribution for past injuries had arrived, but "he had simply un-
derestimated *them*" (p. 16). Choosing to interpret the civil judgment against him literally, he begins work for Houston with a
steadfast single-mindedness that excludes all other concerns. Furthermore, he refuses to compromise his destiny, declining to sell the
cow first to Houston and then to Varner himself, "who was suddenly afraid, afraid for the peace and quiet of the community
which he held in his iron usurious hand, buttressed by the mort-

gages and liens in the vast iron safe in the store" (p. 19). In the face of such frightening determination, Varner's fear is that his judgment against Mink will result in Mink's seeking revenge on Houston or himself. He therefore invokes his power as Mink's landlord and forces him to forego his labor for the cow in order to fulfill his commitment as a tenant to farm Varner's land. When Mink tries to do both, plowing his fields by day and digging post holes at night, it is Houston who takes fright and drives him away. " 'Go back,' Houston said. 'Dont never come on my land again after sundown. If you're going to kill yourself, it wont be here. Go back now. Maybe I cant stop you from working out that cow by daylight but I reckon I can after dark' " (p. 21). While these denials free Mink of the "hurry and haste" to prove himself, such freedom is itself a burden to be borne and endured. Yet it provides him another opportunity to assert his identity as a man, "Because patience was his pride too: never to be reconciled since by this means he could beat Them; They might be stronger for a moment than he but nobody, no man, no nothing could wait longer than he could wait when nothing else but waiting would do, would work, would serve him" (p. 22). When at last his crop is planted and the post holes finished, he permits himself the small luxury of letting Houston wait one night, until the cow has been fed for a final time, before retrieving her.

So carefully has Mink planned the moment at which he will assert his victory over his tormentors that he even takes care to guard against the return of the cow by Houston or the constable. When he ascertains that the cow has not been returned, he is pleased and confident.

> He went to the barn. The cow was not there of course, as he had known. He was glad of it. The whole thing—realizing that even if one of them brought the cow home, he would still have to go out to the barn to make sure—had been good for him, teaching him, before any actual harm had been done, just exactly what They were up to: to fling, jolt, surprise him off balance and so ruin him: Who couldn't beat him in any other way: couldn't beat him with money or its lack, couldn't outwait him; could beat him only by catching him off balance and so topple him back into that condition of furious blind fearless rage where he had no sense. (p. 24)

It is in this state of mind that he approaches Houston to reclaim his cow, only to discover that he has been denied even his small victory. By invoking the pound fee law, Houston claims from Mink two more days of toil and, more important, forces Mink to claim his cow at the end of the working day without the satisfaction of making Houston wait to rid himself of the animal. Mink's attitude now, however, is in direct contrast to the "thin furious rage" (p. 16) in which he made his initial appeal to Varner for justice. Although he is certainly caught "off balance," he stands "quite still; his hand did not even tighten on the coiled rope," and "walking, peacefully and steadily" to find Varner, he thinks not of civil but of clan law and its relationship to the universe dominated by "*them.*" "He thought *If Flem was jest here. . . .* his cousin's absence when he was needed was just one more test, harassment, enragement They tried him with, not to see if he would survive it because They had no doubt of that, but simply for the pleasure of watching him have to do something extra there was no reason whatever for him to have to do" (pp. 26–27). Before seeing Varner, in fact, he prepares the ambush from which he will shoot Houston. When the two extra days are worked out and the pound fee paid, he retrieves his cow and sets out for Jefferson with his last five dollars to buy shotgun shells.

This journey, conceived in vengefulness and motivated by inhumanity, is the prototype for Mink's journey, thirty-eight years later, from Parchman prison to Jefferson to kill Flem. Here, as later, Mink's feelings are a mixture of determination, pride, and regret: determination to be avenged, pride in having planned his vengeance well, and regret for the circumstances that necessitated his revenge. Despite the loss of his money, he goes on doggedly to try to pay with a lie for the shells that he no longer has currency to buy. Although he has five birdshot shells for his ancient gun, he tries to obtain better ammunition because "even if he were guaranteed that they would fire, Houston deserved better" (p. 30). His regret is for Flem's absence: "*Yes* he thought peacefully *if Flem had been here he could a stopped all this on that first day before it ever got started*" (p. 37). In fact, thoughts of Flem pervade this journey as does his obsession with revenge upon Flem in the later one. It is on the way to Jefferson to buy shells that "for the first time he began really to think about his absent cousin" (p.

35), and in so doing he relates Flem's power over *"them"* to his own inadequacy in dealing with the same. As the first shell fails to explode, Mink's inability to deal with his destiny is iterated: "He thought *And even now. They still aint satisfied yet"* (p. 39). The explosion of the second shell, which kills Houston, is, however, an assertion that cosmic justice does exist for those prepared to endure their fate. His injuries avenged, Mink's only regret is that he could not confront Houston "between the roar of the gun and the impact of the shot . . . to say to Houston and for Houston to have to hear it: "I aint shooting you because of them thirty-seven and a half four-bit days. That's all right; I done long ago forgot and forgive that. Likely Will Varner couldn't do nothing else, being a rich man too and all you rich folks has got to stick together or else maybe some day the ones that aint rich might take a notion to raise up and take hit away from you. That aint why I shot you. I killed you because of that-ere extry one-dollar pound fee" (p. 39). The distinction between wealth and poverty provides a metaphor for that between civil law, represented in Varner's judgment, and justice, represented in the murder of Houston. Given Mink's concept of a fundamentally just destiny, the murder is an assertion of his identity as a man and his right, as a man, to at least minimal humanity.

In the course of events that befall Mink as a result of his murdering Houston, the theme of Flem's involvement in Mink's destiny is further developed in terms of the punishment Mink must endure because of Flem's absence. Whether or not Flem could actually have saved Mink from prison is irrelevant. To Mink, Flem has the power to do so by virtue of his position in the community and the obligation to do so as a member of the Snopes clan. Thus, when his months of waiting "in quenchless expectation and hope" (p. 42) for Flem to save him turn out to be futile, and he must admit to himself that *"He* [Flem] *aint coming"* (p. 42), Mink again sets himself upon revenge. His mood is similar to that calm determination which he experienced when informed about the pound fee.

> So now he had peace. He had thought he had peace as soon as he realised what he would have to do about Houston, and that Houston himself wasn't going to let him wait until Flem got

> back. But he had been wrong. That wasn't peace then; it was
> too full of too many uncertainties: such as if anybody would
> send word to Flem about his trouble at all, let alone in time. Or
> even if the word was sent in time, would the message find Flem
> in time. And even if Flem got the message in time, there might
> be a flood or a wreck on the railroad so he couldn't get back
> in time.
>   But all that was finished now. He didn't have to bother and
> worry at all now since all he had to do was wait, and he had
> already proved to himself that he could do that. Just to wait:
> that's all he needed; he didn't even need to ask the jailor to send
> a message since the lawyer himself had said he would come
> back to see him after supper. (p. 42)

Now, however, the waiting and the enduring involve not the
length of one spring planting, as before, but thirty-eight years.

As Mink submitted himself to the law first by digging post
holes and then by foregoing that digging in order to plant his crop,
so he now submits himself to the law again. In place of a justice of
the peace there is now a lawyer to tell him what he must do, and
he takes the lawyer's statement of the terms of his imprisonment
no less literally than he did Varner's statement of the terms under
which he could regain his cow. He believes that "his own lawyer
couldn't lie to him, because there was some kind of rule somebody
had told him about that if the client didn't lie to his lawyer, the
Law itself wouldn't let the lawyer lie to his own client" (p. 48).
Mink thus interprets the lawyer's explanation of the provisions of
parole as the law's commitment to free him eventually and adopts
them as the strict rules by which to govern his life in the penitentiary: "*To do whatever they tell me to do. Not to talk back to
nobody. Not to get into no fights. That's all I got to do for jest
twenty-five or maybe even jest twenty years. But mainly not to
try to escape*" (p. 49). Like Varner, Mink's lawyer is frightened
by the simplistic literalness of his client, whom he perceives to be
"as deadly as a small viper—a half-grown asp or cobra or krait"
(p. 45). When he attempts to have Mink sent to an asylum, from
which there is no release, however, Mink violently resists. "Insanity is an imputation which Mink rejects on every count: he has the
illiterate rustic's horror of being called 'crazy,' and moreover he
has no wish to repudiate his responsibility for the act of vengeance.
His killing of Houston was not an irresponsible or compelled act:

it was an act for which he insists on taking responsibility." [13] To plead insanity would be to deny the one act by which he feels he has proven his right to identity as a man. In addition, he has already committed himself to yet another act of vengeance, expressive of his identity as a member of a clan. He thinks "with a kind of amazement of the time when his only reason for wanting to get out was to go back home and farm, remembering it only for a moment and then no more, because now he had to get out" (pp. 48–49). The sense of necessity that distinguishes wanting from having to do a thing is quite clear and is entirely commensurate with Mink's view of life as predestined: he thinks, *"If a feller jest wants to do something, he might make it and he might not. But if he's GOT to do something, cant nothing stop him"* (p. 49). Ironically, by accepting the penalty set by the law for one murder, and by abiding by the dictates of the law during his imprisonment, Mink is fulfilling his destiny, for the law will be obligated to release him to murder again. *"Yes sir he thought. It looks like I done had to come all the way to Parchman jest to turn right around and go back home and kill Flem"* (p. 51).

In the context of such primitive morality, dominated by Mink's belief in predestined justice and his idealism regarding clanship, Flem's manipulation of Mink's destiny and his violation of blood ties clearly implies that he is amoral. The imputation of amorality is made explicit when destiny and clanship are viewed from the altered perspective of Montgomery Ward Snopes's cynical nihilism. Vickery points out that in *The Mansion* Flem remains largely in the background of the action because "position, status, power, and all the external trappings that accompany them are already in his possession"; further, she contends that "he must fall back on the urge to keep, to protect and conserve." [14] When, in the summer of 1923, however, Montgomery Ward is arrested for dealing in pornography, Flem is still "grazing on up through Jefferson" (p. 57), and what he must conserve are the means and opportunity to achieve his goals: his reputation for respectability and his life. By the scandalous nature of his profession, Montgomery Ward threatens the former, and Mink, simply by having served fifteen years of a twenty to twenty-five year prison sentence, is an imminent threat to the latter. As related by the naive Charles Mallison in *The Town*, the danger to Flem's respectability is primary, and Flem neutralizes it in the guise of a public-spirited citizen whose interest is in "civic virtue" (p. 175). But in *The Mansion*, the narrators are V. K. Ratliff, the shrewd Snopes historian, and Montgomery Ward himself, whom Brooks calls "the only world-weary Snopes, the only detached aesthete of all the Snopeses." [15] In the light of their mature insights into Snopesism, the events surrounding Montgomery Ward's imprisonment for moonshining are expanded to bear directly upon Mink's revenge. Seen into more fully, Flem's attempts to protect his respectability are of secondary concern, veiling his primary purpose which is the preservation of his life. In this, Montgomery Ward is not so much Flem's victim, as in *The Town*, as his instrument. His tempting Mink to a futile escape attempt is planned by Flem, and Mink bears him no grudge, thereby sustaining the theme of Flem's insensitivity to clanship and dramatizing his amorality.

Philosophically, Montgomery Ward is ideally suited to his role. His fully resigned expectation and acceptance of exploitation at the hands of his kinsman Flem is in sharp contrast to Mink's intense faith in the laws of kinship and his deep sense of betrayal when Flem violates those laws. When Montgomery Ward's pornographic studio is closed, Ratliff says that "even in the initial excitement, Montgomery Ward never had one moment's confusion about what was actively happening to him. The second moment after Lawyer [Stevens] and Hub [Hampton] walked in the door, he knowed that at last something was happening that he had been expecting ever since whenever that other moment was when Flem found out or suspected that whatever was going on up that alley had a money profit in it" (p. 52). When it appears that Flem will lose his profit by being "doomed to respectability" (p. 57), Montgomery Ward "even in his extremity . . . had more simple sense and judgment, let alone family pride and loyalty, than to actively believe that ten thousand Lawyer Stevenses and Hub Hamptons, let alone jest one each of them, could a diddled Flem Snopes. In fact, sooner than that foul aspersion, he would believe that Flem Snopes was subject to bad luck too, jest like a human being" (p. 59). When he is told that he will be sentenced to Parchman prison rather than Atlanta because the sheriff "captured five gallons of moonshine whiskey setting in the bottles on the shelf that Montgomery Ward his-self assumed never held nothing but photograph developer" (p. 60), his reaction is "not alarm, not astonishment: jest interest and surprise and even that mostly jest interest" (p. 60). Described in Ratliff's characteristically ironic phrasing, Montgomery Ward's resignation to inhumanity emphasizes Mink's resistance to it, elevating Mink in stature as a principled and starkly moral man. As such, the danger that Mink represents to the amoral Flem is considerably heightened.

The extent of this danger may be gauged in terms of the financial expense to Flem in counteracting it. He is the financial man, the banker dedicated to acquisition of wealth, who values his life only in proportion to the cost of preserving it. As Ratliff points out, his expenditures on Montgomery Ward are not motivated, as the community had supposed, by either clan loyalty or respectability.

> So ever body was wrong. Flem Snopes hadn't spent no two thousand dollars' worth of bond money to purify Montgomery Ward outen the U.S.A. America, and he didn't spent no twenty-five or thirty dollars' worth of white-mule whiskey jest to purify the Snopes family name outen Atlanta, Georgia. What he had done was to spend twenty-five or thirty dollars to send Montgomery Ward to Parchman when the government would a sent him to Georgia free. Which was a good deal more curious than jest surprising, and a good deal more interesting than all three. (pp. 63–64)

Expressed by Montgomery Ward in poker phraseology, Flem's interview with him in the Jefferson jail assumes the aspect of the bartering sessions that typify Flem's mode of operation throughout the trilogy. With typical frugality and lack of waste, Flem spends no more and no less than is necessary for the achievement of his purpose. Economically "chewing his mouthful of nothing" (p. 67), Flem steadily beats Montgomery Ward down to the price that he has himself predetermined as sufficient to gain Montgomery Ward's compliance with his wishes, forcing him to submit by threatening him with exposure to federal prosecution. Presented with the certified letter containing the pornographic post card, Montgomery Ward says, "So it looks like I've been raised. And it looks like I wont call. In fact, it looks like I'm going to pass" (p. 69). For duping Mink into attempting an escape, Montgomery Ward receives a trip to the brothels of Memphis in the company of his halfbrother, Clarence, and "a railroad ticket to wherever you want, and a hundred dollars" (p. 69).

Lacking the faith in himself that sustains Mink, Montgomery Ward accepts these terms as the best of a bad bargain. Nonetheless, he is sensitive to the exploitation of human weakness, and he does not lose sight of the fact that clanship is at issue or that Flem's life is purchased at the cost of twenty years more imprisonment for Mink. Because he is a cynic, however, his judgments of the human condition are often indirect and are most commonly revealed by association with other events in the novel or by the statements that they elicit from others. Thus, while he makes no explicit judgment of Clarence's exploitation of Virgil Snopes's sexual prowess, the episode is given significance by its obvious relationship to Lump's profiteering from Ike's "stock-diddling," in *The Hamlet,* and Flem's ruthless use of the physical love between Manfred and Eula, in *The Town.* The fact that Montgomery Ward is to some extent moved by such conditions is suggested in his sympathetic description of the time-ruined madam, Miss Reba. In her "fat raddled face and body that had worn themselves out with the simple hard physical work of being a whore" (p. 79), Montgomery Ward sees something "that, as they say, shouldn't happen to a dog" (p. 79). Miss Reba's hard lot suggests the lot of Mink, who is later described as "a damn little worn-out dried-up shrimp of a man not as big as a fourteen-year-old boy" (pp. 83–84). Informed of Mink's circumstances, Miss Reba reacts with a passionate outcry expressive of pity for all injured humanity: " 'The poor son of a bitch," she said. . . . 'All of us. Every one of us. The poor son of a bitches' " (p. 82). Montgomery Ward's reaction is to give to Reba and Mink the fifty dollars given him by Flem. Although he gives Miss Reba ten dollars directly, he insists that she herself send the remainder to Mink, "the poorest son of a bitch anywhere at this second" (p. 79). She sends it "from a friend" (p. 82). Back in Jefferson, Montgomery Ward renounces Flem's two thousand dollar bond by returning to jail three weeks early in what he cynically calls "a dry run against my conscience" (p. 83). For the moment, he is free of Flem's control.

> So now I had a set of steel bars between; now I was safe from the free world, safe and secure for a little while yet from the free

Snopes world where Flem was parlaying his wife into the presidency of a bank and Clarence even drawing per diem as a state senator between Jackson and Gayoso Street to take the wraps off Virgil whenever he could find another Arkansas sport who refused to believe what he was looking at, and Byron in Mexico or wherever he was with whatever was still left of the bank's money, and mine and Clarence's father I.O. and all of our Uncle Wesley leading a hymn with one hand and fumbling the skirt of an eleven-year-old infant with the other. (p. 83)

The irony of being free only when in prison is doubled by the fact that Montgomery Ward is in prison so that he can serve as Flem's agent in denying Mink freedom.

In a number of respects, Montgomery Ward's behavior parallels Mink's in similar situations. Both submit to forces they consider to be beyond them, Mink to destiny and Montgomery Ward to Flem, and both reject offers of money that would compromise them as men, Mink from Varner and Houston, and Montgomery Ward from Flem again. In addition, both men have definite ideas of what to expect from their kinsmen. Herein lies the basis for the contrast between them. In the context of their similar actions, the dissimilarity of what they expect from clanship characterizes each by contrast to the other. Beck states the distinction between them in terms of inner strength and inner weakness:

Mink's scruples are simple and his fidelity to them has about it a kind of fierce Anglo-Saxon strictness. Montgomery Ward's more subtle hesitancies have no such authority for him; he is capable of some sentiment but he cannot rise to consistent conduct. Since Mink's behavior is principled (however primitive his concepts) and even his most violent acts are assertions of honor without regard for practical advantage, he retains sturdiness, his will supported by a limited but sufficient sense of *amour propre*. That is something beyond Montgomery Ward, with all his brashness; he seems nauseated at last by his own iniquities. . . . a lack of center leaves him inadequate in a crisis.[16]

Revived by Montgomery Ward's glib lies, Mink's belief in the interdependence of clansmen permits him to convince himself that Flem wants him freed, and he therefore violates the primary law of prison existence—"not to try to escape" (p. 51). Although he realizes when he enters the prison yard in a dress and sunbonnet that his escape will fail, his pride is such that he does not turn back but is "even still walking on past the moment when he knew that he had been sold and that he should have known all along he was being sold" (p. 85). Some measure of the esteem in which he holds personal honor is suggested by the fact that he fights for it: "it took five of them [guards] striking and slashing at his head with pistol barrels and even then it finally took the blackjack to stop him, knock him out" (p. 86). Montgomery Ward, on the other hand, bases his action on his belief in the inevitability of clan inhumanity, which he describes as "the promissory note of breathing in a world that had Snopeses in it" (p. 85). Lacking the capacity for self-assertion, his pride is not in himself but in Mink as a representative of the human condition. He says, "I was proud, not just to be kin to him but of belonging to what Reba called all of us poor son of a bitches" (p. 85). Finally, the measure of his dishonor is the contempt in which he is held by the guard to whom he reports Mink's escape plan. In terms of prison morality, "every convict had a right to try to escape just as every guard and trusty had the right to shoot him in the back the first time he didn't halt. But no unprintable stool pigeon had the right to warn the guard in advance" (p. 85).

Because of these multiple points of reference, the continuing similarities and contrasts between Montgomery Ward and Mink transcend the merely personal and local and constitute an extension and expansion of the theme of retribution established in Mink's concept of a universe dominated by "*them*." Inevitably, this larger view involves Flem, by whose instrumentality the two are juxtaposed. Since both Mink and Montgomery Ward are imprisoned by Flem, their respective reactions as victim and instrument of his amoral machinations bear directly upon him. Mink's commitment to revenge on Flem is the first of these. Montgomery Ward's description of Flem "with the shadow of the cell bars crisscrossing him" (p. 66) in the Jefferson jail furthers the sense of his culpability. That Flem's guilt is beyond all leniency, however, is firmly established by Mink's reaction to his being duped into the attempted escape. Escape not only violates the major law by which Mink has governed his prison existence, but the means of escape, dressed "like a little girl playing mama in the calico dress and sunbonnet" (p. 85), further violates Mink's acute sensitivity to his identity as a man: "he still wanted to believe that a man should be permitted to run at his fate, even if that fate was doom, in the decency and dignity of pants" (p. 85). His betrayal results in a twenty-year extension of his sentence. But despite the fact that Montgomery Ward is the agent of these injuries, and to the amazement of the warden whose orientation is to prison behavior, Mink bears Montgomery Ward no malice.

> So he [Mink] came in. The bruises and slashes from the butts and the blades of the sights were healing fine. The blackjack of course never had showed. "Hidy," he said. To me [Montgomery Ward]. "I reckon you'll see Flem before I will now."
> "Yes," I said.
> "Tell him he hadn't ought to used that dress. But it dont matter. If I had made it out then, maybe I would a changed. But I reckon I wont now. I reckon I'll jest wait." (p. 86)

By forgiving Montgomery Ward, in spite of the active part he has played in Mink's betrayal, Mink demonstrates that the principles which motivate his revenge transcend momentary individual animosities and local prison customs. A larger imperative is at issue: revenge upon Flem Snopes. To this end Mink's fearful capacity for belief and endurance is directed, accentuating with renewed emphasis Flem's amorality.

Typically, Mink assumes full responsibility for his actions. Whereas Montgomery Ward blames his part in Mink's betrayal on his membership in "what you might call a family, a clan, a race, maybe even a species, of pure sons of bitches" (p. 87), Mink accepts the consequences of his escape attempt with calm determination. "'They told me,' he said. 'I was warned.' He stood, not moving, relaxed, small and frail, his face downbent a little, musing, peaceful, almost like faint smiling. 'He [Flem] hadn't ought to fooled me to get caught in that dress and sunbonnet,' he said. 'I wouldn't a done that to him'" (pp. 88–89). The nearly forty years of prison, like the thirty seven and a half days of labor for Houston, result from actions that Mink himself initiates, and as such he can forgive them. The sunbonnet and dress, however, like the pound fee, represent an ultimate and unforgivable injustice imposed upon him undeserved, and the forty dollars he receives "from a friend," one dollar for each year of his prison term, in no

way appeases him. " 'It was Flem,' he said. 'He can afford it. Besides, he never had no money hurt against me. He was jest getting
a holt with Will Varner then and maybe he figgered he couldn't
resk getting mixed up with a killing, even if hit was his blood kin.
Only I wish he hadn't used that dress and sunbonnet. He never
had to do that' " (p. 89). His peacefulness now recalls the peace
he knew while preparing to murder Houston. It results directly
from his certainty that, in a predestined world dominated by
"*them*," his ability to endure, to "wait," will earn him the opportunity for retribution.

In the course of this long term of single-minded "waiting," Mink
is stripped of all human rights except the right to be revenged. No
longer does he contend for survival with his environment.

> He remembered how at first he had cursed his bad luck for
> letting them catch him but he knew better now: that there was
> no such thing as bad luck or good luck: you were either born
> a champion or not a champion and if he had been born a cham-
> pion Houston not only couldn't, he wouldn't have dared, misuse
> him about that cow to where he had to kill him; that some folks
> were born to be failures and get caught always, some folks were
> born to be lied, to and believe it, and he was one of them. (pp.
> 89–90)

As a tenant farmer, he and people of his kind "never had owned
even temporarily the land which they believed they had rented
between one New Year's and the next one. It was the land itself
which owned them, and not just from a planting to its harvest but
in perpetuity" (p. 91). Even in this condition, however, he had
some rights of self-assertion. His satisfaction was in repaying his
"*immolated youth and hope*" (p. 90) with fire, and the repayment
was personal, between the man and the demanding land: "*Every
late February or March we can set fire to the surface of you until
all of you in sight is scorched and black, and there aint one god-
damn thing you can do about it. You can wear out our bodies and
dull our dreams and wreck our stomachs with the sowbelly and
corn meal and molasses which is all you afford us to eat but every
spring we can set you afire again and you know that too*" (p. 91).
In prison, however, "that was past now. He no longer belonged
to the land even on those sterile terms. He belonged to the gov-

ernment, the state of Mississippi" (p. 91). In this situation, Mink is deprived even of that small pleasure he once took in farming well. His labors as a farmer are meaningless, since it does not matter whether the crops grow or not. "All he had to do now was just to keep moving; even the man with the shotgun standing over him neither knew nor cared whether anything came up behind him or not just so he kept moving, any more than he cared" (p. 92). In fact, the only thing that does give Mink's life meaning is his obsession with past injuries: "Parchman just changed the way a man looked at what he saw after he got in Parchman. It didn't change what he brought with him" (p. 92). Dwelling upon Flem's inhumanity, Mink is sustained by his determination to be avenged.

In this context the theme of Mink's isolation from the community, which is first established by his poverty, is extended to suggest an isolation from life itself. Life is something he remembers in terms of passions now years past: the murder of Houston, his trial, his impatience to kill Flem. Instead of experiencing living, he only hears about it: "waiting, he found out that he was listening, hearing too; that he was keeping up with what went on by just listening and hearing even better than if he had been right there in Jefferson because like this all he had to do was just watch them without having to worry about them too" (p. 93). Inured to waiting, he is no longer tortured by the prospect that Flem may not be alive in 1948 for him to kill. Whereas "he could remember how at one time that too had driven him mad" (p. 93), the passion of his frustration is now only regret for the necessity that faces him, the madness, which is "gone too now, into, beneath the simple waiting; in 1948 he and Flem both would be old men and he even said aloud: 'What a shame we cant both of us jest come out two old men setting peaceful in the sun or the shade, waiting to die together, not even thinking no more of hurt or harm or getting even, not even remembering no more about hurt or harm or anguish or revenge.' . . . *But I reckon not* he thought. *Cant neither of us help nothing now. Cant neither one of us take nothing back*" (p. 94). Isolated from life, be becomes a pariah in the prison community also, "a sort of self-ordained priest of the doctrine of non-escape" (p. 94) in a society that guarantees prisoners the right to escape and trustees the right to shoot them. His destiny is to endure imprisonment in order to earn the right to kill Flem, and so certain is he of his inability to change the shape of that destiny that he jeopardizes his life in order to fulfill the letter of the law and endure all that is ordained. Ironically, by thwarting the escape attempt of nine of the ten to whom he is shackled, he lengthens his own prison term and makes his prison existence even more isolated than before. As the warden explains, "I cant let you go around loose inside here, where any of them can get at you. You've only got five more years; even though you didn't stop all of them, probably on a recommendation from me, the Governor would let you out tomorrow. But I cant do that because Stillwell will kill you" (p. 97). Confined alone now, without even the former necessity to "keep moving," Mink's isolation is complete.

In this circumstance, Mink's fidelity to the laws of the government, which owns him, wavers. In terms of civil law he has earned his freedom; yet the law will neither free him to be murdered nor, in the person of Cap'm Jabbo, the guard who saved Mink's life, kill Stillwell and dispel the threat of murder. It is a capricious law, malicious and unreliable. He reasons,

> He had tried himself to escape and had failed and had accepted the added twenty years of penalty without protest; he had spent fifteen of them not only never trying to escape again himself, but he had risked his life to foil ten others who planned to: as his reward for which he would have been freed the next day, only a trained guard with a shotgun in his hands let one of the ten plotters get free. So these last five years did not belong to him at all. He had discharged his forty years in good faith; it was not his fault that they actually added up to only thirty-five, and these five extra ones had been compounded onto him by a vicious, even a horseplayish, gratuitor. (p. 98)

This situation is much the same as that which caused Mink to disavow civil law when his scrupulously kept bargain with Houston was broken by the addition of another two days of labor. Now, as then, he places his faith in that higher agency, superior to civil and social law, which he holds in reserve to forestall despair. Although he comes to call "*them*" by the name "Old Moster," however, it is unlikely that he has undergone a religious conversion. At several junctures in the novel, Mink turns away from civil law after having been fooled by it, and this turning away, no matter what he calls the power to which he turns, emphasizes his isolation. He says that he has reaffirmed his belief in "Old Moster" on his own, telling the warden that "I didn't need no church. . . . I done it in confidence" (p. 100). In addition, the only church group available to him at Parchman is "Jehovah's Shareholders," led by men with whom Mink has nothing in common: "Self-ordained leaders who had reached prison through a curiously consistent pattern: by the conviction of crimes peculiar to the middle class, to respectability, originating in domesticity or anyway uxoriousness: bigamy, rifling the sect's funds for a woman: his wife or someone else's or, in an occasional desperate case, a professional prostitute" (p. 100). The warden gives ample evidence that Mink was not a member of this group. His affirmation of God "in confidence," therefore, is consistent with his independent character and adds yet another dimension to his isolation.

This theological isolation is in perfect harmony with his singleness of purpose and his alienation from society. When his faith in "Old Moster" is rewarded by Stillwell's death in the inexplicable collapse of a deconsecrated church, Mink is thus already established as the fully independent man, unencumbered by traditional social customs, and with faith and motive refined to their essences. As such, he gains his freedom at the moment when he is best prepared to fulfill his destiny. Reentering the world in 1946, after thirty-eight years of imprisonment, he is literally obsolescent, and the trials that he must now undergo are, if anything, more difficult. Yet Stillwell's death provides him with all that he has ever wanted or expected, for he "hadn't asked for justice since justice was only for the best, for champions, but at least a man might expect a chance, anybody had a right to a chance" (p. 94). When Linda Snopes Kohl files a petition for his release, the long-promised opportunity for retribution granted those who can endure is at hand. He accepts it soberly, surprised but still unplacated when he discovers that Flem has made no attempt to thwart his release. Fearful that "his muscles might have lost the agiliy and co-ordination, the simple bold quick temerity for physical risk" (p. 103), and struck with nostalgia at the discovery that the seasons "belonged to him again" (p. 104), he nonetheless puts aside both his fear and his memories to mount the highway toward Jefferson, which, "when his foot touched it last thirty-eight years ago, had not even been gravel but instead was dirt marked only by the prints of mules and the iron tires of wagons; now it looked and felt as smooth and hard as a floor, what time you could see it or risk feeling it either for the cars and trucks rushing past on it" (pp. 103–104). In a world of wars he never heard of, a world of POW camps, "Krauts," and "Japs," Mink discovers that he does not even know how old he is. To determine his age, he uses as a metaphor the one aspect of the world that has not changed: "He thought *Money*. He said: 'If you had twenty-five dollars and found thirty-eight more, how much would you have?'" (p. 106). Money immediately recalls Flem and with him, because of its unvarying value in a changing world, his own steadfast determination for revenge. "*Sixty-three* he thought. *So that's how old I am*. He thought quietly *Not justice; I never asked that; jest fairness, that's all*. That was all; not to have anything for him: just not to have anything against him. That was all he wanted, and sure enough, here it was" (p. 106).

"Linda": "Young Enough and Brave Enough at the Same Time"

THE SECOND section of *The Mansion*, entitled "Linda," focuses upon Flem's amorality from the standpoint of his agency in the exploitation of human love and lovers. As with the parallel stories of Eula-Manfred and Linda-Gavin in *The Town*, the love theme is treated in the first person style of narration, and the narrators are again V. K. Ratliff, Gavin Stevens, and Charles Mallison. Their subject is Linda Snopes Kohl, who is seen "from three main angles, through Gavin, Ratliff, and Charles, and also in refractions produced by their views of each other's views, sometimes in dialogue, sometimes in their subjectively centered first-person recapitulations." [17] Through their presentation of her dilemma, themes that run throughout the trilogy are further developed and extended, creating patterns of recurrent character, action, and event similar to those through which Mink's primitive heroism is projected. Ultimately, the contrast between those possessed of a capacity for love and the impotent Snopes archetype is as revealing of Flem's amorality as that between Mink's high standard for clanship and Flem's insensitivity to it. Beck says, "the Flem-Mink confrontation and the Linda-Gavin Eula involvement are not plot and sub-plot but that plot-paralleling, with essential thematic reciprocations, which is found in much of Faulkner's work." [18] As was the case in the story of Mink, "Linda" focuses upon Flem by indirection. In the recapitulation of events from *The Hamlet* and *The Town* by deeply principled narrators intimately involved in those events, the groundwork is laid for Linda's emergence as the embodiment of a transcendent love, which is ideologically based in a fundamental humanism and which is the antithesis of all that Flem represents. By contrast to Linda and by her antipathy to Flem, his amorality is revealed in yet another respect and is given greater amplitude.

Whereas the pattern of thematic variation in "Mink" is brought about by alternation of perspective, however, the love theme is characterized by metamorphosis. Vickery sees the sexual pattern in the trilogy as moving "from sex to passion to that charitic [*sic*] emotion shared by Linda and Gavin Stevens, from the need to enslave to the desire to liberate." [19] The end result of this metamorphosis is a transcendent or humanistic love, which, according to Vickery, "fuses the moral and emotional, the imaginative and the real, the contemplative and the active into a single response." [20] In Linda this fusion is not forced but instead develops logically from her heritage and her training. Nor is her role in *The Mansion* strained, for her behavior is prepared for, prior to her appearance, by Ratliff's extended consideration of the metamorphosis that love has undergone. By means of Ratliff's speculations, Linda is seen to be a direct lineal descendant of Helen of Troy through Eula, whose mythic sexuality was matched by the godlike McCarron, "that-ere single unique big buck . . . outen the big woods or the high mountain or the tall sky" (p. 120). As such, she inherits an unending capacity for love, but, whereas in Eula this manifests itself in physical sexuality, in Linda it is refined to its spiritual aspect.

The distinction between Eula and Linda is conveyed largely in terms of Gavin's different reactions to them. When he is introduced, in *The Town*, as a romantic young idealist of nineteen, his attraction to Eula is physical and is based on his quixotic desire to protect her who needs no protection. His relationship with Eula is never consummated because he is unsuited for the lover's role that he assumes. Nonetheless, his relationship with Linda, although it is of a different sort, is firmly based in and motivated by his love for Eula. It is established, in fact, "when Eula Varner taken that first one look of hern at Lawyer—or let him take that first one look of hisn at her, whichever way you want to put it—and adopted the rest of his life into that of whatever first child she happened to have, providing of course it's a gal" (p. 114). No longer the nineteen-year-old boy, he approaches Linda not as a suitor protecting her virginity but as a tutor protecting her from Snopeses. His suitability for this role is somewhat reflected in the fact that he served during World War I not with the English but the French army, "them folks that, according to him, spent all their time talking about epicene exactitudes to ladies" (p. 132). His posture now is that of the disinterested humanist, spiritual rather than physical. Ratliff continues,

> Jest to train her up and marry her wasn't it. . . . He had to be the sole one masculine feller within her entire possible circumambiance, not jest to recognize she had a soul still capable of being saved from what he called Snopesism: a force and power that stout and evil as to jeopardise it jest from her believing for twelve or thirteen years she was blood kin when she actively wasn't no kin a-tall, but that couldn't nobody else in range and reach but him save it. (p. 137)

As McCarron matched Eula's sexuality because of his "separate McCarron cover" (p. 128), so Gavin is the appropriate match for Linda, whose "fragile" soul (p. 137) recalls Gavin's own "fragile and what you might call gossamer-sinewed envelope of boundless and hopeless aspiration" (p. 128).

In Ratliff's account of this metamorphosis from sexual to humanistic love, Flem Snopes is seen to be an unchanging and ever-present danger to love in all of its forms. Beginning with his marriage to Eula and his subsequent move to Jefferson, the stages of his relentless rise toward the presidency of the bank have direct reference to the various phases of the love transformation. Having "grazed up Uncle Billy Varner and Frenchman's Bend" (p. 115), Flem leaves the Bend with Eula, who is "still jest being and breathing, setting with the baby in the wagon that day they moved in to Jefferson so Flem could get a active holt on Grover Winbush to evict him outen the other half of that café me [Ratliff] and Grover owned" (p. 127). While Gavin and Manfred de Spain contend for Eula's love, "Flem Snopes grazed gently on up them new Jefferson pastures, him and his wife and infant daughter still living in the tent behind the café and Flem his-self frying the hamburgers now after Grover Winbush found out suddenly one day that he never owned one half of a café neither" (p. 128). Flem moves from café owner to the position of power plant superintendent, an appointment made by Eula's lover, Manfred de Spain, mayor of Jefferson. In the course of their love affair, Mayor de Spain becomes "Banker de Spain," and "at about the same more or less coincidental moment . . . Flem Snopes moved outen being the ex-superintendent of the power plant, into being vice-president of the bank" (p. 135). Ratliff explains that "ever body knowed that the reason Flem Snopes was vice-president of De Spain's bank was the same reason he was ex-superintendent of the power plant: in the one case folks wanting to smile at Eula Varner had to at least be able to pronounce Flem Snopes, and in the other De Spain had to take Flem along with him to get the use of Will Varner's voting stock to get his-self president" (pp. 137–138). In essence, Flem trades his wife's sexual favors to Manfred in return for positions of increased power.

In similar fashion, he trades upon his wife's maternal concern for Linda's reputation and upon Linda's regard for him as her father. Developing along lines that parallel the sexual love of Manfred and Eula, the relationship between Gavin and Linda is constantly threatened by Flem. After losing his contest with Manfred, Gavin convinces himself that he is "disenchanted for good at last of Helen, and so now all he had to worry about was what them Menelaus-Snopeses might be up to in the Yoknapatawpha-Argive community while he had his back turned" (p. 130). His commitment to Linda is based on a combination of this concern with Snopesism and the memory of his lost love for Eula. His efforts to save her "soul" from Snopesism by getting her away from Jefferson, however, are stymied by Flem. Flem dares not let Linda leave him. As Ratliff explains, "all I had to do was jest to imagine my name was Flem Snopes and that the only holt I had on Will Varner's money was through his daughter [Eula], and if I ever lost what light holt I had on the granddaughter [Linda], the daughter would be gone" (p. 139). In order to secure his "holt" on Varner's money, Flem presumes upon Linda's generous feelings for him to force her to will him her share of her grandfather's estate: "Because of course all Helen's children would have to inherit something of generosity even if they couldn't inherit more than about one millionth of their maw's bounty to be generous with" (p. 141). Eula's "bounty" and "generosity" are physical; Linda's are spiritual. Yet Flem exploits both for financial gain. Linda's will provides Flem the opportunity to dispossess Manfred of the bank presidency and leaves Eula no alternative except suicide to protect Linda's "establishment" and "name." Flem's final comment on Eula's sexuality is his viciously ironic inscription on her monument. His reaction to Linda is to dismiss her: "at last Flem leaned out the window and spit and then set back in the car and tells her: 'All right. You can go now' " (p. 149).

The death of the love goddess and the departure of her daughter coincide directly with Flem's achievement of his ultimate goal: the economic domination of his environment. As president of the bank and owner of the bank president's house, "at last even Flem Snopes seemed to be satisfied" (p. 152). Ratliff says of him,

> All he needed to do too after he had done locked up the money and went home was to live in solitary peace and quiet and contentment too, not only shut of the daughter that kept him on steady and constant tenterhooks for years whether she might not escape at any moment to where he couldn't watch her and the first male feller that come along would marry her and he would lose her share of Will Varner's money, but shut of the wife that at any time her and Manfred de Spain would get publicly caught up with and cost him all the rest of Varner's money and bank voting stock too. (p. 152)

Flem's arrival at his long-sought goal signals no end to Snopesian malevolence, however, and his apparent absorption into society as an accepted and trusted member is not meant to depict, as some critics have claimed, the social ills attendant upon a decaying Southern aristocracy.[21] Rather, his accomplishments suggest the ever-increasing scope of his insidious cruelty and the vulnerability of his victims. In thematic terms, his acquisition of the bank and the mansion is accomplished at the expense of human love, and the peace he finds in living in De Spain's mansion is defined in terms of his being rid of Eula and Linda. Furthermore, De Spain is dispossessed of his bank and home not because he is a member of a degenerating aristocracy but because he values his relationship with Eula above material possessions. Flem's agency in this dispossession is yet another sign of his amoral insensitivity to love.

Flem's occupancy of the De Spain mansion is thus entirely commensurate with his repeated destruction of human hopes and desires. By remodeling the mansion to conform to the image of Mount Vernon, Flem exploits Manfred's birthright in the same way that he did his love for Eula. Like Eula's monument, the "colyums" that reach "all the way from the ground up to the second-storey roof" (p. 154) represent only the outward manifestation of respectability, a façade by which Flem consolidates his position in Jefferson. Ratliff comments

> But it was jest the house that was altered and transmogrified and symbolised: not him. The house he disappeared into about four p.m. ever evening until about eight a.m. tomorrow, might a been the solid aristocratic ancestral symbol of Alexander Hamilton and Aaron Burr and Astor and Morgan and Harriman and Hill and ever other golden advocate of hard quick-thinking vested interest, but the feller the owners of that custodianed money seen going and coming out of it was the same one they had done got accustomed to for twenty years now: the same little snap-on bow tie he had got outen the Frenchman's Bend mule wagon in and only the hat was new and different; and even that old cloth cap, that maybe was plenty good enough to be Varner's clerk in but that wasn't to be seen going in and out of a Jefferson bank on the head of its vice-president—even the cap not throwed away or even give away, but sold, even if it wasn't but jest a dime because ten cents is money too around a bank, so that all the owners of that money that he was already vice-custodian of could look at the hat and know that, no matter how little they might a paid for one similar to it, hisn had cost him ten cents less. It wasn't that he rebelled at changing Flem Snopes: he done it by deliberate calculation, since the feller you trust aint necessarily the one you never knowed to do nothing untrustable: it's the one you have seen from experience that he knows exactly when being untrustable will pay a net profit and when it will pay a loss. (pp. 154–155)

Under Flem's ownership, De Spain's ancestral home mocks the respectability for which it once stood, suggesting yet another aspect of Flem's elementally exploitive nature.

Furthermore, the manner in which Flem dwells in the mansion recalls his single-minded acquisition of money and his abhorrence of waste. Although he parrots the two previous presidents of the bank to the extent of maintaining "a black automobile too even if it wasn't a Packard, and a Negro that could drive it too even if he never had no white coat and showfer's cap" (p. 156), these are only adjuncts to his respectable facade. Flem does not ride in the car, and the "showfer" is employed most of the time as a yard boy. Flem never enters "all them big rooms furnished like De Spain left them" but dwells instead in "that one room at the back where when he wasn't in the bed sleeping he was setting in another swivel chair like the one in the bank, with his feet propped against the side of the fireplace" (p. 155). His life in the mansion is literally an extension of his life in the bank, solitary and economical, devoted solely to the consideration of money. He is unchanged in other ways as well. As president of the bank Flem is "watching yet and learning yet" (p. 156) just as he did as Varner's clerk and Manfred's vice-president, exercising "the only kind of humility that's worth a hoot: the humility to know they's a heap of things you dont know yet but if you jest got the patience to be humble and watchful long enough, especially keeping one eye on your back trail, you will" (p. 157). As Vickery correctly points out, Flem's career is expressive of the "theme of permanence in the midst of change." [22]

> What at first appears to be a simple linear presentation of Flem's career is actually circular and self-repetitive. Each successive book thus contributes to the comic view of Flem by using the same pattern of external symbols. As he rises from a tenant farmer to a bank president, he progresses from overalls to a white shirt and a black bow tie and from cap to a suit and . . . [a black felt hat]. Concurrently, his rented room, lunch pail, and horse are ultimately replaced by the mansion, the dining room, and the Cadillac. But the emphasis on the externality of these changes serves to point out the absence of any real progress or achievement. . . . As he sits, feet propped on the ledge built to protect his expensive mantelpiece, he evokes Will Varner sitting on his flour barrel throne wondering what fool had

wanted or needed the baronial splendor of the Old Frenchman Place just to eat and sleep in. While apparently moving not only through space and time but through the economic and social structure of Jefferson, Flem has begun and ended with nothing.[23]

Flem's arrival in De Spain's mansion does nothing to mitigate his fundamental amorality. Rather, it deepens and amplifies that amorality by indicating his complete isolation from human society.

A closely related consideration is the fact that the development of the love theme is related to and dramatized in terms of Flem's rise. His occupancy of the De Spain mansion, but its concomitance with Eula's death, ominously coincides with the ascendance of humanistic over physical love in the metamorphosis of the love theme. Eula is dead, her mythic sexuality never to be reproduced; yet her capacity for love exists in altered form in her daughter, Linda, who now assumes a dominant role in the novel. Unlike Eula, whose lovers suggest her physical plentitude, Linda is "doomed to fidelity and grief. . . . To love once quick and lose him quick and for the rest of her life to be faithful and to grieve" (p. 158). She finds love not in the pastoral confines of Frenchman's Bend but in Greenwich Village, "a little place without physical boundaries located as far as she is concerned in New York City, where young people of all ages below ninety go in search of dreams" (p. 151). Whereas Eula is the object of all men's dreams and takes as lovers the most virile representatives of Southern aristocracy, Linda is herself a dreamer whose lover, Barton Kohl, is "jest another ordinary man that believed if a gal was worth sleeping with she was worth deserving to have a roof over her head and something to eat and a little money in her pocket for the balance of her life" (p. 164). Complementing the "epicence exactitudes" on which Gavin's relationship with Linda was based, Barton Kohl's Marxian socialism provides an ideological basis for her developing humanism. The humanistic spirit in which Gavin liberated her from Snopesism by sending her to Greenwich Village is the same in which she and Barton Kohl join the Loyalists to liberate the oppressed of Spain. Their love goes beyond the merely physical, beyond the desire "to cuddle up together and be what she calls happy" (p. 162). Ratliff says of Linda, "when you are young enough, you can believe. When you are young enough and

brave enough at the same time, you can hate intolerance and believe in hope and, if you are sho enough brave, act on it" (p. 161).

This ideologically based love, expressed in the fidelity and devotion of the lovers to each other and to mankind, is just as antithetical to Snopesism as was the physical love embodied in Eula. By
entering the Spanish Civil War on the side of the Loyalists, Linda
and Barton Kohl demonstrate their opposition not just to Franco
but, as Gavin points out, to all "the hereditary proprietors, the
farmers-general of the human dilemma" (p. 160): Hitler and Mussolini and "the ones right here at home: the organizations with
the fine names confederated in unison in the name of God against
the impure in morals and politics and with the wrong skin color
and ethnology and religion: K.K.K. and the Silver Shirts; not to
mention the indigenous local champions like Long in Louisiana
and our own Bilbo in Mississippi, not to mention our very own
Senator Charence Egglestone Snopes right here in Yoknapatawpha
County" (p. 161). By his machinations in the moral world, Flem
Snopes is himself a member of this group; and his equation with it
gives his amorality a more universal dimension. Gavin's fiercely
personal opposition to Flem is a manifestation of his opposition
to inhumanity in all of its forms. This larger attitude, instilled
by Gavin in Linda, informs her disinterested commitment to
Marxian social justice, which is itself a manifestation of her
transcendent or humanistic love. Linda affirms this love symbolically when, prior to her departure for Spain, she sends McCarron
away in order to be with Gavin. The cigarette lighter she gives
him, inscribed "G L S" (p. 175), joins her initials with his and
represents their spiritual marriage. The entire episode constitutes
a recurrence, in modified context, of the affirmation of physical
love symbolized in Eula's choosing Manfred as her lover rather
than the idealistic Gavin. Moreover, as Eula's sexual relationship
with Manfred was juxtaposed against Flem's impotence, Linda's
spiritual relationship with Gavin is destined to be played out
against the backdrop of Flem's fully established materialism. Following the death of Barton Kohl in Spain, Linda returns to Jefferson, where social tradition severely limits the sphere of her good
works. Because of her close association with Gavin, however, it is
inevitable that she eventually assumes his antipathic posture toward
Flem. Based in the larger context of commitment to principled ex-

istence, Linda's opposition to inhumanity focuses at last on the injuries attributable directly to Flem Snopes, involving her ideologically in the revenge theme established by Mink's theological belief in universal justice.

Like Mink's life in Parchman prison, Linda's life in Jefferson after the Spanish Civil War is one of intense isolation. Vickery points out that she, like Mink, is an anachronism, acting out of "old commitments, compulsions, and regrets." [24] She is a Communist, dedicated to social reform in a postwar world "whose single and principal industry is not just solvent but dizzily remunerative peace" (p. 180). As a widowed war veteran, Linda is comparable to those other veterans, Tug Nightingale and Bayard Sartoris, who returned to Jefferson "with only a third of life over, to know now that they had already experienced their greatest experience, and now to find that the world for which they had so endured and risked was in their absence so altered out of recognition by the ones who had stayed safe at home as to have no place for them in it anymore" (p. 181). Like Linda, Tug went to war for reasons which were basically humanistic, believing that "we cant let them Germans keep on treating folks like they're doing. Somebody's got to make them quit" (p. 185). He is repaid not with admiration for his humanism but with scorn for his anachronistic belief that the world is flat. In similar fashion, Linda is scorned for her insistence on the equal rights of Negroes. Her selfless indifference to community opinion is prepared for by Bayard Sartoris' disinterested recklessness. To Bayard, for whom the war offered an outlet for "the natural blackguardism inherent in men" (p. 189), the death of his twin brother demonstrates "that most people, nearly all people, loved themselves first" (p. 189) and that he is one of them. His reaction is a deep sense of shame, which he counteracts by "trying, in that sullen and pleasureless manner, to find out just how many different ways he could risk breaking his neck that would keep the most people anguished or upset or at least annoyed: that completely un-Sartoris-like capacity for shame which he could neither live with nor quit; could neither live in toleration with it nor by his own act repudiate it. That was why the risking, the chancing, the fatalism" (p. 190). Whereas Bayard's lack of concern for community opinion is self-centered, however, Linda's is a product of her generous idealism. Both attitudes are potentially destructive, but Bayard's threatens only his own life while Linda's poses a threat to the concept of white supremacy on which the traditional social order of Jefferson is based. Accordingly, her alienation from society is greater than either his or Tug Nightingale's. This is made explicit in the varying degrees of responsibility that the three have for their fathers' deaths. Tug's father is an irreconcilable Confederate veteran who dies because of his son's enlistment in the Yankee army: "killed, Uncle Gavin said, by simple inflexibility, having set his intractable and contemptuous face against the juggernaut of history and science both that April day in 1865 [when Lee surrendered] and never flinched since" (p. 187). Bayard's father, "who hated cars yet gave up his carriage and pair to let Bayard drive him back and forth to the bank" (p. 189) despite a weak heart, becomes his unwitting son's victim in an automobile accident. Flem's death, however, is purposely arranged by Linda, who recognizes in him the inhumanity that caused her mother's death and that threatens the humanistic principles which she attempts to perpetuate.

With her return to Jefferson, then, Linda becomes part of the recurrent pattern of isolation and revenge established in the section of *The Mansion* that is devoted to Mink. Her reaction to unbearable injury, an altered form of Mink's, gives added scope and intensity to the ever-present sense of Flem's amorality and prepares the way for the conjunction of their steadily converging stories. Through the informed speculations of Ratliff, Charles Mallison, and Gavin, the possible motives for Linda's return are thoroughly investigated. Under their concerned yet tentative scrutiny, prospects are presented and revised as new evidence is brought forth by observation, dialogue, and direct experience in what Beck describes as the "analytical narrowing down [which] creates, within the total fictional illusion, the differing but converging dimensions of appearance and actuality." [25] In the process, Linda is revealed not as a grotesque figure but, as Brooks points out, as a woman of "force and dignity; she never becomes the shrill and frenetic embodiment of a cause." [26] In large part, this is due to the many facets of her character, which emerge from the inquiries of the narrators and which are preserved despite her increasing isolation and discriminating purpose. Often described in terms of paradoxes, Linda is lacking in feminine softness; yet there is a distinct physical attractiveness about her. Charles Mallison says that she is "the same tall girl too tall to have a shape but then I dont know: women like that and once you get their clothes off they surprise you even if she was twenty-nine years old now" (p. 198). Her voice is "that dry harsh quacking voice that deaf people learn to use" (p. 199), but her eyes are "so dark blue that at first you thought they were black. . . . Fine eyes too, that probably if you were the one to finally get the clothes off you would have called them beautiful too" (p. 198). Her handshake is hard and masculine, and Charles notices that she is "a nail-biter" (p. 199); yet she kisses Gavin publicly, and Charles imagines his uncle writing on her pad, *"Vale not these cherry lips with vacant speech But let me drink instead thy tender Yes"* (p. 200). Although he cynically describes her as a war "hero," he is capable of seeing her sympathetically as well: "immured, inviolate in silence, invulnerable, serene" (p. 203).

As such, Linda lives figuratively in that state between adolescence and adulthood, which Gavin finds so attractive and in which he began forming her mind. Immobilized in time by her deafness, Linda is "no mere moment's child but the inviolate bride of silence, inviolable in maidenhead, fixed, forever safe from change and alteration" (p. 203). This perception, clearly indicative of virginity, immediately recalls Linda's earlier, spiritual relationship with Gavin. When she does not do so, Charles considers and then rejects the possibility that Gavin and Linda are secret lovers: "Hc [Gavin] would have to find the ways and means; all she would bring would be the capability for compliance, and what you might call a family precedence. Except that she wasn't her mother, not to mention Gavin not being Manfred de Spain" (p. 211). Because Linda lacks Eula's mythic sexuality, "that one matchless natural advantage which her mother and Manfred de Spain had" (p. 211), the love between Linda and Gavin must be based on "continence. To put it crudely, morality" (p. 212). As Linda's relationship with Barton Kohl clearly shows, however, she does not value continence in itself, and Charles is forced to revise his theory again when he sees Linda and Gavin discussing not love but their mutual opposition "to people like Hitler and Mussolini" (p. 218). Listening to her quacking voice, he admits: "There was no passion, no heat in it; and, what was worse, no hope. I mean, in bed together in the dark and to have more of love and excitement and ecstasy than just one can bear and so you must share it, murmur it, and to have only that dry and lifeless quack to murmur, whisper with" (p. 217). Recalling Gavin's prediction that "her doom would be to love once and lose him and then to mourn" (p. 219), Charles sadly says, "So she was lost; she had even lost that remaining one who should have married her for no other reason than that he had done more than anybody else while she was a child to make her into what she was now" (p. 219).

By calling Linda "lost," Charles clearly means that she has abandoned herself to the loveless ritual of life in Flem's mansion and to a futile adherence to the precepts of her dead husband's communism. In both cases, the sense of her isolation is increased, and she is seen to be a woman alienated from family and traditional society as well as from married love. Charles imagines her Christmas dinner with Flem,

> ... with him at one end of the table and Linda at the other and the yardman in a white coat serving them—the old fish-blooded son of a bitch who had a vocabulary of two words, one being No and the other Foreclose, and the bride of silence more immaculate in that chastity than ever Caesar's wife because she was invulnerable too, forever safe, in that chastity forever pure, that couldn't have heard him if he had had anything to say to her, any more than he could have heard her, since he wouldn't even recognize the language she spoke in. The two of them sitting there face to face through the long excruciating ritual which the day out of all the days compelled; and nobody to know why they did it, suffered it, why she suffered and endured it, what ritual she served or compulsion expiated—or who knows? what portent she postulated to keep him reminded. Maybe that was why. I mean, why she came back to Jefferson. Evidently it wasn't to marry Gavin Stevens. Or at least not yet. (pp. 215–216)

Flem's respectability demands that he and his daughter dine together on Christmas day. The ritual meal is simply another instance of his exploitation of ceremony. The suggestion that Linda suffers and endures this ceremony in fulfillment of a private ritual, however, immediately juxtaposes her in opposition to Flem and constitutes the first in a series of darker portents that signify Flem's doom. As Brooks points out, Linda has returned to see justice executed on Flem, and the special quality of her hatred for him stems from injuries no less real than those suffered by Mink. "Linda as a young girl had craved his love and approval and had—as she knows now—been deliberately tricked into feeling a kind of gratitude and affection for him. Her realization of this betrayal and her knowledge of the coldly despicable motivation which allowed him to use a child's affection in this manner provide two reasons for her feelings toward her supposed father. She knows too that he pitilessly used her mother and was at least indirectly responsible for her death." [27] It is these injuries of which, by her presence in Flem's mansion, she reminds him. The private ritual she serves is the ritual of revenge.

The public manifestation of the antagonism between Flem and Linda is expressed in terms of the opposition between capitalism and communism. As noted earlier, Linda's concept of Marxian social justice effectively alienates her from the white population of Jefferson, among whom, Charles says,

> there was one concert of unanimity, no less strong and even louder at the bottom, extending from the operators of Saturday curb-side peanut- and popcorn-vending machines, through the side-street and back-alley grocers, up to the department-store owners and automobile and gasoline agencies, against everybody they called communists now—Harry Hopkins, Hugh Johnson and everybody else associated with N.R.A., Eugene Debs, the I.W.W., the C.I.O.—any and everybody who seemed even to question our native-born Jefferson right to buy or raise or dig or find anything as cheaply as cajolery or trickery or threat or force could do it, and then sell it as dear as the necessity or ignorance or timidity of the buyer would stand. (p. 214)

Her alienation from this group, of which Flem is decidedly a member, carries forward the sense of her increasingly active yet obliquely rendered antipathy to him. As communism is the outer aspect of her deeply principled humanism, so her opposition to capitalism is the public aspect of her private compulsion for revenge. It is this complementary balance between ideology and private commitment in Linda that makes her more than the mere embodiment of a cause and leads Brooks to note that, "if Linda's vengeance is in a sense inspired by a personal passion, it seems to be also abstract and almost disinterested." [28]

Vickery points out that, although there are no serious economic threats to Flem in *The Mansion*, the facade of respectability upon which his economic domination of Jefferson is based leaves him most vulnerable. He is in a trap of his own making. There is a fine irony in the fact that, "having forced Eula into that suicide which reasserted in the eyes of society that Linda was his daughter, he has made it necessary to continue the charade unless and until Linda herself chooses to terminate it." [29] As long as she lives with him, he is bound to treat her publicly as his daughter, despite the fact that her every action threatens his hold on his domain. When she decides that she wants whiskey, he does not dare let her drive alone to the moonshiner because she is too deaf to hear the horns of other cars. Charles explains,

> So now he had not one dilemma but three: not just the bank president's known recognisable car driving up to a bootleg joint, but with him in it; then the dilemma of whether to let every prospective mortgagee in Yoknapatawpha County hear how he would sit there in the car and let his only female child walk into a notorious river-bottom joint to buy whiskey, or go in himself and with his own Baptist deacon's hand pay out sixteen dollars' worth of his own life's blood. (pp. 221–222)

Her meetings with the only other Communists in Jefferson, the Finnish immigrant laborers, are not discreetly held but take place in Flem's own "capitalist parlor." They talk of "the emancipation of man from his tragedy, the liberation at last and forever from pain and hunger and injustice, of the human condition" only two doors away from Flem, "the capitalist himself who owned the parlor and the house, the very circumambience they dreamed in, who had begun life as a nihilist and then softened into a mere anarchist and now was not only a conservative but a tory too: a pillar, rock-fixed, of things as they are" (p. 222). Insofar as actually liberating man from his straitened condition, Linda's meetings are futile. Nonetheless, they pose a substantial threat to the reputation of the capitalist who must permit them to be held in his house.

Linda further threatens Flem's standing in the community by her attention to Jefferson's Negroes. Growing logically out of her commitment to liberate man from "pain and hunger and injustice," Linda's attempts to provide equal educational opportunities for

Negro children in a white Southern town are as futile as her less specific dreams. Although vain, however, her project is firmly based in her ideology and at the same time has direct reference to her personal compulsion for revenge. She plans to hold her tutoring sessions for Negroes in "her sitting room in her father's house" (p. 223). Charles finds further portents in her persistence and thinks "how suppose she were docile and amenable and would have obeyed him [Flem], but it was he, old Snopes, that didn't dare ask, let alone order, her to quit. You didn't know why of course. All you could do was speculate: on just what I.O.U. or mortgage bearing his signature she might have represented out of that past which had finally gained for him that back room in the bank where he could sit down and watch himself grow richer by lending and foreclosing other people's I.O.U.'s" (p. 227). Thus, while Linda's concern for the minority group is completely in keeping with her socialism, it is also, like the Christmas dinner ritual, a "portent she postulated to keep him [Flem] reminded." While amplifying her isolation from society, it deepens her vengefulness.

Flem's response is typical of his devious manipulation of human hopes and dreams and testifies to the fact that Snopesism as a malevolent force still exists. Just as, in *The Town*, Flem exploited Linda's generosity in order to gain the bank presidency and rid himself of Eula, he now exploits her humanism to retain his respectable facade and rid himself of her. The product of her humanism is isolation, the sense of not belonging to the community, and it is greatly increased by the cross burned on the lawn and the words *"Nigger Lover"* (p. 226) and "KOHL COMMUNIST JEW" (p. 228) scrawled on the sidewalk. Viewing Linda's activities from the standpoint of Flem's ruthless amorality, Charles Mallison says that "those words on his sidewalk he had to walk through every time he left home were no more portents and threats of wreckage and disaster to him than any other loan he had guessed wrong on would be an irremedial disaster, as long as money itself remained unabolished. That the last thing in the world he was thinking to himself was *This is my cross; I will bear it* because what he was thinking was *All I got to do now is keep folks thinking this is a cross and not a gambit*" (p. 229). Later, Gavin Stevens adds, *"It was he himself probably who scrawled*

Jew Communist Kohl on his own sidewalk at midnight to bank a reserve of Jefferson sympathy against the day when he would be compelled to commit his only child to the insane asylum" (p. 240). In working out her vengeance against Flem, Linda is thus still subject to victimization by him. In this situation she is clearly reminiscent of Mink, who was directly threatened with commitment to an asylum and whose prison sentence Flem had lengthened in order to preserve his own life. As Mink perseveres in revenge, so does Linda. When Charles Mallison tells Ratliff that Linda is not going to marry Gavin, he answers prophetically: " 'That's right,' he said. 'It will be worse than that' " (p. 232).

Flem's strategy here, although it is defensive, is no less amoral than his ruthless acquisitiveness in *The Hamlet* and *The Town*. In fact, it is completely commensurate with his posture throughout *The Mansion*, which is to keep and conserve what he has acquired. Moreover, his efforts along these lines emphasize the danger to him in those whom he manipulates. When, with the approach of World War II, communism becomes a national threat, Flem steals Linda's Communist Party card and instigates action against her by the FBI in the hope that she will be imprisoned as an enemy of the government. In both motive and event the theft constitutes a recurrence of Flem's use of Montgomery Ward Snopes to betray Mink. Like Montgomery Ward, the FBI man, Gihon, is clearly Flem's agent. Physically he is "gray, negative as a chameleon, terrifying as the footprint on Crusoe's beach" (p. 234), giving him almost a family resemblance to the alien Flem, whose eyes are "the color of stagnant pond water" and whose hair "didn't have any color at all" (p. 198). As Montgomery Ward betrayed Mink by falsely assuming the posture of a loyal clansman, Gihon justifies his investigation on the grounds of a patriotism that Gavin finds "quite cold, quite impersonal" (p. 235). Mink is made to forego his strict adherence to prison law, and by attempting to escape he loses his status as an imminent threat to Flem and becomes a jail bird again. Linda is asked to compromise her loyalty to her Communist friends, which, Gavin cynically notes "will whitewash her from an enemy into a simple stool pigeon" (p. 236). In both cases Flem is behind the manipulations. Mink's determination to kill him poses a literal threat to Flem's life; but because Flem defines life solely in terms of economic domination, which requires that his respectability be unassailable, Linda too is a mortal threat to him. He therefore attempts to forestall her in the same way that he did Mink. In the process the recurrent pattern of events closely associates Mink and Linda, binding them together in motive and involving her more deeply in the theme of revenge as Flem's mortal enemy.

Not surprisingly this darker aspect of Linda's character in large part escapes Gavin Stevens. To some extent this is due to its oblique rendering: the "portents" of a deep compulsion, which Charles sees, and Ratliff's veiled forebodings are not sufficient to portray Linda as an overt avenger. A more important consideration, however, is the foundation of romantic idealism, on which Gavin's relationship to Linda is based and from which standpoint they view each other. When he returned from World War I, she filled a gap in his life left by his lost love for her mother; and his self-sacrificing commitment to preserve her from Flem's influence was based on his assertion, in *The Town*, that "nothing cannot remain anywhere since nothing is vacuum and vacuum is paradox and unbearable" (p. 135). In *The Mansion*, after Linda's return from the Spanish Civil War, it is Gavin who fills the gap in her life left by the death of Barton Kohl. Just as, after losing Eula in *The Town*, he refuted the poet's notion "that Fancy passed me by And nothing will remain" (p. 135), so now she says, "What line or paragraph or even page can . . . [poets] compose and write to match giving your life to say No to people like Hitler and Mussolini?" (p. 218). Gavin's answer, by its idealism, constitutes a reaffirmation of his earlier commitment to protect Linda: "She's right. She's absolutely right, and thank God for it. Nothing is ever lost. Nothing. Nothing" (p. 218). This is the same context in which, years before, Gavin failed to see that Linda, as heiress to her mother's estate, represented a threat to Flem's economic ambitions. Now, as then, he regards her as Flem's helpless victim. Although he briefly considers that Flem has stolen her Communist party card *"to defend his very existence before she destroyed it,"* he quickly dismisses the idea: *"You know better. He will use it to destroy her"* (p. 240).

It is typical of Gavin's idealism and his concern for Linda that at times when he perceives her to be in the gravest danger, he urges her to leave Jefferson. Because this protectiveness is so often

linked with what Beck calls "Gavin's refusal of women's favors
offered under duress of any kind," [30] leaving Jefferson is associated
throughout the trilogy not only with freedom from the immediate sphere of Flem's amoral influence but also with the liberation
of lovers to fulfill their own destinies. In *The Town*, after refusing Eula's offer of her body, Gavin himself left Jefferson and
returned to find a spiritually fulfilling love with Linda. Likewise,
in *The Town*, his insistence that Linda leave Jefferson is coupled
with his refusal to marry her. His oath to Eula that he will marry
Linda only "if or when I become convinced that conditions are
going to become such that something will have to be done, and
nothing else but marrying me can help her" (pp. 332–333) frees
Linda to fulfill her destiny as a lover with Barton Kohl. By this
means, Gavin consistently rejects the ritual of love, whether physical or social, and affirms what Beck calls "his romantic regard
for women [and] . . . his idealistic faith in love itself and the
possibilities of its realization." [31]

In the modified context of *The Mansion*, this pattern of events
recurs and becomes one vehicle for the steadily converging themes
of love and revenge. Whereas in *The Town* it was Linda's destiny
as the daughter of the love goddess to find love herself, in *The
Mansion* she has found and lost that love and is doomed "to
fidelity and grief." Her destiny now as Eula's daughter is to avenge
her mother's death and the injuries that she has herself incurred.
In order to do so, however, she must, like Mink, disencumber herself of all other passions and commitments so that she can single-
mindedly concentrate on revenge. Just as Mink repays his debt to
society and gains his liberty by selflessly enduring the harsh regi-
men of Parchman prison, Linda repays her long dependence
upon Gavin and gains the freedom to fulfill her destiny by re-
enacting the ritual offering of marriage and physical love. When
Gavin urges her to "*Leave here Go away*" (p. 236), Linda replies,
"I just must be where you are" (p. 238). This is not dependence
on her part but generosity: she says, "I wont depend" (p. 238).
Her offer to marry him is made not for her sake but for his, and
his idealistic refusal is based on the fact that marriage with a
woman "doomed to love once quick and lose him quick" would
be false (p. 158). For the same reason he refuses her offer of her
body. Her use of "the hard brutal guttural" word for love (p.

238) emphasizes that a merely sexual relationship would also be false: he writes on her pad, *"what shocks is that all that magic passion excitement be summed up & dismissed in that one bald unlovely sound"* (p. 239). Although he perceives that "she looked out of or across . . . the immeasurable loss, the appeaseless grief, the fidelity and the enduring" (p. 239), he does not realize that these are for the memory of her mother as well as Barton Kohl, and he assures her *"we are the 2 in all the world who can love each other without having to"* (p. 239). She promises to leave Jefferson not, as Gavin supposes, to escape Flem's influence, but rather to free Gavin to love as he once freed her. " 'Yes,' she said. 'Then you can marry. . . . You must. I want you to. You mustn't miss that. Nobody must never have had that once. Nobody. Nobody' " (pp. 240–241). That she has repaid Gavin for her long dependence on him and is now free to pursue her darker destiny is clear from the fact that she confidently sends him away: "Yes, go. You see, I'm all right now, I'm not even afraid anymore" (p. 241).

This self-sufficiency in Linda is dramatically demonstrated by her life as a tool checker in the Pascagoula shipyards during the Second World War. Here, building ships for Russia (p. 245), she casts off the last vestiges of her sexuality and reaffirms her ideological commitment to oppose inhumanity in all of its forms. Gavin says, "she could wear overalls again, once more miniscule in that masculine or rather sexless world engaged, trying to cope with the lethal mechanical monstrosities which war has become now, and perhaps she was even at peace again, if peace is possible to anyone" (p. 246). In like manner, Mink reaffirmed his determination to kill Flem, facing the warden after his escape attempt "small and frail, his face downbent a little, musing, peaceful, almost like faint smiling" (p. 88).

When Gavin visits Linda in Pascagoula, they enact the ritual of the wedding night but without physical consummation. Their separate rooms, arranged for by Linda, put a wall between them that signifies not only the ultimate refinement of their spiritual love but also the separateness of their destinies. By making Gavin promise that he will marry, Linda frees him at last of his oath to Eula. Symbolized in the beautiful shell she gives him, her gift of marriage constitutes a return of that gift which he gave her as a girl. Once this debt to him is repaid, Linda can become fully independent. She therefore says, "That's what I want you to do for me. I want you to marry. I want you to have that too. Because then it will be all right. We can always be together no matter how far apart either one of us happens to be or has to be" (p. 252). Having married her own first love, Linda encourages and approves Gavin's marriage to his, Melisandre Backus Harriss. As Linda has suggested, their destinies do lead them in different directions: while Gavin returns to Jefferson to marry Melisandre, Linda remains in Pascagoula to work for the defeat of Hitler. In terms of her relationship to Flem, Linda's independence and the unalterable opposition to inhumanity that her occupation suggests are most significant. As the final interview between Charles Mallison and Ratliff clearly indicates, Gavin's marriage is yet another portent of Linda's private compulsion.

> So when I [Charles] saw Jefferson next I was in uniform, long enough to call on the squire and his dame among his new ancestral white fences and electric-lit stables and say Bless you my children and then run Ratliff once more to earth.
> "He cant marry her now," I said. "He's already got a wife."
> And you never thought of *soberly* in connection with Ratliff either. Anyway, not before now, not until this time. "That's right," he said. "She aint going to marry him. It's going to be worse than that." (p. 256)

In the intense atmosphere of love affirmed, Flem's exploitation of love increases the amorality of his aggressions. The opposition between him and Linda is thereby intensified. In her is his destruction.

"Flem": "Just To Hate Evil Is Not Enough"

IN THE final section of *The Mansion*, entitled "Flem," the steady narrowing down of sensibilities through which Flem's amorality is revealed throughout the trilogy culminates in the obsessed consciousness of Mink Snopes. Brooks comments that "the whole last third of the novel is dominated by Mink. In those last chapters even the scenes laid in Jefferson are keyed to the somber, intensely personal world of Mink, who, undaunted by every kind of difficulty and handicap, makes his way from Parchman to Memphis to Jefferson and on into Flem Snopes's sitting room, where he puts a bullet into Flem's brain." [32] As has often been noted, this journey is in certain respects picaresque, and Mink's encounters with good men and bad imbue him with a definite heroism. Millgate asserts that "Mink more and more compels our reluctant admiration, and in displaying so great a capacity for dignity and endurance even in a man otherwise utterly vicious and degraded Faulkner makes a magnificent gesture of admiration and faith towards mankind as a whole." [33] Of central significance to the thematic unity of the trilogy, however, is the fact that the admirable qualities in Mink are evoked by his will to destroy Flem Snopes, and his emergence as an heroic figure intensifies by contrast the sense of Flem's elemental amorality. The pervasive somberness that Brooks finds in the "Flem" section of *The Mansion*, then, is not due solely to concentration on the personal world of Mink but is equally attributable to the brooding sense of Flem Snopes as a malevolent presence.

Nor is Mink the only character whose dignity and endurance provide the contrast by which Flem's amorality is expressed. Linda too has achieved that heightened state of disinterested individual responsibility which characterizes Mink's commitment to revenge, and her ideological response to Flem's exploitation of her own and her mother's capacity for love is no less extreme than Mink's personal response to Flem's betrayal of the tenets of clanship. Her thirty-eight years of life as Flem's nominal daughter coincide chronologically with the thirty-eight years of Mink's imprisonment, both having begun in 1908 and ended in 1946, and her isolation from the traditional social attitudes of Jefferson complements Mink's literal obsolescence in the postwar world into which he emerges from Parchman prison. Moreover, it is Linda who frees Mink from Parchman, and in those chapters dealing with her petition to the governor for Mink's release she is heroically imaged as a "knight" (p. 350). Therefore, Mink's journey toward Jefferson and his ultimate revenge not only dominates the final section of *The Mansion*, as Brooks points out, but also relate to the entire trilogy. In the context of the populous fictional background against which Flem's amorality is juxtaposed, Kerr's contention that Flem's death results from no single injury but from his cumulative inhumanity provides a significant insight into the gathering patterns of recurrence and repetition on which the structure of the trilogy is based. She says that "Flem's fate overtakes him: Eula, through Linda, and all of the rejected Snopeses, through Mink, defeated the impotent Flem who found nothing but an empty respectability to reward his striving, who did not flee from Mink because Flem was his own fate, Mink but the instrument." [34]

While this broader aspect of Mink's journey amplifies themes that pervade the entire trilogy, it in no way minimizes its significance to *The Mansion* itself. Structurally, this journey coincides with Mink's trip from Frenchman's Bend to Jefferson and back, previous to his murder of Jack Houston, and balances the opening and closing sections of the novel. As Vickery notes, "the pattern of action recalled [from *The Hamlet*] in 'Mink' is imposed on the 'Flem' section of *The Mansion*." [35] At the same time the parallels in motivation and event between these two journeys allow for the increasingly intense expression of the dominant themes of isolation and retribution. Whereas the murder of Houston follows thirty-eight days of labor for the cow and two for the pound fee, the murder of Flem marks the end of thirty-eight years of imprisonment. In the former case the preparatory journey covers only a few miles and is accomplished in one day and one night. The second journey, covering many miles and encompassing the time between Mink's release on September 26 and his own death on October 3, reflects the more elemental nature of Flem's injury to him and dramatically demonstrates the effects of the terrible metamorphosis that he has undergone in Parchman. Both journeys take Mink into the alien milieu of cities, but his trials in Memphis in 1946 are more excruciating and require of him a more extreme adjustment than do the problems he faces in Jefferson in 1908. Whereas his alienation in Jefferson is based primarily on his poverty as a tenant farmer, in Memphis this is compounded by his age, his prison record, and his literal obsolescence in the modern world. Justified in terms of his fully developed independence and rendered in all of its aspects in the most minute detail, Mink's solitary journey becomes the ultimate vehicle for the revelation of Flem's amorality, a precise complement to the corresponding reduction of sensibilities through which Flem is perceived.

From the outset of Mink's journey, two aspects of his character are immediately obvious: he is perfectly honest, and he is driven by an inner compulsion that approaches religious fervor. Both of these qualities are directly related to his isolation. Stopping to eat at a small country store, Mink discovers "to his shock and for the moment unbelief, possibly in his own hearing, . . . that the tin [of sardines] would now cost him twenty-six cents—the small flat solid-feeling tin ubiquitous for five cents through all his previous days until Parchman" (p. 259). Fearful that the slightest deviation from absolute honesty may return him to prison and unwilling to gamble his opportunity for revenge against his need for money with which to buy a gun, Mink reminds the storekeeper when he believes that the man has neglected to charge him for the soft drinks:

> Because the two empty bottles were still sitting on the counter in plain sight; he thought rapidly *If I could jest pick up the change and git outside before he notices them*—if not an impossibility, certainly a gamble he dared not take, had not time to risk: to gamble perhaps two dollars against a shout, a leap over the counter to bar the door until another sheriff came for him. So he said, not touching the change: "You never taken out for the sody." (p. 261)

In contrast to Mink's honesty, the storekeeper exploits his unfamiliarity with the modern world by overcharging him. Whereas the storekeeper easily succumbs to the temptation to make an extra fifty cents, Mink desperately resists the temptation to gratify his appetite for Coca Cola, telling himself, *"Be a man, Be a man. You got to be a man. You got too much to do, too much to resk"* (p. 262). So severe are his circumstances and so extreme his determination to be avenged that even the most insignificant gratifications threaten his purpose and must be repressed. As Brooks points out, Mink "allows nothing to alter his purpose or, even for a moment, to shake his faith that he can put a bullet into Flem Snopes and settle their account. This conception of honor, so hair-raising in its single-minded purpose, is something literally out of this world—certainly out of the world of the twentieth century. Mink's desire for revenge is almost as selfless and detached as that of a character in an Elizabethan revenge play." [36]

This self-reliance and faith in the ultimate equity of the universe elicits from the Reverend J. C. Goodyhay and his congregation a sympathetic response that lends a certain evangelical rectitude to Mink's intensely personal commitment to revenge. Brooks explains that Goodyhay's religion is indigenous to the South and that his congregation is a small, partially urbanized Holiness group with roots in the traditional Southern Baptist church. Although battered pickup trucks and prefabricated houses have replaced the wagons and tenant farms of forty years before, the religion is basically unchanged. In Brooks' words "It embodies the same account of man and of his relation to God that has dominated this segment of society for two hundred years. It is highly personal. It emphasizes the will. It is finally a religion of the Holy Ghost in which power is communicated directly to men without any mediation of the sacraments and which calls for an answering response and resolve on the part of the sinner." [37] This theological stance closely approximates Mink's belief in a primitive Jahweh, who assures an equity in human affairs by dispensing justice to those capable of enduring the trials set for them. So intense is Mink's belief in the efficacy of his own will that it is easily recognizable to those of like orientation. Sister Beth Holcomb says, "You look like a preacher" (p. 264), and Goodyhay's response is the same: "Hell, you're a preacher" (p. 266). While these assessments are not literally true, they are figuratively expressive of the nature and depth of Mink's determination to justify his identity as a man by killing Flem, who denied his humanity by betraying him. The similarities between Goodyhay's GI Christ in Marine battle dress and Mink's concept of a supreme power whom he now calls "Old Moster" further the sense that his compulsion is characterized by a nearly religious fervor. Moreover, Mink's implicit association with Southern Baptist evangelism provides yet another point of contrast between him and Flem, whose position as deacon in the Baptist church is merely an aspect of his respectable facade. Mink's elemental personal morality, deeply rooted in the ancestral theology of his land, reveals by contrast Flem's alien nature.

Between Thursday, September 26, and Sunday, September 29, Mink makes no physical progress toward Jefferson and Flem. Yet during his three-day sojourn with Goodyhay he is severely tested by a series of events that constitute a recurrence of past trials, and as such they increase his stature by further defining his concept of honor and his will to endure. Fearful that because of rising prices he will not have enough money to buy a gun, he is forced to seek work, subordinating his pride in himself as an independent man to his need to justify himself as a human being. He thinks,

> *So I will have to stop somewhere and ask for work and I aint never asked no man for work in my life so maybe I dont even know how* thinking *And that will add at least one more day, maybe even more than one* thinking quietly but still without despair *I'm too old for this. A feller sixty-three years old ought not to have to handle such as this* thinking, but without despair: quite indomitable still *But a man that's done already had to wait thirty-eight years, one more day or two or even three aint going to hurt.* (p. 264)

Ironically, his payment from Mrs. Holcomb for raking leaves and from Goodyhay for carpentering is not in money but in food, which he had earlier determined to do without in order to conserve what funds he has. In similar fashion, preparatory to murdering Houston, Mink abjured the necessities of life, which his last five dollars guaranteed, in order to spend the money on shells for his gun. In both cases his decision results in loss of the money. The five dollars is lost in the mail carrier's wagon on the way to Jefferson, and his ten-dollar bill is stolen by Goodyhay's migrant worker, Dad. Mink endures even this vicissitude, however, with honor and absolute honesty. As he previously resisted the temptation not to pay for the Coca Cola, he now rejects the much greater temptation to steal Goodyhay's automatic pistol. *"If I jest had that for two days I wouldn't need no ten dollars* thinking *I done been robbed in good faith without warning; why aint that enough to free me to rob in my turn. Not to mention my need being ten times, a hundred times, a thousand times more despaired than ara other man's need for jest ten dollars* thinking quietly peacefully indeed now *No. I aint never stole. I aint never come to that and I wont never"* (p. 274). The intensity of Mink's need and the magnitude of the temptation that faces him immediately evoke the object of his revenge, Flem Snopes.

The evocation of Flem Snopes as a felt presence at this juncture is substantially strengthened by the developing contrast between Mink's relationship to Flem and his relationship to Goodyhay. Both relationships are based primarily on promises: as Mink's clansman, Flem has an implicit obligation to save him from imprisonment, and as Mink's employer and host Goodyhay makes an explicit promise to return the stolen ten dollars. In each case Mink must faithfully wait a prescribed time for their fulfillment. Whereas Flem ignores the blood ties of clan loyalty and treats Mink inhumanly, Goodyhay responds fully to the spiritual ties that he senses between Mink and himself and treats him with humanity and compassion. Echoing Miss Reba's passionate outcry of pity for all injured humanity, Goodyhay prays "on his knees but no more, his head up, the coldly seething desert-hermit's eyes not even closed, . . . 'Save us, Christ, the poor sons of bitches' " (p. 271). His congregation is made up of "a passel of free-loading government-subsidised ex-drafted sons of bitches acting like whatever had caused the war not only actually happened but was still going on, and was going to keep on going on until somebody did something about it" (p. 272), and he promises the return of Mink's ten dollars in the same spirit in which Montgomery Ward asked Miss Reba to send forty dollars to Mink, "the poorest son of a bitch I can find" (p. 79). Finally, Goodyhay's sermon is very nearly a statement, in rough theological terms, of Mink's own philosophy.

> "All right," Goodyhay said. "Anybody that thinks all he's got to do is sit on his stern and have salvation come down on him like a cloudburst or something, dont belong in here. You got to get up on your feet and hunt it down until you can get a-hold of it and then hold it, even fighting off if you have to. And if you cant find it, then by God make it. Make a salvation He will pass and then earn the right to grab it and hold on and

fight off too if you have to but anyway hold it, hell and high water be damned." (p. 279)

Because of Goodyhay's kept promise, Flem's unfulfilled obligation is avenged. Most of the money with which Mink eventually purchases the gun that kills Flem comes literally from the Reverend J. C. Goodyhay's collection plate.

Although the relationship between Goodyhay and Mink suggests a fundamental spiritual kinship, which is in direct contrast to Flem's inhuman insensitivity to man and God, Goodyhay's impulse is evangelistic and outward whereas Mink's is personal and inward. Goodyhay is vocal while Mink is secretive. It is indicative of his extreme isolation from society that even in the presence of Goodyhay's congregation Mink feels himself to be "alien, not only unreconciled but irreconcilable" (p. 281). The congregation shares in the experience of World War II, and the anguish of that experience provides a common ground for membership. Thus, a Negro woman who lost her son and a white prostitute who lost her husband sit side by side with the veterans themselves, and Mink senses "that identity, similarity among them even beyond the garments they wore—more battle jackets, green army slickers, one barracks cap still showing where the officer's badge had been removed" (pp. 276–277). For Mink, however, World War II has little or no meaning, and he finds nothing to move him in Goodyhay's vision of Christ on Guadalcanal. Rather, he identifies with "the two oldish couples, man and wife of course, farmers obviously, without doubt tenant farmers . . . old, alien too, too old for this, unreconciled by the meager and arid tears which were less of tears than blisters" (pp. 281–282). As Brooks says, the basis of Goodyhay's and Mink's philosophy of existence is the same, but their worlds are forty years apart. Sitting in Goodyhay's church, Mink is utterly solitary. Brooks explains that "all he is really concerned with here is that Brother Goodyhay will make good on his promise to raise the ten dollars that he needs to get on to Memphis to buy the gun." [38]

Here, as elsewhere, Mink's isolation from society in its varying aspects reflects directly the singleness of his purpose. At the same time his elemental kinship with the moral world justifies his cause and deepens the sense of Flem Snopes's amorality. Beck emphasizes that below the "plain surface" of Mink's plight there lies "a tension controlled this side of desperation only by his indomitable will. The submerged emotion is always felt, however, and one means of its conveyance is in the sense of setting, suggested as to its impact upon this poor little old man bent on murder. Faulkner has given the nightmare of Mink's impeded obsessive progress through space and circumstance an almost surrealistic expression." [39] This is nowhere plainer than in Mink's approach to Memphis,

> . . . not only after forty-four years but under the matchless condition: at night, the dark earth on either hand and ahead already random and spangled with the neon he had never seen before, and in the distance the low portentous glare of the city itself, he sitting on the edge of the seat as a child sits, almost as small as a child, peering ahead as the car rushed, merging into one mutual spangled race bearing toward, as though by the acceleration of gravity or suction, the distant city; suddenly off to the right a train fled dragging a long string of lighted windows as rapid and ephemeral as dream; he became aware of a convergence like the spokes of a gigantic dark wheel lying on its hub, along which sped dense and undeviable as ants, automobiles and what they told him were called buses as if all the earth was hurrying, plunging, being sucked, decked with diamond and ruby lights, into the low glare on the sky as into some monstrous, frightening, unimaginable joy or pleasure. (p. 283)

Faced with surviving in such a setting, Mink verges upon despair. He thinks, "*I been away too long; when you got something to handle like I got to handle, and by yourself and not no more to handle it with than I got, not to mention eighty more miles to go yet, a man jest cant afford to been away as long as I had to be*" (p. 283). He is sustained, however, by his unswerving resolve, what Beck calls his belief in "endurance as life's irreducible integer." [40] He assures himself, "*A man can get through anything if he can jest keep on walking*" (p. 289).

In this largely inimical city, Mink is guided by experiences long forgotten but now instinctively remembered. "Without warning the city spun, whirled, vertiginous, infinitesimal and dizzying, then as suddenly braked and immobilized again and he not only knew exactly where he was, but how to pass the twelve hours" (p. 285). Leaving the "wan anonymous faces thronging about him, hurrying and myriad beneath the colored glare" (p. 285), he takes refuge in the Confederate Park where he had spent the night on trips to the Memphis brothels forty-four years before. It is vacant, silent, a "backwash" of the modern city into which "he seemed to have blundered, strayed, and then abandoned, betrayed by having had to be away from it so long" (p. 286). From the Confederate Park he moves to other landmarks of his youth: Court Square, "where he would be sheltered from the River air by the tall buildings themselves" (p. 287), and the train depot with "the same hollowly sonorous rotunda through which he had passed from the Jefferson train on the three other times he had seen Memphis" (p. 288). His geographic orientation to the city is complemented by a recurrence of the events of his overnight stay in Jefferson in 1908 prior to the murder of Houston. In Jefferson his night walk was lighted by "the lights from the drugstore falling outward across the pavement, staining the pavement with dim rose and green from the red- and green-liquid-filled jars in the windows" (p. 32). In Memphis he moves through a "circumambience . . . [which] flashed and glared luminous and myriad with color and aloud with sound: . . . a clutch of winking red green and white lights slid across the high night itself" (p. 284). On both occasions Mink seeks out a train depot in which to sleep, encountering generous and ungenerous men along the way. A telegraph operator let him sleep in the Jefferson depot, perceiving him to be "as forlorn and defenseless as a child" (p. 36). In Memphis, "waiflike and abandoned . . . but no more pitiable than a scorpion" (p. 287), he is given fifty cents for a bed by a policeman. A Jefferson movie-house manager sent him away because he lacked the price of admission; a Memphis plainclothesman rousts him out of the depot as a vagrant. In Jefferson he walked to the Negro section at the outskirts of town. In Memphis he walks "the vacant side streets and alleys" (p. 289) of the slums and buys his breakfast at a Negro owned store. Jefferson's Commercial Hotel, which "in two years his cousin Flem would own . . . though of course Mink didn't know that now" (p. 32), finds an analogue in a Memphis whorehouse, "the actual housefront (he didn't know it of course and probably wouldn't have recognized her either, but his younger daughter was now the madam of it) which he had entered with his mentor that night forty-seven years ago" (p. 290).

These instinctually remembered landmarks and recurrent events create a definite sense of the presentness of the past that corresponds precisely to Mink's intensely felt sense of injury at the hands of Flem Snopes. As Vickery points out, for Mink, as for Flem and Linda, "time has in effect stopped; they are anachronisms whose motives, responses, and actions derive from a vanished past. Mink's imprisonment keeps him unaware of the changing world and free of its influences. . . . Hence his actions are the result of drives and emotions arising out of Frenchman's Bend forty years earlier." [41] An aspect of completion is given Mink's parallel journeys, moreover, by their circularity of structure. Whereas Mink's stay in Jefferson began with his attempts to buy shells, his purchase of a gun terminates his stay in Memphis. In the first case his efforts were thwarted by the fact that he was obliged to lie about his motives to Ike McCaslin, a moral man who "*wont know how to believe a lie even if I could tell him one*" (p. 31). In the second, Mink is successful because of his absolute honesty, and it is the pawnbrokers, "blue-jowled as pirates" (p. 291), who supply Mink with a lie by which they justify selling him a gun. The pawnbrokers tell him, "That's a genuine bulldog dectective special forty-one, the best protection a man could have. That's what you want, aint it—protection?" (p. 291). Beginning and ending with Mink's attempts to arm himself for revenge, the events of his visits to Jefferson and Memphis form a circle, providing, as Vickery says, "a metaphor of the juxtaposition of discrete action against continuing plot and of archetype against history." [42] At the time of his departure from Memphis, Mink is no better armed than at his approach to Jefferson in 1908. In place of the ancient shotgun with which he was forced to kill Houston, he now acquires a pistol, which resembles "a cooter. . . . snub-nosed, short-barrelled, swollen of cylinder and rusted over, with its curved butt and flat reptilian hammer it did resemble the fossil relic of some small antediluvian terrapin" (p. 291). Isolated from society, his obsolescence imaged by the antiquated and unreliable weapons, which are the only ones he can command, Mink is sustained in each case by his indomitable will to assert his own humanity.

The more waiflike Mink appears and the more ill equipped to accomplish his end, the larger looms this obsessive capacity for endurance and compulsion to be avenged, and the deeper flows the impulsion of Flem's amorality. Flem has money, power, and position. Mink has only his faith in the ultimate equity of human affairs, faith that he will be afforded an opportunity to "get his own just and equal licks back in return" (p. 6). But this is enough. Once possessed of the almost pitiable gun, "he was all right; he stepped out into the full drowsing sunlight of early fall, into the unsleeping and passionate city. He was all right now. All he had to do now was to get to Jefferson, and that wasn't but eighty miles" (p. 293). Significantly, this same phraseology is used by Linda in order to signify her preparedness to avenge herself on Flem. At Pascagoula, when Gavin has promised to marry, she tells him, "I'm all right now" (p. 253).

The sense of completion, however temporary, with which this phase of Mink's journey closes is emphasized by the narrative turn from the intensely personal world of Mink's obsessive antagonism toward Flem to the public one of Ratliff's, Gavin's and Charles Mallison's opposition to amorality in general. Brooks comments that the comic episodes included here, involving Clarence Snopes's defeat by Ratliff and Old Meadowfill's eccentric resistance to Orestes Snopes, constitute "minor victories in the war against Snopesism [and] may be said to lead up to the major victory with which the novel ends." [43] The method by which this is accomplished, however, transcends the mere paralleling of event, the personal and the overt being bound inextricably together by repetitions of character, action, and episode, which, in Vickery's view, "dramatically juxtapose the permanence of myth against the fluidity of history." [44] While the comic interludes, following the surrealistic rendering of Mink's sojourn in Memphis, may startle, Beck explains that

> The antithetical modes [are] deeply interfused. With Faulkner the comic is not a relaxing interlude to make way for a renewed tensing in pity and terror; it is rather the lighter side of the grotesque, almost a picturesqueness of the absurd, with humor the regulative medium of both judgment and compassion. Thus there are thematically relevant points to all the jests, recurrent irony frames event in the perspective of detachment, and even

slapstick episode wears the aura of anarchic folly as its darker
abstraction. The opalescent mode, comprising extremes, manifests a supreme artistic synthesis, structure and texture truly
composed, because concurrently and correlatively hit upon and
evolved by an imagination capable of sustaining a continuously
operant interaction between instance and implication. Everything
counts, and the parts are not merely relevant, but related, in an
intensified dramatic continuum.[45]

The impact of Snopesism upon the moral world is Faulkner's subject, and it is an indicator of his true realism that the reactions of
the moral community cover the entire range of human emotion.

Chapter thirteen of *The Mansion* is particularly relevant to
Mink's obsession because of the similarities between Clarence
Snopes's career in politics and Flem's rise to the presidency of the
bank. Both are protégés of Will Varner, adopted for his convenience into the social structure of Frenchman's Bend and dependent in varying degrees upon his patronage in their ascension to
positions of power. Flem moves from the position of clerk in the
Varner store to a partnership and ultimately to the vice-presidency
of the bank in which Varner has the controlling interest. Clarence moves "steadily onward and upward from being old Varner's privately appointed constable in Varner's own private Beat
Two, then supervisor of the Beat and then elected out of the
entire county by means of old Will's diffused usurious capacity
for blackmail, to be the county representative in Jackson: and now,
1945, tapped by all the mutually compounding vote-swapping
Varners of the whole congressional district for the House of Representatives in Washington itself" (pp. 296–297). Like Flem, he is
"unprincipled and without morals" (p. 297), but whereas Flem
is possessed of an inscrutable intelligence and intuition for self-
aggrandizement, Clarence has only "his blind instinct for sadism
and overreaching, . . . dangerous only to someone he would have
the moral and intellectual ascendency of" (pp. 297–298). Nonetheless, he prospers for awhile under Varner's direction, becoming,
as did Flem before him, "a little careful of his public dignity, not
for the sake of his constituency but because even he knew a damn
sight better than to take chances with old Will Varner's standards
of *amour-propre*" (p. 298). Like Flem's, Clarence's success is based
in large part on his instinct.

. . . not merely to beat, hammer men into insensibility and submission, but to use them; not merely to expend their inexhaus-
tible numbers like ammunition or consume them like hogs or
sheep, but to use, employ them like mules or oxen, with one eye
constant for the next furrow tomorrow or next year; using not
just their competence to mark an X whenever and wherever old
Will Varner ordered them to, but their capacity for passion and
greed and alarm as well, as though Clarence had been in the business of politics all his life instead of those few mere years as a
hick constable. And, as Charles's uncle said, doing it all by simple
infallible instinct, without preceptor or example. Because this
was even before Huey Long had risen far enough to show their
own Mississippi Bilbo just what a man with a little brass and
courage and no inhibitions could really accomplish. (p. 301)

Ratliff's opposition to Clarence's further exploitations of human
dignity, while it is comic in mode, is no less committed than Mink's
determination to be avenged on Flem.

Ratliff's action against Clarence is undertaken in spite of Gavin's assertion that "we are just too old. Call it just tired, too tired
to be afraid any longer of losing. Just to hate evil is not enough.
You—somebody—has got to do something about it. Only now it
will have to be somebody else. . . . Because it wont be us" (p.
307). In effect, the obstacles that Ratliff faces are the same faced
and overcome by Mink: old age, weariness, and lack of energy.
Yet as Mink's hatred is unimpaired, so is Ratliff's good will. His
simple reply to Gavin's pessimistic assessment of their situation
indicates that he at least is prepared to continue the struggle
against evil, and as such it constitutes an assertion of the continually regenerative nature of morality. " 'Maybe,' Ratliff said"
(p. 307). The remark is closely analogous to Mink's determined assertion in Memphis that "*A man can get through anything if he
can jest keep on walking*" (p. 289). By means of a ploy reminiscent of the goat trade in *The Hamlet*, when Ratliff acted because Tull and Bookwright could think of no way to punish
Flem for usury, Ratliff ousts Clarence from the Congressional race
by dampening the senator's trouser legs with dog urine and relying on the nature of dogs to do the rest. When Clarence is publicly
embarrassed, Will Varner withdraws his support of his candidacy,
declaring that "I aint going to have Beat Two and Frenchman's
Bend represented nowhere by nobody that ere a son-a-bitching

dog that happens by cant tell from a fence post" (p. 319). Told in
the tall-tale tradition, Ratliff's account of the political rally is
overlaid with that subtle irony, which, according to Beck, "voices
the several characters' quietly insistent ethical protests, made the
more impersonal by cool laconicism and the more pointed by
wit. . . . In Faulkner's massive over-all composition . . . [the]
elements of the tragic will seem the constant from which the recurrent comedy is thrown back as a shaped echo." [46] Charles Mallison's penetrating analysis of Ratliff's moral self-sufficiency pierces
the veil of irony, projecting precisely the attitude that dominates
Mink's existence. Charles says, "So what you need is to learn
how to trust in God without depending on Him. In fact, we need
to fix things so He can depend on us for a while. Then He wont
need to waste Himself being everywhere at once" (p. 321).

The serious moral overtones of this tall-tale comedy lead logically into the darker comedy of the Meadowfill episode. Here the
comic mode is made the vehicle for a gathering sense of cumulative
Snopesian inhumanity and greed, evoked by the numerous resem-
blances between present events and past Snopes iniquities. By
permitting Jason Compson to outsmart himself in search of easy
money, Flem acquires the ancestral Compson estate, renames it
Eula Acres, and divides it into lots for a GI housing development.
In similar fashion, in *The Hamlet*, he acquired the Old Frenchman place from Will Varner by marrying Eula and turned the
worthless property to a profit when Ratliff, Bookwright, and Armstid outsmarted themselves by succumbing to the lure of buried
treasure. Armstid's insanity is reflected here in Jason's "coldly
seething indefatigable outrage" (p. 327); and old Meadowfill,
himself a victim of a "false deed" (p. 335) to real estate, stones
the boys who rob his decaying orchard, thus matching Armstid's
pursuit, with a shovel in hand, of marauding boys. Whereas Armstid's madness is mocked by Flem, who spits at it, Meadowfill's
apoplectic anger is cultivated by Flem's agent, Orestes Snopes, and
their feud over a trespassing pig recalls that of Mrs. Hait and
I.O. Snopes over a trespassing mule in *The Town*. In both I.O.'s
and Orestes' feuds, moreover, Gavin Stevens is involved in the role
of legal witness. Flem hires him to witness the transaction by
which I.O. is ousted from Jefferson, freeing Flem of any scandalous association with him. In *The Mansion* Orestes pays him to

witness the fact that he has given away his pig, thereby freeing himself of suspicion when Meadowfill is shot trying to kill the animal. Flem uses his resultant facade of respectability to further his rise toward the bank presidency, and Orestes hopes to use his aura of innocence to enhance his chances of gaining control of Meadowfill's valuable property. Although Gavin is powerless to halt Flem's machinations, he does thwart Orestes' plans by a clever bit of detective work, thus demonstrating that he, like Ratliff, has in some measure learned "how to trust in God without depending on Him." Insofar as Clarence is Flem's counterpart and Orestes, Flem's agent, both Ratliff and Gavin strike blows against Flem by their actions, involving themselves anew as lesser but no less committed figures in the developing pattern of retribution. Based on lifetimes of dedication to the principles of moral existence, their behavior in fundamentally comic situations complements Mink's obsessive behavior and evokes, in altered respect, the growing sense of the presentness of the past. As Ratliff says of their encounters, "As soon as you look, you see right away it aint nothing but jest another Snopes" (p. 349).

It is characteristic of the trilogy that this steadily modifying evocation of the past in the present is expressive of the motives underlying immediate action, which itself turns inevitably upon the continuing conflict between morality and amorality. As Beck correctly points out, "In the era of Flem Snopes's long progression from hamlet to mansion not only do familiar county folk reveal themselves further, sometimes surprisingly; the present brings past event into drastic reassessment, discovering behind the former overt action more of motive and mood." [47] For this reason a special sense of foreboding surrounds Linda's return to Jefferson in 1945 after four years of resisting Nazism by laboring in the Pascagoula shipyards. Linda, like Mink, is a figure at once pathetic and heroic, and to Charles Mallison, who also witnessed her return from the Spanish Civil War in 1937, she seems no less alienated but somehow fiercer than before. With "a really splendid dramatic white streak in her hair running along the top of her skull almost like a plume," she seems to him to be a "knight [who] had run out of tourneys and dragons, the war itself had slain them, used them up, made them obsolete" (p. 350). Having run out of wars with the defeat of Hitler and Mussolini and denied the opportunity to work for social reform by the postwar affluence of Jefferson's Negroes, Linda falls back, much as Mink did in the course of his imprisonment, on that hostility toward Flem that Charles Mallison earlier sensed as a "ritual she served or compulsion expiated" (p. 216). As before, she forces Flem to jeopardize his respectability by defending it, making him drive weekly to Jake-leg Wattman's illegal distillery: "for respectability, the look of things . . . he still wasn't going to let her drive alone fifteen miles to a bootlegger's joint and buy a bottle of whiskey" (p. 356). In similar fashion, the necessity to defend his life against Mink by keeping him in prison results in unavoidable peril to Flem when Mink is finally released.

Such similarities to Mink darken the sense of Linda's purpose and forward the convergence of her destiny with his. With Linda, however, the justification of motive and conduct is achieved not in a surrealistic vacuum, as with Mink, but in a populous moral world where motive is sensed as to its broader implications and conduct is open to speculation and interpretation. Characteristically, this justification is based on the continuing contrast between Gavin and Flem in their relationships to Linda. Now married to Meli-sandre Backus Harriss, Gavin lives with his wife in the old Backus homestead, "transmogrified by the old New Orleans gangster's money as old Snopes had tried to do to the De Spain house with his Yoknapatawpha County gangster's money and failed since here the rich and lavish cash had been spent with taste so that you didn't really see it at all but merely felt it, breathed it, like warmth or temperature" (p. 358). Visiting in Gavin's home, Linda is "still happy, satisfied; and that other thing which Charles had sensed, recognized: proprietorial. As if Linda herself had actually invented the whole business: his Uncle Gavin, his Aunt Melisan-dre, Rose Hill" (p. 357). At the door of "the cold mausoleum in which old Snopes had immolated that much of his money with-out grace or warmth," however, Linda is cold and abrupt, her hand "hard and firm like a man's since after all it was a ship riveter's or at least an ex-ship riveter's" (p. 359). Possessed of an uneasy foreboding, Charles recalls Ratliff's assertion that "she aint going to marry him [Gavin]. It's going to be worse than that" (p. 360), and Ratliff iterates his warning when he attributes Lin-da's restlessness to the fact that "she has done run out of injustice. . . . So she will have to think of something, even if she has to invent it" (p. 361). His final assessment of Linda's humanism implies a judgment of Gavin as well and portends Gavin's deeper involvement in the theme of retribution.

> "I aint worried about her," Ratliff said. "She's all right. She's jest dangerous. I'm thinking about your uncle."
> "What about him?" Charles said.
> "When she finally thinks of something and tells him, he will likely do it," Ratliff said. (p. 361)

Based on their mutually protective spiritual love, Gavin's involvement in Linda's destiny engages him also in Mink's and Flem's. The ultimate intrusion of this reality on Gavin's idealized scheme for protecting Linda and Gavin's ability finally to cope with it brings the development of Flem's amorality to a head by demonstrating the rejuvenatory character of the moral world.

The part that Gavin plays in Linda's efforts to free Mink from prison has seemed to some critics to be so completely a reversal of form as to be literally Snopesian.[48] In light of the patterns of repetition and recurrence that pervade the trilogy and the sincerity of Gavin's often misguided idealism, however, his compliance with Linda's plans signifies no collusion. In fact, it is perfectly in keeping with the nature of his long relationship with Linda and his inclination to see people as being better than they are that Gavin should misconstrue Linda's motives in having Mink pardoned and agree to assist her. For himself, he has no illusions as to the mortal danger in which Mink's release will place Flem. " 'Mink?' he said. 'Mink?' He thought rapidly *Oh hell, not this* thinking rapidly *Nineteen . . . eight. Twenty years then twenty more on top of that. He will be out in two more years anyway. We had forgotten that. Or had we*" (p. 366). Nonetheless, he accedes on humanitarian grounds when Linda argues that "two years of life are not important. . . . two years of jail are" (p. 368). Assuming that her motives are merely merciful, Gavin represses his desire to warn her and acts in accordance with his old instinct to protect her. "He wrote *I love you* thinking rapidly *If I say No she will find somebody else, anybody else, maybe some jackleg who will bleed her to get him out then continue to bleed her for what the little rattlesnake is going to do the moment he is free*" (pp. 368–369). In order to shield Linda from such exploitation and the painful knowledge of the possible consequences of her mercifulness, Gavin insists that Mink's pardon be contingent upon his acceptance of a quarterly remittance, in return for which he must promise to leave Mississippi and not return. As Longley points out, "Gavin's personal passion for justice makes him want to see Mink released, and his attorney's passion for red tape, contracts, and paper work makes him believe the agreement will work." [49]

Gavin's activities are thus neither Snopesian nor collusive but morally informed and independent, however legalistically idealistic. Rejecting Ratliff's assertion that he has remained silent about the potential danger in releasing Mink because "You jest wanted to keep your own skirts clean," he claims instead that "It was because I not only believe in and am an advocate of fate and destiny, I admire them; I want to be one of the instruments too, no matter how modest" (p. 368). Because his motives are beyond reproach, he assumes he will be successful, much as Mink and Linda assume they will be. In the face of Ratliff's foreboding hints of disaster, Gavin's effusive self-confidence is in ironic contrast to Linda's transcendent humanity and Mink's darker, elemental trust in his own will to endure. Their iron advocacy of fate and destiny has been tempered in the furnaces of war and prison, his, only in idealistic lapses into quixotism. Circulating the petition for Mink's pardon, Gavin thus assures Ratliff that it is harmless.

> "Go on," Stevens said "Sign it. I'm going to take care of . . . [Mink's vengefulness] too. What do you think I am—a murderer?"
>
> "Not yet anyway," Ratliff said. (p. 369)

While Mink gambles his revenge on his will to endure and Linda her impulse for justice on the same, Gavin remains naively certain of the efficacy of his own cleverness.

> So Stevens would have—indeed, intended to have—nothing but progress to report to his client [Linda] after he sent the documents in to the state capital and the rest of the summer passed toward and into fall. . . . Indeed, he felt he could almost select the specific day and hour he preferred to have the pris-

oner freed, choosing late September and explaining why to
his client on the pad of yellow office foolscap, specious, voluble,
convincing since he himself was convinced. . . . not explaining
to Linda his reasons why the little child-size creature who must
have been mad to begin with and whom thirty-eight years in
a penitentiary could not have improved any, must not come back
to Jefferson; hiding that too behind the rational garrulity of the
pencil flying along the ruled lines—until suddenly he would
look up (she of course had heard nothing) and Ratliff would be
standing just inside the office door looking at them, courteous,
bland, inscrutable, and only a little grave and thoughtful too
now. (p. 371)

At a similar juncture, in *The Town*, Gavin idealistically refused
to marry Linda, expressing with equal speciousness his concern
that she should find a fulfilling love, and unwittingly involved
himself thereby in the interlocking fates of Manfred, Eula, and
Flem.

Now, as at that earlier time, the basic fault with Gavin's perception of reality lies in his dangerous over simplifications of motive and conduct. Like Mink, Linda has cause to hate Flem, for
he had a part in her mother's death, and Ratliff says that if she
knew how dangerous Mink was, she would "grab a-holt of . . .
[Gavin] and go to Parchman and take him out tonight and have
him back in Jefferson by breakfast tomorrow" (p. 373). Just as
Gavin fails to perceive that Linda is potentially vengeful, so he
also fails to credit Mink with sanity. Despite his continued insistence on Mink's madness, however, he bases his confidence in
his scheme on the assumption that Mink will act rationally and
accept the money offered him, giving up his revenge in return for
freedom and a life of ease. He tells the warden, "He will know
that the only sane thing to do is to accept the money and the
pardon, since to refuse the pardon because of the money, in two
more years he not only wouldn't have the two thousand dollars,
he might even be dead" (p. 375). In addition, the scheme by
which Gavin is confident of preserving Flem's life is essentially a
business transaction; yet Gavin enters into it without the advice
or consent of that master trader whose life is at stake and who,
by his transaction with Montgomery Ward, has already demonstrated the ability to neutralize Mink's threat. Because of his idealistic enthusiasm for causes and his penchant for romantic general-

izations, Gavin fails to see, as Ratliff does not, that the release of
Mink involves "fate, and destiny, and luck, and hope, and all of
us mixed up in it—us and Linda and Flem and that durn little
half-starved wildcat down there in Parchman, all mixed up in the
same luck and destiny and fate and hope until cant none of us
tell where it stops and we begin" (pp. 373–374). Such is the impact of Flem's amorality on the moral world that it impinges upon
all of its aspects, threatening each humane action, making potentially disastrous each generous oversight, and coloring the lives
and destinies of all those committed to principled existence. As
Beck points out, "Stevens' championing of Linda is more than
quixotic, as principled chivalrous response to moral challenge. The
larger-looming element of the grotesque, stemming from fictional
conventions particularized by Faulkner's adaptations of style, also
represents both the aggressor's deviation from the humane and
the distortions produced by extreme resistance to aggression.
Irony, as concomitant of the grotesque, becomes medium of the
tragicomic, comprehending the contradictory involvements of
human affairs." [50] Gavin's errors of perception and the resultant
ironies that so anguish him project the archetypal amorality of
Flem Snopes, whose centrality to the trilogy is rendered "by invariable opaqueness and intransigence contrasted to the concerned subjectivity and tentativeness of disinterested opponents." [51]

Seldom in the trilogy is this insistent contrast so overt as in the
setting forth of Gavin's and Flem's reactions to Mink's release
from Parchman prison. Emphasized by his sudden turn from self-
assurance to self-doubt, Gavin's response to the news that Mink
has left Parchman without the money intended to insure against
his return to Jefferson is tortured in the extreme. For the first
time Gavin sees that fate and destiny are more than mere abstrac-
tions and that Mink's freedom literally represents a mortal danger
to Flem. His self-searching recognition of his own culpability in
that danger sets him in desperate motion, barely forestalling despair.

> He recrossed the Square rapidly, thinking *Yes, I really am a
> coward, after all* when that quantity, entity with which he had
> spent a great deal of his life talking or rather having to listen to

(his skeleton perhaps, which would outlast the rest of him by a few months or years—and without doubt would spend that time moralising at him while he would be helpless to answer back) answered immediately *Did anyone ever say you were not?* Then he *But I am not a coward: I am a humanitarian.* Then the other *You are not even an original; that word is customarily used as a euphemism for it.* (pp. 378–379)

In contrast to Gavin's acute, self-recriminating awareness of the moral significance in the failure of his clever scheme, Flem's interest is in the business aspect of the transaction. When frantically, "almost in one breath," Gavin blurts that Mink has not taken the money and thus refused the bargain, Flem is concerned only with the terms of the deal.

"How much was it?" Snopes said.
"What?" Stevens said.
"The money," Snopes said.
"Two hundred and fifty dollars," Stevens said.
"Much obliged," Snopes said. (pp. 379–380)

Although Stevens assumes full responsibility for the danger in which Flem has been placed and, still trying to protect Linda, becomes almost confessional, Flem imposes no penance upon him.

"Are you going to tell Linda?" [Stevens said].
"Why?" Snopes said.
"Yes," Stevens said. Then heard himself say in his turn: "Much obliged." Then, suddenly indeed this time: "I'm responsible for this, even if I probably couldn't have stopped it. I just talked to Eef Bishop. What else do you want me to do?" *If he would just spit once* he thought.
"Nothing," Snopes said.
"What?" Stevens said.
"Yes," Snopes said. "Much obliged." (p. 381)

So little do these antipodal characters have in common that, in confrontation with Flem's imperviousness, even Gavin's frantic verbosity is stilled.

This passivity suggests no honor in Flem, and certainly it cannot be construed as bravery. With his feet propped on Colonel Sartoris' desk as against the Adam mantel in the old De Spain mansion, Flem is simply insensitive to, because incapable of comprehending, Gavin's intense sense of moral responsibility and guilt. Even in the throes of an acute awareness of his own cowardice, Gavin finds nothing admirable in Flem's attitude, and he thinks of Mink's revenge as Flem's "just fate" (p. 382). Although he does everything in his power to stop Mink, he does so not for Flem but to protect Linda from the knowledge that "her act of pity and compassion and simple generosity murdered the man who passes as her father whether he is or not or a son of a bitch or not" (p. 391). Never doubting that Linda is innocent of intrigue and therefore safe from a malevolent destiny, Gavin convinces himself that Mink must be dead because "God Himself is not so busy that a homicidal maniac with only ten dollars in the world can hitchhike a hundred miles and buy a gun for ten dollars then hitchhike another hundred and shoot another man with it" (p. 389). His illusion is based on his generous feelings for Linda and his belief that the moral world is fundamentally beneficent. However, his animosity toward Flem is real enough. He tells Ratliff, "I'm not really an evil man. . . . I wouldn't have loaned Mink a gun to shoot Flem with; I might not even have just turned my head while Mink used his own. But neither am I going to lift my hand to interfere with Flem spending another day or two expecting any moment that Mink will" (p. 393). Yet it is Gavin himself and not Flem who spends the following days expecting Mink; and when Sheriff Bishop offers the theory that Mink is dead, "Stevens knew that he himself had never believed it. . . . 'Yes,' Stevens said, 'you're probably right,' thinking quietly *We wont stop him. We cant stop him—not all of us together, Memphis police and all. Maybe even a rattlesnake with destiny on his side dont even need luck, let alone friends*" (p. 394). The next day, looking at "the somber black-and-white-and-violet convolutions of tulle and ribbon and waxen asphodels fastened to the locked front door [of the bank]" (p. 395), Gavin tells the Memphis friend who has called to say that Mink's pistol is harmless, "The pistol was here last night. It functioned" (p. 395). More than the desperation of his initial self-searching, the sardonic terseness and impersonality of this comment from one characteristically so effusive indicates the depth of his despair. In terms of Gavin's idealized perception of Linda's innocence, Flem threatens her with disillusionment more severely in death than during his life.

Citing the fact that Mink's success is revealed prior to the description of the last days of his journey from Memphis to Jefferson and into Flem's back room, Brooks comments that "Faulkner is thus not playing for gross suspense as to the event" [52] and suggests that this sequence of events has direct thematic relevance. In chapter sixteen of *The Mansion*, the emphasis is on Gavin's reaction to his involvement in Flem's destiny; in chapter seventeen, on Mink's reaction. As Brooks correctly says, "Since we already know that he has succeeded, we are left free to concentrate on Mink's hopes, fears, and actions as he fulfills his own life by ending Flem's." [53] The result is a set of interlocking responses to amorality, in which Gavin's idealism and Mink's vengefulness, brought to bear on the same subject and during the same period of time, amplify and deepen the impact of Flem Snopes upon the moral world. Beck says that such counterpointing is the primary mode for the development of thematic unity in the trilogy and represents "the complexity of experience itself." He adds,

> The trilogy's structure is freely elaborated, yet purposefully so; its intricate multiform design is progressively effective. The narration renders both dramatic and meditative variations on the theme of ubiquitous evil and its opposition. The causes and effects of that struggle are boldly delineated in their extremes by the grotesque not as incidental device but as a contouring and a coloration of the subject. The wheel of time, spun back and forth with masterly control, turns up facets of the truth, apprehensions the more intense for never being reduced to conventional definition, and forever struck across by the slanting light of irony. Ethical evaluation is constantly evoked, never imposed, as plot feeds more than curiosity, implying that whatever the fate of individuals, for mankind the end is not yet, nor is the outcome assured.[54]

As individuals, Gavin and Mink are antithetic; yet in their common opposition to Flem, despite its different forms, they represent the complexity of the interaction of good and evil.

As does Gavin in comparable circumstances, Mink discovers as he approaches his goal that he has oversimplified his situation.

THE MANSION

Once armed and away from Memphis, he thinks that "only geography [stands] between him and the moment when he would walk up to the man who had seen him sent to the penitentiary without raising a finger, who had not even had the decency and courage to say No to his bloodcry for help from kin to kin, and say, 'Look at me, Flem,' and kill him" (p. 396). As he draws closer to Jefferson, however, he finds himself "confronted by an almost insurmountable diffusion of obstacles" (p. 396). He must avoid being recognized, gather information about Linda in order to ascertain the extent to which he can depend on her deafness, and test his pistol. Ironically, the first two problems are solved by Gavin's having arranged for Mink to be released during the cotton-picking season, when he would be able to find "familiar work," work with which Mink has "the strongest emotional ties" (p. 371). The remoteness of the farm where he takes work as a cotton picker guarantees his obscurity; and the Negro owner, who has benefited from Linda's concern for human rights, assures him that "she's deaf. You dont need to dispute it" (p. 401). Crediting his good fortune in finding the farm to the justness of his cause, Mink says that "it was as if Old Moster Himself had said, 'I aint going to help you none but I aint going to downright hinder you neither'" (p. 403). The same faith carries him through the successful test of the pistol. Although the second shell fires, the first did not, and Mink thinks, "*Maybe the last one wont shoot neither, . . . but for only a moment, a second, less than a second, thinking No sir. It will have to. It will jest have to. There aint nothing else for it to do. I dont need to worry. Old Moster jest punishes; He dont play jokes*" (p. 407). It is this darker aspect of fate and deeper sense of justice that Gavin ignores when, at a similar juncture, he declares, "By God, God Himself is not so busy that a homicidal maniac with only ten dollars in the world can hitchhike a hundred miles and buy a gun for ten dollars then hitchhike another hundred and shoot another man with it" (p. 389). Ratliff's answering comment that it all depends "on who God wants shot this time" (p. 389) is borne out as Mink follows the railroad tracks into Jefferson, "the track, the right-of-way . . . his path into town where the privacy of freedom it had taken him thirty-eight years to earn would not be violated" (p. 406). Not only does the railroad represent freedom, but it also provides a symbol of the imminent danger that

Mink represents to Flem. Mink enters "the first quiet edge-of-town back street beneath the rigid semaphor arms of the crossing warning" (p. 407).

In this final stage of his journey, Mink's ultimate emergence as a man fated to fulfill himself by avenging ancient wrongs is rendered not only by comparison and contrast to Gavin Stevens but also by the underlying and insistent imposition of the past on the present. Here, as in his sojourn in Memphis, the events surrounding the murder of Houston thirty-eight years before are established as the archetype for revenge, upon which Mink unconsciously relies in preparing himself to murder Flem. Evoked at intervals by memories undefined as to time or circumstance, Mink's sensed associations with his past become the basis for his almost instinctual reactions to present imperatives. His declaration that *"Old Moster jest punishes He dont play jokes"* (p. 398) is evoked when "for a moment, a second something nudged at his memory" (p. 398). It constitutes a reflexive return in time of need to his old faith, which at the time of the Houston crisis was in *"them—they—it."* Not only does memory sustain him in the face of excruciating doubts, but it also provides him a safe route to Jefferson. By following the highway he would be faced with "the constant risk of passing the people who from that old Yoknapatawpha County affinity would know who he was and what he intended to do" (p. 404). He decides to follow the railroad tracks instead when, seeing a train trestle, he is reminded of that unrestricted freedom with which he watched the trains during a night spent in the Jefferson depot "thirty-eight or forty years ago, just before he went to Parchman in fact—this occasion connected also with some crisis in his affairs which he had forgotten now; . . . some crisis of the constant outrage and injustice he was always having to drop everything to cope with, handle, with no proper tools and equipment for it" (p. 405). Finally, his vague memory of having succeeded in similar moments of adversity sustains him when he faces Flem. As in the murder of Houston, Mink's first shell misfires, and "again that faint something out of the past nudged, prodded: not a warning nor even really a repetition: just faint and familiar and unimportant still since, whatever it had been, even before it had not been strong enough to alter anything nor even remarkable enough to be remembered; in the same second he had dismissed it" (pp. 415–416).

Recurring in the modified context of Mink's second vengeful murder, forgotten situations and events elicit from him those familiar
responses to inhumanity that project his elemental human dignity.
Endurance merits revenge. Faith translates into action. Mink rolls
back the cylinder to fire again not with despair but confidence:
"Hit's all right he thought *Hit'll go this time: Old Moster dont
play jokes* and cocked and steadied the pistol again in both hands,
his cousin not moving at all now though he was chewing faintly
again, as though he too were watching the dull point of light on
the cock of the hammer when it flicked away" (p. 416).

The death of Flem Snopes, banker, Baptist deacon, and respect-
ed citizen of the town of Jefferson, must be traced to his dark inner
life as usurer, betrayer, and amoral alien in the moral world. In
response to these traits in Flem, the cousin he betrayed in *The
Hamlet* and the nominal daughter he exploited in *The Town* fix
upon his destruction in *The Mansion*. Their revenges, motivated
by deep personal injury and justified by transcendent moral in-
junctions, clearly project the self-destructive element inherent in
the Snopesian principle of unremitting inhumanity. It is entirely
consistent with this principle that Flem's toleration of Linda's
presence in his mansion and his failure to take steps against Mink's
release from Parchman result finally in his passive acceptance of
death. Mink "didn't need to say, 'Look at me, Flem.' His cousin
was already doing that, his head turned over his shoulder. Otherwise he hadn't moved, only the jaws ceased chewing in midmo-
tion. . . . [he] appeared to sit immobile and even detached too. . . .
not moving at all now though he was chewing faintly again" (pp.
415–416). As Beck states, "It is scarcely out of a sense of dignity or
with any appearance of it that Flem fails to resist Mink under those
circumstances; his inertness most emphatically marks an absence in
him not only of heroism in the ancient mold but of primary human
traits and responses. What makes Flem so peculiarly pernicious is
this seemingly congenital insensitivity, the basis of his literal inhumanity." [55] In their conclusive confrontation, it is not Flem but
Mink who, by his fortitude, is imbued with human dignity. The
assistance that Linda renders Mink brings to bear against Flem the
additional force of her ideological humanism. Together, their actions define the unpalliated amorality of an aggressor whose successes are so excruciatingly injurious as to elicit from his victims

the responses that destroy him. As Brooks correctly says, Flem Snopes "runs out his string in lethargy and inertia" and faces death with "a kind of reptilian coldbloodedness or even the torpor of the bloated leech." [56]

Consistent with the concerned tentativeness, which is the characteristic mode for all interpretations of motive and action in the trilogy, the projection of the total impact and the implications of Flem's death is accomplished through the separate impressions and perceptions of Gavin Stevens and V. K. Ratliff. Beck describes their speculations as being based upon "recollection and expectation; recollection . . . draws upon anything from the insistent past; simultaneously expectation compounds (out of the immediate experience and its affinities for anything precedent) an apprehension, a fear, a hope, or a desire, becoming an intention." [57] As such, inquiry not only explains events from multiple perspectives but becomes the medium through which the various witnesses' responses to events are recorded. In the case of Flem's death, the scope of response is indicated by the fact that, when Mink fires the shot which kills Flem, "it seemed to him, Mink, that the report of the pistol was nothing but that when the chair finished falling and crashed to the floor, the sound would wake all Jefferson" (p. 416). Acuity of response is conveyed through the reactions to Flem's death of Gavin and Ratliff, who, as sensitive and committed proponents of the principles of moral existence, not only represent Jefferson but also are deeply involved with Linda and, by having circulated and signed her petition, with Mink and Flem as well. In them, recollection spans the experience of the entire trilogy, and expectation is premised on that total experience.

Despite his defeats, Gavin's positive role in *The Mansion* is fully sustained by the consistently generous nature of his expectations. Millgate argues that "it is largely through his humanity, his sensitivity both to the promise of life and to its pity, that we apprehend the book's deeper levels of suffering and anguish. And it is largely in terms of his own demanding scale of values, his high estimation of man's possibilities, that the characters of the novel, himself among them, are ultimately judged." [58] Therefore, when Gavin is forced by incontrovertible fact to acknowledge Linda's willful part in Flem's murder and to seek out Mink to give him the money to escape, he is not compromising his standards of morality but demonstrating a capacity for compassion that is completely in keeping with his character throughout *The Town* and *The Mansion*. Just as Mink's act of vengeance is elevated to transcend the merely personal by the assistance Linda renders him, so Gavin's assistance to them both, given at moments when he is most aware of the paradoxes between his idealism and reality, is in recognition of their grievous injuries and condones their deed as morally justified. It is only at the funeral of the man who "had no auspices either: fraternal, civic, nor military: only finance . . . belonging simply to Money" (p. 419) that Gavin is described as being one of "the publicly bereaved" (p. 421). In contrast, his grief for Linda and Mink is deep rooted and acute and his actions in their behalf consciously assertive.

Unlike Ratliff, who has noted the dark portents in Linda's life throughout *The Mansion* and hinted at their dangerous consequences, Gavin has stoutly defended her intentions as innocent and shielded her from disillusionment by assuming responsibility for Mink's release. So powerful is his belief in her essential goodness that, despite his attempts to equivocate, he nearly flounders at the discovery that the foreign car she has purchased to leave Jefferson in was ordered in July, at the moment Mink's release was assured. At first he is terrified by his discovery, reading in the passion of the farewell kiss from Linda an offer of payment for the disillusion she has caused him. By refusing her pity, however, he reasserts the values of mutual trust and devotion on which their relationship is based and reestablishes their love as humane in spite of its consequences to Flem. When, referring to Gavin's loss of "her mother first, then her," Linda says, "You have had nothing" (p. 424), Gavin "could have written *I have everything. You trusted me. You chose to let me find you murdered your so-called father rather than tell me a lie.* He could, perhaps should have written *I have everything. Haven't I just finished being accessory before a murder.* Instead, he wrote *We have had everything*" (p. 425). Although he is grieved by Linda's involvement in Flem's death and does not understand her motives, his reaffirmation of their love exonerates her of cruelty or inhumanity.

Gavin's discovery of what Linda has done is expanded by Ratliff's perception of her motives, which, based on his recollection of the portents in her life, gives a second perspective on events and carries forward the partial and progressive investigation of reality. Taking his cue from Flem's failure to defend himself against Linda, Ratliff likens their relationship to a game of "Give-me-lief" (p. 430). Flem's "lief" was the revelation of Eula's love affair with De Spain, which caused Eula's death, and Linda's was the release of Mink, which causes Flem's. Ratliff further speculates that Linda had Mink freed rather than wait two years for his release because "someday her maw would be saying to her, 'Why didn't you revenge me and my love that I finally found it, instead of jest standing back and blind hoping for happen-so? Didn't you never have no love of your own to learn you what it is?' " (p. 431). Having responded earlier to Eula's capacity for love and wept because he failed her by not being "brave enough to accept it" (*The Town*, p. 359), Gavin now sheds tears of compassion for Linda, whom he has failed by being unable, despite his efforts, to protect from the necessity of engineering the killing of Flem. Through a combination of Gavin's discoveries and Ratliff's shrewd interpretation of them in terms of his own perceptions, the reality of Flem's death is seen into more fully and its impact on the moral world recorded in the anguished response of sensitive witnesses. Contrasted to Linda's dispassionate role in the murder of Flem Snopes, Gavin's grief suggests a depth of suffering in her that is its own justification for murder.

Viewed in the light of Gavin's compassionate lament for her, Linda's criminal act is clearly elevated to the level of an intense assertion of those moral values that inform her existence. In the final scene of the novel, Mink is similarly elevated by Gavin's humane generosity toward him. Founded on his recognition of Linda's suffering, Gavin's response to Mink here is in direct contrast to his previous fears concerning the "homicidal maniac" (p. 389) and serves to emphasize the qualities of dignity and endurance that sustain Mink through his long imprisonment and tortuous journey. Just as he followed figuratively Ratliff's analysis of Linda's motives, so Gavin now literally follows his sure lead across the overgrown farmyard in Frenchman's Bend, "choked fiercely with rose vines long since gone wild again" (p. 432). In the dark "cave" of the fallen foundation, Mink is revealed "by the faint wavered gleam" of "the gold initialled lighter" (p. 432) given to Gavin by Linda at the time of her marriage and inscribed "GLS" with both of their initials. As the symbol of their spiritual love here suggests, his fully realized acceptance of Linda's part in the murder and his compassion for her permit Gavin literally to see Mink's condition in the same generous light that she does. Linda surprised Mink in the course of his revenge and assisted his escape from Flem's mansion. Gavin finds him "blinking up at them like a child interrupted at its bedside prayers" (p. 432) and gives him the money to leave Mississippi with the concerned warning that "You cant stay here. . . . If we knew where you were, don't you know the sheriff will think of this place too by tomorrow morning?" (p. 432). Whereas he previously imposed conditions on the freedom he offered Mink, he now gives him the money without obligation; even the amount is the same. Mink asks, "You mean when I take it I aint promised nobody nothing?" and Gavin answers, "Yes. . . . Take it" (p. 433). As though reminding Gavin of that transcendent nobility inherent even in so frail a concept of personal morality as Mink's, Ratliff himself lights their departure from Mink's den as Gavin climbs "the fading earthen steps again, once more up and out into the air, the night, the moonless dark, the worn-out eroded fields supine beneath the first faint breath of fall, waiting for winter. Overhead, celestial and hierarchate, the constellations wheeled through the zodiacal pastures: Scorpion and Bear and Scales; beyond cold Orion and the Sisters the fallen and homeless angels choired, lamenting" (p. 433).

This striking image encompasses both a culmination of recollections from the entire narrative, marking the final convergence after Flem's death of the lives of Linda, Gavin, and Mink, and an expectation of Mink's approaching victory in death. When Gavin and Ratliff leave Jefferson on the evening of October 3 in search of Mink, "the sun had crossed the equator, in Libra now" (p. 417). In the zodiac, Libra is represented by the sign of the scales and is bounded on either side by Virgo, the virgin, and Scorpio, the scorpion. Throughout *The Mansion*, Linda is imaged as a virgin, "the inviolate bride of silence, inviolable in maidenhead" (p. 203), who frees love from its ritual enactment. Mink is consistently portrayed as a stinging reptile or insect: "a half grown asp or cobra or krait" (p. 45), a "rattlesnake" (p. 394), a "fer-de-lance" (p. 393), "a scorpion" (p. 287). As a lawyer, Gavin is logically associated with the scales of justice. The immediate proximity of these three signs in the zodiac clearly suggests the intricate involvement of the characters so imaged in each other's fate. In addition, their active opposition to Flem is condensed into the eight days of Mink's journey, which covers the time between September 26 and October 3. During the entire course of this journey, Libra is the dominant zodiacal sign, signifying not only Mink's and Linda's commitment to justice but also the justness of their commitment. Although Gavin does not seek retribution in Flem's death, his association with the sign of Libra is warranted by the fact that it is he who mediates with both Linda and Mink and who purposely chooses autumn as the season in which Mink is released. Finally, the inclusion of "Scorpion" and "Scales" with the constellations "Bear," "Orion," and "the Sisters" (the Pleiades) implies that Mink, by enduring the trials set for him and accomplishing his just end by killing Flem, will join that select company, "himself among them, equal to any, good as any, brave as any, being inextricable from, anonymous with all of them: the beautiful, the splendid, the proud and the brave, right on up to the very top itself among the shining phantoms and dreams which are the milestones of the long human recording—Helen and the bishops, the kings and the unhomed angels, the scornful and graceless seraphim" (pp. 435–436). Distorted, hardened, and numbed by Flem's betrayal of his humanity, Mink finds community at last in death. The heights that he attains in death bespeak forever the depths of amorality in him whom he endured a lifetime to kill.

Conclusion

"Equal to Any, Good as Any,
Brave as Any"

WITH the death of Flem Snopes, Faulkner brought to a close a chronicle on which he had labored intermittently for nearly four decades. From the time of its inception in the mid-1920s to the publication of *The Mansion* in 1959, the period of the trilogy's creation encompasses and extends beyond that period of productivity between 1929 and 1940 commonly known as Faulkner's major years. In addition, as a unified trilogy, it is Faulkner's most extended work. For these reasons alone, aside from questions of literary merit, the Snopes trilogy is deserving of critical attention as a historical index to the development of Faulkner's thought and art. Here are the multitude of characters, familiarly Faulknerian in nature as well as in name, who represent the work of a lifetime. Tulls, Bookwrights, Armstids, and McCaslins supply the populous fictional background against which the drama is played. Gavin Stevens and Charles Mallison, refined to meet the unique demands of "the Snopes dilemma," are joined in their struggle against Flem Snopes, himself a character original to the trilogy, by other new characters: Eula Varner, her daughter Linda, and V.K. Ratliff. Critical opinion to the contrary, it is hardly remarkable that characters from other Yoknapatawpha novels and stories appear in the Snopes trilogy. In fact, it is typical of Faulkner to involve characters from one work in another of similar theme, a notable example being Quentin Compson's roles in both *The Sound and the Fury* and *Absalom, Absalom!* Furthermore, both *The Hamlet* and *The Town* incorporate previously published material in interlocking episodes organic to the narrative. What may seem surprising is that, in a novelist given to portraying evil in the Gothic grotesque tradition to dramatize its implications for moral man, Flem Snopes should be confined exclusively to the trilogy and its source stories. While this may be accounted for by Faulkner's statements that the story of the Snopeses was conceived not as a single novel in the Yoknapatawpha saga but as an independent, several volume "chronicle," it is more likely that Flem, Faulkner's most terrifying monster, evolved from the author's previous portraits of villains to dominate his own unique milieu.

Faulkner entitled his earliest Snopes manuscript "Father Abraham" (1925–26), and he continued to use that biblical image to describe Flem in *Sartoris* (1929), where Flem is briefly mentioned as bringing his clan to Jefferson "like Abraham of old." [1] Although biblical allusions abound in the trilogy, however, by 1940 when *The Hamlet* was published, Faulkner had abandoned them in describing Flem and his tribe, probably because they were too humanizing. He took instead the tack he had taken with Popeye in *Sanctuary* (1931) and adopted as Snopes images inanimate objects and predators. Popeye's eyes are "like rubber knobs," and his features have "that vicious depthless quality of stamped tin." [2] Flem's eyes are "the color of stagnant water" (p. 22), and his face is "as blank as a pan of uncooked dough" (p. 23). Both are impotent. While the immediate dehumanizing effect is much the same in both cases, Faulkner failed to sustain in Popeye the extended portrait of unrelieved inhumanity that he achieved in Flem, and Popeye vacillates between being a modern gangland robot and a pitiable creature of his ruinous environment. Unlike Popeye, Jason Compson in *The Sound and the Fury* (1929) is fully and consistently drawn, and the insensitive, self-seeking cruelty that he projects is in many respects Snopesian. As ambitious, conniving, and treacherous as he is, however, his capacity for emotion makes him recognizably human. Even his exploitation of his niece, Quentin, is in some ways justified by his jealous outrage at her mother, whereas Flem's vicious treatment of Linda is motivated solely by his coldly opportunistic adherence to self-advancement. This singleness of purpose in Flem, transcending even considerations of family and clan, is strongly reminiscent of Thomas Sutpen's uncompromising constancy to his dream in *Absalom, Absalom!* (1936). Like Flem, Sutpen rises from poverty to wealth largely by his ability to use people for his own purposes; yet Faulkner endowed him with a capacity for heroic vision that he expunged from his portrait of Flem. In Sutpen's grand design, the acquisition of money is incidental to establishing his own dynasty and avenging himself upon the aristocracy of the antebellum South. To Flem, money is everything. In him, Sutpen's ambition manifests itself as animal appetite, Sutpen's imagination, as craft, and Sutpen's industry, as intrigue. The baseness of his design mirrors his unresponsiveness to human imperatives and deprives him of human dimension.

The measure of Faulkner's achievement in creating Flem Snopes, however, does not rest solely, or even primarily, on his ability to evolve from other villains and render whole the embodiment of undiluted inhumanity. No less important than establishing the fact that Flem is amoral must be a consideration of the artistic purpose he serves by being amoral. Richard P. Adams provides considerable insight into this larger problem by his investigation of Faulkner's statement that "life is motion." Adams says, "If we conceive of motion as a stream (an image often used by Faulkner) we find that its power cannot be felt by someone moving with it, or in it, as living people normally do. If, however, some object, or better if some person, can be made to stand still against its flow, the result will be a dramatic and possibly disastrous manifestation of its energy." [3] Flem is such a person. His suitability for this obstructive role is affirmed by Adams's further contention that "the better Faulkner's characters are in their moral alliance with life or in their natural adjustment to its pace and rhythm, the less they are able to do for the esthetic success of his work. Those who serve him best are the discontented, the maladjusted, the desperate, and the morally bad." [4] Of all Faulkner's characters, none is so completely out of tune with the rhythms of life as Flem Snopes, none so totally incapable of adjustment to its pace. Existing as a point of stasis in the midst of motion, he threatens to arrest by his amorality the flow of moral life. In the Snopes trilogy, the sharply separate reactions of principled individuals so threatened are made simultaneous by the unchanging nature of the ag-

226   CONCLUSION

gressor, and together they dramatize the depth and scope of the
moral universe of Yoknapatawpha County. To this end, Flem's
presence is a necessity.

Nowhere in the trilogy are the effects of Flem's immutable stag-
nancy on the limitless energy of life more clearly depicted than
in Faulkner's treatment of love. Together with his contention that
"life is motion," his repeated emphasis on fidelity to the truths
of the human heart suggests that moral life is characterized by a
process of growth springing from inner convictions and imperatives. Vickery finds evidence that this is so in the fact that Faulkner seldom imposes upon his characters traditional social standards or predetermined patterns of behavior. She points out that
"moral and social dimensions emanate from the character and not
vice versa." [5] In *The Hamlet*, love is defined in terms of the un-
adorned primal force embodied in Eula and projected by her
mythic sexuality. Eula is totally unaffected by her contemporary
scene, and her growth is attuned to the rhythms of nature and
recorded in the symbolically private world of her own body,
where she seems to listen "in sullen bemusement, with a weary
wisdom heired of all mammalian maturity, to the enlarging of her
own organs" (p. 95). Immobile herself, her moral development is
given a sense of natural motion by the seasonal images through
which she is portrayed. To depict the full range and complexity
of love's pervasive force, moreover, Faulkner places other lovers
in chronologic juxtaposition to Eula. The most striking of these
is the idiot, Ike, whose instinctive sensory responses lead to his
idyll with the cow in a pastoral setting overflowing with cease-
less natural motion and "loud with hymeneal . . . choristers" (p.
165). Through the backward and forward movement of the narrative, the vitality of Ike's idyll extends the scope and depth of
the "priapic hullabaloo" (p. 121) of Eula's last summer, which
culminates in her union with McCarron.

With the interjection of Flem Snopes, however, the narrative
tone, formerly so rich with the rhythm of love, is stilled to
mourning, and summer dies into fall. Eula's marriage to Flem at
the moment of her own fulfillment signals the outside imposition
on love of standards of propriety, and the stultifying effect of
such standards is symbolized in the fact of Flem's impotence. Concurrently, Ike is deprived of his cow, and as he is given a statue

in its place, so Eula's face hardens to a "mask" (p. 147), and she is thereafter in the novel imaged as a piece of sculpture. The cessation of motion, however dramatic and pronounced at this juncture, is nonetheless temporary, and in *The Town* love revives under the overlying romantic scrutiny of Gavin Stevens. His idealization of Eula as Helen, Semiramis, and Lilith renews her aura of timeless sexuality, and her "fated" alliance with Manfred de Spain, characterized by mutual fidelity, becomes a source of universal pride to the community. But the force of their love is felt primarily as an undercurrent, surfacing only when Flem places himself in their path. Insensitive to the morality of love, Flem adopts the surface righteousness and respectability of the town "founded by Aryan Baptists and Methodists, for Aryan Baptists and Methodists" (p. 306) and rises to the presidency of the bank by threatening the lovers with public exposure. Such challenges, however, are not permitted to go unanswered. Gavin romantically fancies himself in the role of Eula's spiritual husband and Linda's spiritual father, and his harried, generous responses to their endangerment are brimming with moral energy. He senses as only the innately moral man can that Flem represents a serious obstruction to their continued moral growth, and his efforts are aimed directly at removing that obstruction. While his repeated failures in this cause serve to define the frightening proportions of his adversary, his readiness to renew the conflict is evidence of the rejuvenative nature of morality.

When, through Flem's machinations, Eula is driven to suicide and Manfred is banished, the rhythm of love is again temporarily halted, and all that remains of the love goddess is her carved face beneath the viciously cryptic inscription on her tombstone: "A Virtuous Wife Is a Crown to Her Husband Her Children Rise and Call Her Blessed" (p. 355). By this inscription, Flem attempts to impose on her memory the artificial definition of love that she transcended in life. Yet the social formality that Flem's gesture represents, like his merely legal marriage to Eula, is insufficient to permanently still the rhythm of love. The carving of her face, selected by Gavin, conveys remembered passion and holds out the promise of love's continuance. In *The Mansion*, that promise is fulfilled through Linda, who, as Eula's natural child and Gavin's spiritual child, combines her mother's boundless capacity for love with her mentor's sensitivity to amorality and his determination to affirm moral freedom no matter what the sacrifice. Firmly grounded in the demands of the heart, her ideological commitment to human rights transcends social tradition as did her mother's sexuality and represents the culmination of the metamorphosis of love from its physical to its philosophical state. Just as the pace of response to Eula is quickened by the juxtaposition of other love stories to create an overriding sense of physical motion, Linda's philosophical orientation to love is in tune with those ideological movements to free man from oppression that result in the Spanish Civil War and World War II. Together with her energetic work for social freedom in Jefferson, her active participation against fascism in both of these conflicts places her in the mainstream of human progress.

To Flem Snopes, however, progress is signified only by the acquisition and retention of money, and his capitalism is as obstructive to Linda's sort of love as was his impotence to Eula's. Imaged with Franco, Mussolini, and Hitler as one of "the hereditary predators, the farmers-general of the human dilemma" (p. 160), Flem, as much as they, both threatens and is threatened by the humanistic impulse represented in Linda. The maintainance of his fortune depends upon his ability to remain in a position of power from which he can hold man in usurious economic bondage, and to that end he assumes the facade of respectability. Linda's indifference to artificial concepts of respectability is as much a danger to his position as her commitment to human freedom is to his methods, and each of his attempts to halt her good works elicits from her a more dramatic counterreaction, be it assisting Negro schools, organizing Communist meetings, or laboring in the Pascagoula shipyards. The energy and motion of Linda's moral life is manifested at its most intense, however, as, with the gradual disappearance of the causes she espouses, she fixes more and more steadily on Flem Snopes as the propagator of all inhumanity. The sense of moral determination that characterizes her single-mindedness is conveyed through the portents connected with her continued residence in Flem's mansion, and it is reinforced by the parallel development of Mink's inexorable journey toward Jefferson. Given scope by Linda's transcendent humanistic love and depth by Mink's intensely personal determination to assert his individual human identity, their murder of Flem is a strictly a moral act, symbolizing the simultaneous accumulation of the multitude of separate responses to amorality throughout the trilogy.

With the death of Flem Snopes, the rhythm of love set in physical motion by Eula in *The Hamlet* and metamorphosed into its philosophical dimension in Linda in *The Town* and *The Mansion* is given final spiritual definition by Mink's ascent into heaven. There, "equal to any, good as any, brave as any" (p. 435), Mink joins "the shining phantoms and dreams" (p. 436) of which Eula, as "Helen," is now one. As Beck correctly says, "To look into the mansion is to look out upon the town and back to the hamlet—and beyond." [6] The unrelieved amorality of Flem and the opulence and complexity of the moral universe that his machinations uncover clearly show the measure of Faulkner's achievement. Unified in theme, as in structure, by the sustention of dramatic tension between morality and amorality, motion and stasis, the trilogy must ultimately be judged Faulkner's most extended and comprehensive statement of the nature of man and the outcome of his struggle.

Notes

Introduction

1. "Nobel Prize Address," *The Faulkner Reader: Selections from the Works of William Faulkner* (New York, 1954), p. 3.
2. *Faulkner in the University: Class Conferences at the University of Virginia, 1957–1958*, ed. Frederick L. Gwynn and Joseph L. Blotner (Charlottesville, Va., 1959), p. 88.
3. Ibid., p. 267.
4. "Nobel Prize Address," pp. 3–4.
5. Warren Beck, *Man in Motion: Faulkner's Trilogy* (Madison, Wis., 1961), p. 81.
6. *Faulkner in the University*, p. 282.
7. *The Mansion* (New York, 1959). All subsequent references are to this edition.

Part 1

1. *Faulkner in the University*, p. 15.
2. *The Faulkner-Cowley File: Letters and Memories, 1944–1962*, ed. Malcolm Cowley (New York, 1966), pp. 25–26.
3. Michael Millgate, *The Achievement of William Faulkner* (New York, 1963), pp. 180–200.
4. Beck, *Man in Motion*, p. 10.
5. Irving Howe, *William Faulkner: A Critical Study*, 2nd ed. (New York, 1962), p. 59.
6. *The Hamlet*, 3rd ed. (New York, 1964). All subsequent references are to this edition.
7. Beck, *Man in Motion*, pp. 66–67.
8. Ibid., p. 19.
9. Ibid., p. 68.

10. Cleanth Brooks, *William Faulkner: The Yoknapatawpha Country* (New Haven, Conn., 1963), pp. 182, 402–406.
11. Ann L. Hayes, "The World of *The Hamlet*," *Carnegie Series in English* 6 (1961): 13.
12. Brooks, p. 176.
13. Beck, *Man in Motion*, p. 32.
14. Ibid., p. 82.
15. Ibid., p. 83.
16. T. Y. Greet, "The Theme and Structure of Faulkner's *The Hamlet*," in *William Faulkner: Three Decades of Criticism*, ed. Frederick J. Hoffman and Olga W. Vickery (East Lansing, Michigan, 1960), p. 339.
17. Brooks, p. 180.
18. Melvin Backman, *Faulkner: The Major Years* (Bloomington, Ind. 1966), p. 150.
19. See especially Greet, p. 340. He contends that with the appearance of the cow, "Hoake, the goddess' consort, is with sudden and tragic irony replaced by Ike Snopes, idiot; and the 'shape of love' is transformed grotesquely into that of a cow."
20. Millgate, p. 187.
21. Backman, p. 154.
22. Brooks, pp. 183–184.
23. Ibid., p. 185.
24. Hayes, p. 10.
25. Howe (p. 249) says that "precisely because he is so impressive, it comes as something of a shock when Ratliff finally succumbs to avarice—or perhaps to the 'game' of his struggle with the Snopeses— and allows himself to be taken in by Flem. Suddenly, without sufficient warning or preparation, Ratliff proves as gullible as Flem's other victims." He sees Ratliff as being "marred at the end of *The Hamlet*" (p. 251). Brooks (p. 188) says that Ratliff's defeat is the result of a temporary suspension of those humane qualities that permitted him to act successfully against Snopeses in the past: "Ratliff apparently can defeat Flem Snopes only when he is acting in disinterested fashion for the sake of honor or for the sake of someone else, like the idiot Ike. When he himself sniffs the scent of easy money, he loses his caution and eventually finds that he has been trapped." Hayes finds Ratliff's gulling a thematic success insofar as it firmly establishes him as a member of the community to which Flem is completely alien, but she adds that "only the character of Ratliff leaves us uncertain and dissatisfied that things could have turned out this way" (p. 11).
26. Millgate, p. 199.
27. Ibid.
28. Beck, *Man in Motion*, p. 186.

Part 2

1. Malcolm Cowley, "Introduction to *The Portable Faulkner*," in *Three Decades of Criticism*, p. 94.

2. Alfred Kazin, "Mr. Faulkner's Friends, the Snopeses," *New York Times Book Review*, 5 May 1957, p. 1.
3. Ibid.
4. Ibid., p. 24.
5. Ibid., p. 1.
6. *The Faulkner-Cowley File*, p. 26.
7. *Faulkner in the University*, p. 107.
8. Ibid., p. 193.
9. Beck, *Man in Motion*, p. 34.
10. *Faulkner in the University*, p. 108.
11. Olga W. Vickery, *The Novels of William Faulkner: A Critical Interpretation*, 2nd ed. (Baton Rouge, La., 1964), p. 182.
12. Ibid.
13. James F. Farnham, "Faulkner's Unsung Hero: Gavin Stevens," *Arizona Quarterly* 21 (Summer 1965): 116–117.
14. *Faulkner in the University*, p. 140.
15. Ibid.
16. Millgate, p. 236.
17. *Faulkner in the University*, p. 116.
18. *The Town* (New York, 1957). All subsequent references are to this edition.
19. Vickery, p. 184.
20. Ibid.
21. John L. Longley, Jr., *The Tragic Mask: A Study of Faulkner's Heroes* (Chapel Hill, N. C., 1963), p. 49.
22. Ibid., p. 37.
23. Longley, *Tragic Mask*, p. 38.
24. Ibid.
25. Farnham, p. 116.
26. Ibid., p. 123.
27. Longley, *Tragic Mask*, p. 45.
28. Beck, *Man in Motion*, pp. 15–16.
29. Longley, *Tragic Mask*, p. 42.
30. Vickery, p. 183.
31. Farnham, p. 118.
32. Ibid., p. 119.
33. Longley, *Tragic Mask*, p. 151.
34. Beck, *Man in Motion*, p. 136.
35. Ibid., p. 31.
36. Ibid., p. 32.
37. Beck, *Man in Motion*, p. 192.
38. Longley, *Tragic Mask*, p. 44.
39. Farnham, p. 124.
40. Beck, *Man in Motion*, p. 113.
41. Longley, *Tragic Mask*, p. 150.
42. Vickery, p. 190.
43. Millgate, p. 238.
44. Ibid., p. 243.
45. Ibid., pp. 238–239.
46. Robert Penn Warren, "William Faulkner," in *Three Decades of Criticism*, p. 118.

47. Stevens Marcus, "Snopes Revisited," in *Three Decades of Criticism*,
    p. 384.
48. Millgate, pp. 236–237.
49. Howe, p. 284.
50. Ibid., p. 286.
51. Ibid., p. 289.
52. Ibid.
53. John L. Longley, Jr., "Galahad Gavin and a Garland of Snopeses,"
    Virginia Quarterly Review 33 (Autumn 1957): 627.
54. Brooks, p. 201.
55. Howe, p. 288.
56. Beck, *Man in Motion*, p. 29.
57. Ibid., p. 79.
58. Ibid., p. 51.
59. Ibid., p. 52.
60. See especially Hyatt H. Waggoner, *William Faulkner: From Jefferson
    to the World* (Lexington, Ky., 1966), p. 233. Assuming that Gavin is
    Speaking for Faulkner, Waggoner says that "in *The Town* we are
    invited to see the symbol of soulless modernism [Flem] as properly
    to be pitied, not hated; invited easily, quickly, abruptly, with no
    dramatic embodiment of the new perspective."
61. Millgate, p. 239.
62. Beck, *Man in Motion*, p. 85.
63. Andrew Lytle, "*The Town:* Helen's Last Stand," *The Sewanee Review*
    65 (Summer 1957): 482.
64. Joseph Gold, *William Faulkner: A Study in Humanism, from Metaphor
    to Discourse* (Norman, Okla., 1966), p. 148.
65. Ibid., pp. 148–149.
66. Vickery, p. 182.
67. Waggoner, p. 236.
68. Beck, *Man in Motion*, p. 11.
69. Brooks, p. 204.
70. Ibid.
71. Ibid.
72. Millgate, p. 243.
73. Ibid., p. 244.

Part 3

1. *Faulkner in the University*, p. 107.
2. Elizabeth M. Kerr, "Snopes," *Wisconsin Studies in Contemporary
   Literature* 1 (Spring and Summer 1960):68.
3. Vickery, p. 194.
4. Ibid., p. 202.
5. Longley, *Tragic Mask*, p. 46.
6. Brooks, p. 223.
7. Beck, *Man in Motion*, p. 28.
8. Ibid., p. 27.
9. Theodore M. Greene, "The Philosophy of Life Implicit in Faulkner's
   The Mansion," *Texas Studies in Literautre and Language* 2 (Winter
   1961): 412.

10. Brooks, p. 230.
11. Beck, *Man in Motion*, pp. 78–79.
12. Vickery, p. 195.
13. Brooks, p. 230.
14. Vickery, pp. 202–203.
15. Brooks, p. 230.
16. Beck, *Man in Motion*, p. 78.
17. Warren Beck, "Faulkner in the Mansion," *Virginia Quarterly Review* 36 (Spring 1960): 280–281.
18. Beck, *Man in Motion*, p. 29.
19. Vickery, p. 192.
20. Ibid., p. 206.
21. See especially Peter Swiggart, *The Art of Faulkner's Novels* (Austin, Tex., 1962) and Gold, who contends that "Flem's relationship to the mansion is symbolic of all that has happened to him. Society has shown him what it demands, what it values: the impressive, phony exterior, the appearance of wealth and superiority and solidity" (p. 163). Swiggart says that Flem's residence in the antebellum mansion, together with his insensitivity to Linda's attempts to aid Negroes, represents "the degeneration of the white aristocracy, the rise of Snopesism, and the white Southerner's gradual recognition of his latent sense of racial guilt" (p. 203). He adds that, in *The Mansion*, "Snopesism is brought more in line with actuality, but at the expense of its fictional *raison d'être*" (p. 196).
22. Vickery, p. 194.
23. Ibid., pp. 194–195.
24. Ibid., p. 201.
25. Beck, *Man in Motion*, p. 37.
26. Brooks, p. 226.
27. Ibid., p. 227.
28. Ibid.
29. Vickery, p. 203.
30. Beck, *Man in Motion*, p. 112.
31. Ibid.
32. Brooks, p. 219.
33. Millgate, p. 250.
34. Kerr, p. 77.
35. Vickery, p. 195.
36. Brooks, p. 232.
37. Ibid., p. 17.
38. Ibid.
39. Beck, *Man in Motion*, p. 176.
40. Ibid., p. 175.
41. Vickery, p. 201.
42. Ibid., p. 193.
43. Brooks, p. 235.
44. Vickery, p. 197.
45. Beck, *Man in Motion*, p. 199.
46. Ibid., p. 200.
47. Ibid., p. 26.
48. See especially Anthony West, "A Dying Fall," *The New Yorker* 5 December 1959. West contends that, as Gavin's behavior becomes

Snopesian, "Flem Snopes becomes the passive victim of a scheme in which Mink Snopes is used as a thing" (p. 238).
49. Longley, *Tragic Mask*, p. 47.
50. Beck, *Man in Motion*, p. 8.
51. Ibid.
52. Brooks, p. 238.
53. Ibid.
54. Beck, *Man in Motion*, p. 3–4.
55. Ibid., p. 81.
56. Brooks, pp. 229–230.
57. Beck, *Man in Motion*, pp. 191–192.
58. Millgate, p. 249.

Conclusion

1. *Sartoris* (New York, 1929), p. 172.
2. *Sanctuary* (New York, 1931), pp. 4, 2.
3. Richard P. Adams, *Faulkner: Myth and Motion* (Princeton, N. J., 1968), p. 5.
4. Ibid., p. 14.
5. Vickery, p. 295.
6. Beck, *Man in Motion*, p. 203.

Bibliography

Adams, Richard P. *Faulkner: Myth and Motion.* Princeton, New Jersey, 1968.

Backman, Melvin. *Faulkner: The Major Years.* Bloomington, Indiana, 1966.

Beck, Warren. "Faulkner in the Mansion." *Virginia Quarterly Review* 36 (Spring 1960): 272–292.

Beck, Warren. *Man in Motion: Faulkner's Trilogy.* Madison, Wisconsin, 1961.

Brooks, Cleanth. *William Faulkner: The Yoknapatawpha Country.* New Haven, Connecticut, 1963.

Cowley, Malcolm, ed. *The Faulkner-Cowley File: Letters and Memories, 1944–1962.* New York, 1966.

Cowley, Malcolm. "Introduction to *The Portable Faulkner.*" In *William Faulkner: Three Decades of Criticism.* Edited by Frederick J. Hoffman and Olga W. Vickery, pp. 94–109. East Lansing, Michigan, 1960.

Farnham, James F. "Faulkner's Unsung Hero: Gavin Stevens." *Arizona Quarterly* 21 (Summer 1965): 115–132.

Faulkner, William. *The Hamlet.* 3rd ed. New York, 1964.

Faulkner William. *The Mansion.* New York, 1959.

Faulkner, William. "Nobel Prize Address." in *The Faulkner Reader: Selections from the Works of William Faulkner,* pp. 3–4. New York, 1954.

Faulkner, William. *Sanctuary.* New York, 1931.

Faulkner, William. *Sartoris.* New York, 1929.

Faulkner, William. *The Town.* New York, 1957.

Gold, Joseph. *William Faulkner: A Study in Humanism, from Metaphor to Discourse.* Norman, Oklahoma, 1966.

Greene, Theodore M. "The Philosophy of Life Implicit in Faulkner's *The Mansion.*" *Texas Studies in Literature and Language* 2 (Winter 1961): 401–418.

Greet, T. Y. "The Theme and Structure of Faulkner's *The Hamlet.*" In *William Faulkner: Three Decades of Criticism.* Edited by Frederick J. Hoffman and Olga W. Vickery, pp. 330–347. East Lansing, Michigan, 1960.

Gwynn, Frederick L. and Joseph L. Blotner, eds. *Faulkner in the University: Class Conferences at the University of Virginia, 1957–1958.* Charlottesville, Virginia, 1959.

Hayes, Ann L. "The World of *The Hamlet.*" *Carnegie Series in English* 6 (1961): 3–16.

Howe, Irving. *William Faulkner: A Critical Study.* 2nd ed. New York, 1962.

Kazin, Alfred. "Mr. Faulkner's Friends, the Snopeses." *New York Times Book Review,* 5 May 1957, p. 1.

Kerr, Elizabeth M. "Snopes." *Wisconsin Studies in Contemporary Literature* 1 (Spring and Summer 1960): 66–84.

Longley, John L., Jr. "Galahad Gavin and a Garland of Snopeses." *Virginia Quarterly Review* 33 (Autumn 1957): 623–628.

Longley, John L., Jr. *The Tragic Mask: A Study of Faulkner's Heroes.* Chapel Hill, North Carolina, 1963.

Lytle, Andrew. "*The Town:* Helen's Last Stand." *The Sewanee Review* 65 (Summer 1957): 475–484.

Marcus, Steven. "Snopes Revisited." In *William Faulkner: Three Decades of Criticism.* Edited by Frederick J. Hoffman and Olga W. Vickery, pp. 109–124. East Lansing, Michigan, 1960.

Millgate, Michael. *The Achievement of William Faulkner.* New York, 1963.

Swiggart, Peter. *The Art of Faulkner's Novels.* Austin, Texas, 1962.

Vickery, Olga W. *The Novels of William Faulkner: A Critical Interpretation.* 2nd ed. Baton Rouge, Louisiana, 1964.

Waggoner, Hyatt H. *William Faulkner: From Jefferson to the World.* Lexington, Kentucky, 1966.

Warren, Robert Penn. "William Faulkner." In *William Faulkner: Three Decades of Criticism.* Edited by Frederick J. Hoffman and Olga W. Vickery, pp. 382–391. East Lansing, Michigan, 1960.

West, Anthony. "A Dying Fall." *The New Yorker,* 5 December 1959. pp. 236–243.

Index